ART AND DOCTRINE

The Descent from the Cross. Joseph of Arimathea lowers the Saviour's body to be received by Nicodemus (left); The Entombment (centre); Christ proclaims the good news to imprisoned spirits; one, still unrepentent, is seen behind red hot bars (right).

Fairford Church, Gloucestershire. *(Royal Commission on Historical Monuments)*

ART AND DOCTRINE:

ESSAYS ON MEDIEVAL LITERATURE

ROSEMARY WOOLF

EDITED BY
HEATHER O'DONOGHUE

THE HAMBLEDON PRESS
LONDON AND RONCEVERTE

Published by The Hambledon Press 1986

35 Gloucester Avenue, London NW1 7AX (U.K.)

309 Greenbrier Avenue, Ronceverte
West Virginia 24970 (U.S.A.)

ISBN 0 907628 53 2 (cased)
0 907628 54 0 (paper)

British Library Cataloguing in Publication Data

Woolf, Rosemary E.
Art and doctrine.
1. English literature – Middle English, 1100-1500 –
History and criticism
I. Title II. O'Donoghue, Heather
820'. 9'001 PR281

Library of Congress Cataloging-in-Publication Data

Woolf, Rosemary.
Art and doctrine.

Includes index.
1. English literature – Middle English, 1100-1500 –
History and criticism – Addresses, essays, lectures.
2. Anglo-Saxon literature – History and criticism –
History and criticism – Addresses, essays, lectures.
I. O'Donoghue, Heather. II. Title
PR166.W6 1986 820'. 9'001 84-133363

Printed in Great Britain by WBC Print Ltd., Bristol

CONTENTS

ACKNOWLEDGEMENTS

The articles reprinted here first appeared in the following places and are reprinted by kind permission of the original publishers.

I *Review of English Studies*, n.s. 4 (1953), 1-12.

II *Studies in Old English Literature in Honor of Arthur G. Brodeur*, ed. S.B. Greenfield (Oregon University Press, 1963), 187-99.

III *Medium Aevum* (1958), 137-53.

IV *Speculum* (1957), 805-25.

V *Critical Quarterly* (1959), 150-7.

VI *Essays in Criticism*, 12 (1962), 111-25.

VII *Review of English Studies*, n.s. 13 (1962), 1-16.

VIII *Modern Language Review*, 50 (1955), 168-72.

IX *Medium Aevum*, 38 (1969), 55-9.

X *Piers Plowman: Critical Approaches*, ed. S.S. Hussey (Methuen, London/ Barnes and Noble, New York, 1969), 50-75.

XI *Anglo-Saxon Poetry: Essays in Appreciation for John C. McGalliard*, ed. Nicholson and Frere (University of Notre Dame, 1975), 192-207.

XII *Anglo-Saxon England*, v (1976), 63-81.

XIII *J.R.R. Tolkien Scholar and Storyteller: Essays 'In Memoriam'*, ed. Mary Salu and Robert T. Farrell (Cornell University Press, 1979), 221-45. Copyright ©1979 by Cornell University. Used by permission of the publisher, Cornell University Press.

XIV *Continuations and Beginnings. Studies in Old English Literature*, ed. E.G. Stanley (Nelson, Edinburgh, 1966), 37-65.

INTRODUCTION

THESE pieces by Rosemary Woolf span exactly a quarter of a century, from the first article published in 1953 to her death in 1978; the article on Gower and Chaucer was published posthumously in 1979. They deal with many of the major works of Old and Middle English literature, and range from specialized scholarly points of detail to much more general, but no less authoritative, surveys of whole genres of medieval literature. Many of the essays are now regarded as definitive contributions to their subject; some remain controversial. None has been refuted or superseded.

The strength and quality of these articles remains constant: it rests on Rosemary Woolf's balanced fusion of literary criticism and historical scholarship in her approach to medieval literature. The documentation which underpins her critical insights seems now to represent an ideal norm in medieval literary studies, but it was less the fashion when Rosemary Woolf's articles first began to appear in print.

For the greater part of this century, English medieval literature was written about by critics who believed in keeping learning and scholarship quite distinct from the business of literary criticism, and who treated medieval literature with an easy familiarity and affection, little concerning themselves with what is now seen as the unfamiliar and even alien cultural and intellectual background of the period. Of course, fine critics such as Kittredge were not unscholarly; their approach was deliberately unhistorical. Kittredge writes of Chaucer, for instance, that he is 'the most modern of English poets . . . For he knew life and loved it, and his speciality was mankind as it was and is.'

Naturally there was a reaction against these critical methods, and Rosemary Woolf's work can be seen as part of the move away from what might be termed the 'commonsensical' or 'armchair' school of medievalist criticism. The strongest reaction came from critics such as Robertson and Huppé, who advanced the belief that medieval literature can only be read with reference to the intellectual traditions of the time—in particular, in the manner of biblical exegetes, detailing the spiritual associations of words, phrases and motifs in the same way as did the Latin and medieval glossers of Scripture. But Rosemary Woolf did not altogether resemble the Robertsonians in their pure but narrow form of historical criticism. Her application of extra-textual learning is always subservient to the text itself: she uses it to develop an understanding of period, to dispel readings based on historical ignorance or misunderstanding, and, fundamentally, as the soundest basis from which to attempt literary judgements.

The polarity evident in critical approaches to medieval literature—between, to put it crudely, the scholars and the critics—arises from a pervasive duality in medieval literature itself. Most extant English medieval works are religious and didactic, and from this at least the Robertsonians draw justification for their treatment of medieval literature as if it were Scripture. What one critic has called 'the age old balancing of Belief and Literature' in the Middle Ages is a complex and virtually ever-present aspect of all the creative arts of the period. 'Art for Doctrine's sake' is truer of the Middle Ages than 'Art for Art's sake', but the relationship, the balancing act, between the two is not predictable or one-sided. Rosemary Woolf's strength is to be receptive to a work's literary aims, and knowledgeable about its didactic ones; to see clearly the relationship between the two, and exactly how one enriches or cramps the other. Her full-length critical works, *The English Religious Lyric in the Middle Ages* (1968) and *The English Mystery Plays* (1972), deal with two genres in Middle English in which a sensitive understanding of the duality I have outlined is crucial. In the introduction to her book on Mystery Plays, Rosemary Woolf declared a twofold aim: to investigate in a scholarly way the sources and background of the cycles, and to demonstrate the dramatic value of the plays themselves. Similarly, the nature of lyric poetry demands delicate handling if rigorous scholarly analysis is not to spoil its effects, and dissipate such ephemeral qualities as charm and freshness. Rosemary Woolf's two books have been accepted as classic studies, and it is the combination of learning and insight which has ensured their success. This combination distinguishes the articles in this volume, wide in range and varied in scholarly level and tone as they are.

Rosemary Woolf's first published article, 'The Devil in Old English Poetry', illustrates the range of her scholarship. Its central concern is the adaptation of secular heroic convention to Christian subject matter, and, accepting a critical consensus that the attempt is not normally very successful, she investigates one notable exception, the presentation of the Devil. She draws parallels between Old English and Old Norse, assessing Germanic tradition and characteristically extends her range to consider Shakespeare's Iago and Milton's Satan in an attempt to isolate and define what is distinctive and fruitful in the Old English poetic treatment of evil. 'The Fall of Man in *Genesis B* and the *Mystère d'Adam*' explores the presentation of Satan in Old English poetry, comparing the Old English poem with a twelfth-century Anglo-Norman play. Her concern is not with establishing a link between the two—which would merely be a scholarly curiosity—but to analyse what 'stimulated both writers to produce a work quite out of keeping with the literary style of their respective periods'. The exceptional quality of the two works is seen to reside in the two authors' compassion for Eve, who, unusually in medieval literature, is both sinful and sympathetic. Such a presentation is doctrinally tricky, but successful in literary terms.

Another early article, 'Doctrinal Influences in *The Dream of the Rood*', is also inspired by the remarkable literary quality of a work; Rosemary Woolf here makes a straight application of historical scholarship to one of the finest Old English poems, describing the background of contemporary religious thought in relation to the genesis of the poem. Crucially, the background material does not diminish or overload a literary appreciation. Rosemary Woolf acknowledges that 'the exigencies of a complex and rigid doctrine have provoked a magnificent response' which could 'never have been inspired by uncharted freedom', but does not suggest that the poem's 'meaning' can be simply elucidated by reference to the theological background.

In 'The Ideal of Men Dying with their Lord in the *Germania* and in *The Battle of Maldon*' Rosemary Woolf presents, as the culmination of a review of relevant texts in Old Norse, medieval Latin and Old English, a radical challenge to accepted views on *The Battle of Maldon*. She sees the much admired last stand of Byrhtnoth's retainers not as a final flourish of the Germanic 'heroic code' in English, but as a new and strange idea, perhaps borrowed from Old Norse literature. Her view has not been refuted, though it presents a challenge to conventional critical wisdom about the poem. Her short note 'The Lost Opening to the *Judith*' also confronted traditional views: she maintains that only a little of the Old English poem is missing. Part of her evidence is based on the conventions of numbering techniques in manuscripts, but, characteristically, a comparison of *Judith* with its biblical source illuminates the very different concerns of the Anglo-Saxon author, suggesting that the whole poem in Old English would have been short and dramatic, and would have dealt only with Judith's murder of Holofernes.

'*The Wanderer*, *The Seafarer* and the genre of *Planctus*', a close reading of the two most familiar Old English 'elegies', concerns what is perhaps the most difficult area for critics of Old English poetry: the relationship between Christian and secular heroic conventions and ethics apparently mingled in so much Old English literature. The piece on saints' lives—a comprehensive survey of the whole genre in Old English, with an account of its historical development as well as its artistic strengths and weaknesses—also concerns itself with the fundamental question of the balance between Christian and secular aims in literature, showing how Old English saints' lives could present martyrdom as a heroic conflict between good and evil, and miracles as 'propagandist evidence of God's power' which at the same time might serve the less pious interests of an audience and 'delight a taste for the marvellous', as the medieval romancer did.

Like her pieces on Old English literature, Rosemary Woolf's essays on the later period are concerned to describe the extent of doctrinal influence on literature, and to assess the degree of historical knowledge necessary for the reader to understand and appreciate it. Her essay 'The Effect of Typology on the English Medieval Plays of *Abraham and Isaac*' is a most convincing demonstration of the role played by 'extra-literary'—in this case doctrinal—matters in the genesis of the Mystery Plays. With reference both to exegetical sources and to the visual arts of the period, Rosemary Woolf maintains that Abraham's sacrifice would be familiar to a medieval audience as a type of the Crucifixion, and further that certain distinctive aspects of the Abraham and Isaac plays are the result of the dramatist's desire to highlight this typological relationship. This piece has perhaps been the most influential of all Rosemary Woolf's short works, for it is not only persuasive with regard to the particular plays under discussion, but also suggested ways of looking at whole cycles of Mystery Plays, ways which are now widely accepted.

Piers Plowman, with its high concentration of scriptural reference and quotation, and its shifting allegories and associations, has frequently been the object of the minute analyses of the Robertsonian school of exegetical criticism. However, in one of her two pieces on the poem, 'Some Non-Medieval Qualities of *Piers Plowman*', Rosemary Woolf deals with much more general and, equally, more fundamental concerns, attempting to define the peculiar nature of

Langland's allegorical method, and suggesting that it constitutes a new departure from the precise and sustained correspondences which distinguish conventional medieval allegory. She also deals with the difficult matter of the first person voice in medieval literature—a problem taken up subsequently by several critics. The status of the personal voice in a medieval work is also the concern of 'Chaucer as a Satirist in the General Prologue to the *Canterbury Tales*', an introduction to Chaucer's satirical methods which is notable for its clear distinction between Chaucer the acidly acute poet and Chaucer the innocently uncritical pilgrim; Rosemary Woolf correctly diagnosed the failure to be clear about this distinction as the weakness in so much early criticism of the Prologue. The conclusion of 'Some Non-Medieval Qualities of *Piers Plowman*' presents a stylistic analysis of part of a speech by Christ to the Devil towards the end of the poem. Rosemary Woolf notes the scriptural echoes in these lines, and refers in passing to her own article 'The Theme of Christ the Lover-Knight in Medieval English Poetry', a detailed account of the literary presentations of spiritual responses to the Crucifixion, drawing on lyrics, sermons, the *Ancrene Wisse*, and various Latin sources. But, writing of *Piers Plowman*, she freely acknowledges the limitations of her own methods, writing of the provision of scholarly background: 'The magnificence of the lines is scarcely illuminated by it.'

The other article on *Piers Plowman*, 'The Tearing of the Pardon', is by contrast an example of the usefulness of historical knowledge to illuminate a difficult literary crux—here, the controversial scene in which Piers receives what appears, and he expects, to be a pardon, which he tears up in anger. The article comprises an examination of the context of this scene, as a means of determining its significance and an investigation of what the term 'pardon' might have meant to a contemporary audience. The essay remains an important contribution to the continuing debate on the matter.

Rosemary Woolf's last article, 'Moral Chaucer and Kindly Gower', can be seen as a development of her short, introductory piece on Chaucer's satire, for in reversing Coleridge's and Arnold's characterization of Chaucer as 'kindly', and Chaucer's own description of Gower as 'moral', it refutes critical assumptions about Chaucer's sweetness and liberality in matters of morality. The essay is a revealing account of the two poets' attitudes towards sexual sin in their major works, and shows how Gower's compassion for his sinners can blur moral issues, while Chaucer's moral revulsion is expressed in 'a wholesome tone [which] enables the sin to stand out undisguised'. The piece is based on illustrations of how the two poets adapted their source materials to accommodate their responses towards sexual transgressions. The short essay 'In a Fryht as Y con fare Fremede' is a detailed analysis of one medieval love lyric which is identified as a pastourelle.

Rosemary Woolf's criticism, as well as being informed and authoritative, can also be pithy and light. Her articles are full of eminently quotable 'one-liners'—that *Piers Plowman* is 'insusceptible of illustration', for example. She makes frequent and telling reference to later literature, and often to less high-brow varieties, as when she writes drily but justly that 'nowadays anyone who likes the fantasies of science fiction or the highly conventional form of the detective story would [yet] be outraged by the saint's life'.

I

THE DEVIL IN OLD ENGLISH POETRY

THE view that the heroic convention was never satisfactorily adapted to Christian themes has become a commonplace in the critical theory of Old English poetry. It is moreover, a just opinion for, even when allowance has been made for a different and more receptive response from a ninth-century audience than from one of the present day, it must be admitted that the presentation of subject-matter from conflicting standpoints cannot at any date be entirely convincing. The heroic formulae were, however, usually merely decorative, for any more integral use of the old style would have resulted in deep-rooted incongruity; but, nevertheless, even this superficial usage is unsatisfactory: the apostles, for instance, even though they are the apostles of Apocryphal tradition, rather than of the New Testament, are ill at ease in their disguise of Germanic retainers, *Cristes þegnas*.

To this generalization the devil is an exception. Because of the characteristics already attributed to him by the Church Fathers, he had natural affinities with characters in both northern mythology and northern literature. Christ triumphant and his disciples and saints must have seemed foreign to a people whose ancestors had worshipped boastful, quarrelling gods, themselves doomed by fate to be destroyed. But there was a counterpart to the devil, not only in Loki of northern mythology, 'vársinna ok sessa Óðins ok ása', 'goða dólgr',[1] but also in certain characters native to Germanic literature: the devil's common role of tempter was paralleled in the part played by the wicked counsellor who incited his master to evil-doing; whilst by an almost metaphorical treatment the terms used of persons and situations derived from heroic society could be applied to Satan, for his disobedience to God had an intrinsic likeness to the revolt of a *þegn* from his lord, and his subsequent punishment of being an outcast from heaven was a fate of which the exile of a *þegn* from his natural place in his lord's hall might well appear the earthly shadow.

[1] *Skáldskaparmál*, 16. 'The evil companion and bench-mate of Oðin and the gods', 'the enemy of the gods'.

Now whilst there is no evidence that at any historical date the Anglo-Saxons knew of Loki,[2] the similarities between him and the devil are undoubtedly sufficiently marked to deserve comment; in fact, according to the investigations of Grimm, Loki was at one time popularly associated with the devil.[3] Moreover, in accordance with patristic tradition, the devil is generally identified with heathen gods in Old English poetry.[4] Idols are never mere wood and stone, but evil and deceitful objects, animated by the devil. In some points, too, Christian tradition about Satan and northern tradition about Loki coincided: Loki so enraged the gods by his evil deeds which culminated in the death of Baldr, that, after capturing him, they placed him in a cave, where he was to lie bound until *Ragnarøkr*, just as Satan, on the authority of Revelation XX. 2, and elsewhere, was said to lie bound in hell, until he should be loosed before the Day of Judgement. Loki, moreover, like many of the Norse gods and heroes who were shape-shifters, could alter his appearance, as, for instance, when he transforms himself into a mare in order to lure away the giant's horse Svaðilfari: and so in *Solomon and Saturn* the devil appears as a bird, dragon, and wolf, the latter two derived no doubt respectively from the dragon of Revelation and the wolf of the parable; in *Guþlac* the devils assailing the saint turn themselves into human and serpent shape,[5] whilst in *Juliana* and, presumably, in *Genesis B*,[6] the devil disguises himself as an angel of light in order to make his temptation more convincing, a hypocritical device, to which Eve through credulity succumbs, whereas Juliana's faith is so strong that she remains undeceived and unshaken by the insinuating persuasiveness of her temper. This power of self-transformation is

[2] The total absence of reference to heathen gods by proper names in Old English literature makes it impossible to determine clearly what mythological figures were known to the Anglo-Saxons, or had been worshipped by them. That some tradition remained seems certain from the mention of the *feðerhama* [feather-covering] and *hæleðhelm* [a helmet which makes its wearer invisible], which must be of mythological origin. It is beyond the scope of this essay, however, to pursue mythological speculation. I intend only to point out interesting resemblances between Loki and the devil, without insisting on any actual influence.

[3] Grimm, *Teutonic Mythology*, trans. J. S. Stallybrass (London, 1882–8), xii.

[4] Cf. F. Klaeber, 'Die christlichen Elemente im Beowulf', *Anglia*, xxxv (1912), 249.

[5] *Guþlac*, 907 ff. In the *Vita S. Guthlaci* of Felix, from which Guþlac II is almost certainly derived, the devils transform themselves into many terrifying animal shapes, a lion, a bear, a bull, etc.

[6] The poet is apparently following two different traditions here. In l. 491 the devil 'wearþ hine þa on wyrmes lic' [changed himself into the shape of a serpent], whereas at ll. 656 f. Eve refers to him as 'þes boda sciene, / godes engel god' [this bright messenger, / good angel of god]. This confusion occurs also in the *Apocalypse of Moses*.

therefore common to both mythology and Christian belief, although the angel-of-light disguise is of specifically Christian origin, as it appears, for instance, in the *Vita Adae et Evae* and the *Apocalypse of Moses*, and is stated as a doctrine with biblical support by Gregory I in his *Moralia* (Lib. xxix, Cap. xxx): 'Transfigurat enim se velut angelum lucis (ii. Cor. xi, 14), et callida deceptionis ante plerumque proponit laudabilia, ut ad illicita pertrahat' ['He transfigures himself into an angel of light, and puts forth before the multitude clever praising pieces of deception, so as to lead to ill-doing'].

The devil in Old English poetry is twice referred to as the hobbler.[7] Loki himself was not lame, but the semi-divine smith Weland was, possibly because a man, strong but crippled in the leg, would be likely to take up the occupation of a smith, or possibly because he had been hamstrung in order to prevent his escape from bondage. The devil's lameness, however, was more probably caused by his fall from heaven, just as was Hephæstus', who had been 'thrown by angry Jove / Sheer o'er the crystal battlements'. Fable told how he had alighted on the island of Lemnos, but Milton, preserving the orthodox identification of heathen gods with devils, maintained that he had dropped long before with Satan to hell.

There are two pieces of mythological property associated with the devil, which seem to have no origin in Christian history or legend: a *feðerhama*[8] and a helmet of invisibility.[9] The former has been compared to the *fjaðrhamr* of Weland, by Mr. Timmer, who claims that the poet 'has given some of the features [of the Weland story] to Satan's helper'.[10] But the only other resemblance stated is the motive of vengeance. Now although, in the *Þiðrikssaga af Bern*,[11] the *fjaðrhamr* is used by Weland to accomplish his mission of revenge, in the *Vǫlundarkviða*[12] it is probably used instead for his escape: furthermore, the types of vengeance are quite dissimilar: Weland's on Niðhad is of a real and terrible kind, whilst the devil's, directed at man, is only a malicious pin-prick at the Almighty. The resemblance to Loki is in fact much more marked. Detachable wings or shoes

[7] *Hellehinca, Andreas*, 1171; *adloma, Guþlac*, 912. Both words have been disputed. But the difficulty of supplying plausible emendations together with their mutual corroboration seems sufficient to substantiate them.

[8] *Genesis B*, 417.

[9] *Hæleðhelm, Genesis B*, 444; *heoloþhelm, The Whale*, 45.

[10] *The Later Genesis*, ed. B. J. Timmer (Oxford, 1948), note to l. 417.

[11] Chs. 57–90. This is a later version of the Weland story.

[12] Cf. *Die Edda*, ed. R. C. Boer (Haarlem, 1922), note to the *Vǫlundarkviða*, stanza 27.

were, of course, common features of both Germanic and classical myth; in the latter there were the winged shoes of Hermes, and the wings of Icarus, although these were not made of feathers; whilst in the former, there was the *fjaðrhamr* of Freyja lent, at Þorr's request, to Loki in order that he might journey to Jǫtunheim to recover the hammer Mjollnir; and Loki also possessed shoes which enabled him to fly through the air. The *hæleðhelm*, though clearly of mythological origin, is not associated with Loki. It is, however, reminiscent of Pluto's helmet, forged by the Cyclops, and, in Germanic mythology, of the *tarnkappe* won by Siegfried from the dwarf Alberich in the *Niebelungenlied*,[13] and of the head-covering used by the elves for the same purpose of rendering the wearer invisible.

Yet too much stress must not be laid on these mythological trimmings; it is not, for instance, the fact that both Loki and the devil make use of a *feðerhama* which is chiefly interesting, but a more fundamental similarity. That is, on broad grounds, that Loki too is the 'foe of the gods', in other words Satan (derived from the Hebrew for 'adversary'), *Godes andsaca*, he who is to lead the forces of evil at the end of the world, whilst, more specifically, it is that he also delighted in giving evil advice for evil's sake. When the gods, according to Snorri, asked each other in their consultation who had advised them to make their disastrous bargain with the *jǫtunn*, whereby they were in danger of losing Freyja, and with her the sun and moon, 'en þat kom ásamt með ǫllum, at þessu myndi ráðit hafa sá er flestu illa ræðr, Loki Laufeyjarson'.[14]

But Loki was not the only person *sá er flestu illa ræðr* in Germanic story. There were human beings of this type too: Bikki,[15] Sibeck,[16] and Bolviss,[17] and in Old English literature probably Unferð. Attempts have, of course, been made to clear Unferð's name from the charge of malicious scheming at the Danish court, but these attempts at whitewashing do not convince. Unferð's ambiguous position at Heorot, his former fratricide, and his significant association with prophetic references to later treachery in the Scylding dynasty, together suggests overwhelmingly that, in some version of the story of Hroðgar and Hroðulf, Unferð took the same part as did Bikki at the

[13] *Aventiure*, iii. 97, and ibid. vi. 337.

[14] *Gylfaginning*, ch. xlii: 'And they all agreed that he must have advised this, who gives most evil counsels, Loki Laufeyjarson.'

[15] *Vǫlsunga Saga*, ch. xli.

[16] *Þiðrikssaga af Bern*. The name in its Old English form, Sifeca, appears in *Widsiþ*, 116.

court of Eormenric. For the purpose of comparison with the devil, however, the behaviour of Unferð is too hypothetical, and it is better therefore to make use of the most famous of all Germanic wicked counsellors, Bikki, whose history was almost certainly known to the Anglo-Saxons, for they knew of the evil deeds of his master Eormenric, as both *Beowulf*[18] and *Widsiþ*[19] testify, and they knew his name, for it appears in place-names, such as Biccanhlew, Biccanpol, and others.

The devil is clearly the counterpart to, or rather the archetype of, those who, to quote Coleridge's well-known comment on Iago, act out of 'motiveless malignity', who commit, according to common belief, the sin against the Holy Ghost which will not be forgiven. It is therefore possible to trace parallels between their courses of behaviour. Bikki is notorious for the evil advice which he gave to Randver, son of Eormenric, that he should take Swanhild, his father's destined bride, for himself, and for his evil advice to Eormenric that he should have Swanhild trampled to death by wild horses; whilst, according to the author of the *Vǫlsunga Saga*, this latter incitement to a brutal vengeance was only the worst of many bad counsels, for *marg ill ráð hafdi hann honum áðr kennt.*[20] In the same way Satan is remembered for his disastrous advice to Eve, but is also portrayed in Old English poetry as the constant giver of bad advice. His evil suggestions range from the encouraging of men drunk with beer to renew old grudges[21] to the occasion when he

> forlærde ligesearwum, leode fortyhte,
> Iudea cyn, þæt hie god sylfne
> ahengon, herga fruman.[22]

Both the devil and Bikki show an equal resourcefulness when their immediate plans go astray. Thus when the wild horses will not harm Swanhild because of her beauty, before Eormenric can intervene, Bikki swiftly devises the method of covering her face; whilst in the same way, when the first method of killing Juliana has failed, the devil, before Heliseus has time to relent or fear the angelic intervention, advises him to try again to put the saint to death, this

[17] Saxo Grammaticus, *Gesta Danorum*, bk. vii.
[18] l. 1201.
[19] l. 88, etc.
[20] *Vǫlsunga Saga*, ch. xlii: 'Many evil counsels had he given him previously'.
[21] *Juliana*, 483 ff.
[22] *Elene*, 208 ff. 'Seduced with wiles, led astray the people, the race of the Jews, so that they crucified God himself, creator of armies.'

time by means of burning oil.

It is interesting to notice how Bikki's love of evil for its own sake puzzled later writers. In Saxo's version of the story, therefore, Bikki is given a motive, although it is briefly and unconvincingly stated.[23] It is, moreover, generally agreed that the incident alluded to, the slaying of Bikki's brothers by Eormenric, is a later addition to the story, a mere repetition of Eormenric's other crimes, such as the slaying of his nephews the Harlungs: whilst, according to Chambers, the enmity between Eormenric and Bikki, who is said to be the son of the Livonian king, reflects racial quarrels of a later age.[24] The same effort to rationalize this type of evil-doing may be seen again in the medieval treatment of Judas. Unable to accept the Gospel narrative, which assigns to Judas no motive for his betrayal of Christ, except, by implication, an evil delight in betraying for evil's sake, for 'Satan had entered into him', men of the Middle Ages found in John xii. 3–6[25] the basis of an explanation, which was apparently popular and is to be found, for instance, in the thirteenth-century ballad of Judas and in the York Mystery plays, that Judas as bearer of the moneybag felt himself cheated over what seemed to him the waste of the pot of precious ointment, since this might have been sold for 300 pieces of silver, of which he could rightfully have claimed a tithe; hence his willingness to sell Christ for thirty pieces of silver: a trivial excuse, but one which would leave him with some shred of motive. In the same tradition of villainy, Iago in his soliloquies makes an ineffectual attempt through his pretended jealousy of Othello to justify his logically motiveless actions to himself, and Bradley, unable to accept this diabolical state of mind, labours to find some rationality in him.

The character of the devil is precisely similar. At the beginning, before he has been damned for innumerable centuries, he deludes himself, as in *Genesis B*, that he will be happier if he can bring about the downfall of man, but in the poems which describe him after the coming of Christ, that is in the second period defined by Gregory I,[26]

[23] *Gesta Danorum*, bk. viii.

[24] *Widsith*, ed. R. W. Chambers (Cambridge, 1912), p. 20.

[25] Maria ergo accepit libram unguenti nardi pistici pretiosi, et unxit pedes Jesu, et extersit pedes ejus capillis suis; et domus impleta est ex odore unguenti. Dixit ergo unus ex discipulis ejus, Judas Iscariotes, qui erat eum traditurus: Quare hoc unguentum non veniit trecentis denariis, et datum est egenis? Dixit autem hoc, non quia de egenis pertinebat ad eum, sed quia fur erat, et loculos habens, ea quae mittebantur, portabat. (*Biblia Sacra Vulgatae Editionis.*)

[26] Gregory I had classified the devil's life into three periods. For a detailed study of this see C. Abbetmeyer, *Old English Poetical Motives derived from the Doctrine of Sin* (Minneapolis, 1903).

no justification for his actions is suggested. The devil tempts because it is his nature to tempt. There is no possibility of any relief from torment, any more than for Marlowe's Mephistopheles or Milton's Satan, for *'fyr biþ ymbutan / on æghwilcum, þæh he uppe seo'*,[27] in other words, whichever way he flies, he carries hell-fire with him.

From the human point of view, then, Satan is the wicked counsellor, a supernatural manifestation of a type of evil-doer, already familiar to the Anglo-Saxons. But from the divine point of view he is the rebel and outcast or, by an almost inevitable form of imagery, the faithless retainer and eternal exile. It has already been pointed out how superficial and unsatisfactory is the treatment of the apostles as retainers of the Lord: from one aspect alone are they *milites Christi* [soldiers of Christ]. The application of the heroic code to the devil in *Genesis B*, however, is extremely interesting because it is integral. The Anglo-Saxons were, of course, familiar with the Augustinian doctrine that the devil had fallen through pride, the *engles oferhygd*,[28] and yet pride was a prominent characteristic of Germanic heroes: not the pride of Guþlac, over which the fiends taunt him, which depends upon a complete reliance on God, but the pride of Beowulf who *strenge getruwode, / mundgripe mægenes*,[29] and who, despite a pious acknowledgement of God's assistance, would scarcely have been content to ascribe to him the glory of his victories.[30] This poetic dilemma is solved in *Genesis B* by the use of the lord-retainer relationship with reference to God and Satan. The Anglo-Saxons clearly had quite as rigid a conception of a hierarchic system as had the Elizabethans, but whereas in the sixteenth century, under the influence of the Neoplatonists who had spread the Aristotelian idea of a universal order, a chain of being was imagined which stretched 'from the foot of God's throne to the meanest of inanimate objects',[31] in Anglo-Saxon times it was not extended above or below human society, and the idea could therefore only be applied to the supernatural world by analogy. In other words, whilst

[27] *Christ and Satan*, 263 f. 'There is fire surrounding every person, though he may be on high.'

[28] *Genesis B*, 328. Dr Sisam in 'Notes on Old English Poetry', *R.E.S.*, xx (1946), 257 f. has suggested that *engles* should be emended to *egle*. I quote here, however, from the manuscript as its reading is by no means inadmissible.

[29] ll. 1533 ff. 'trusted in his strength, in his powerful hand grip'.

[30] Cf. *Beowulf*, 1384 ff. It might be argued, however, that at ll. 1657 ff. Beowulf acknowledges assistance from God. But such a passage as this seems out of keeping with the general tone of the poem, and anyway does not contradict the fact that Beowulf was, in the word of the dirge, *lofgeornost* [most eager for renown].

[31] E. M. W. Tillyard, *The Elizabethan World Picture* (London, 1943), ch. iv, p. 25.

Milton could depend upon his readers recognizing Satan's rebellion as a violation of the natural order, an Anglo-Saxon poet could only arouse this comprehension in his audience by the use of imagery drawn from contemporary society.

The Anglo-Saxon emphasis on a fixed and ordered relationship may be seen in *Beowulf* itself. Beowulf after his fight with Grendel was already great enough to bring to the minstrel's mind a famous hero such as Sigemund, and by his complete cleansing of Heorot, he won for himself measureless fame. Were a man's social honour to depend only on personal achievements, there would be no need or point for Beowulf's payment to Hygelac of such elaborate homage on his return home to the land of the Geatas. When he professes Hygelac to be his superior, this sentiment must spring from a courteous acknowledgement that, although he has achieved braver deeds than Hygelac, the King is rightfully his lord. Now the use of the lord-retainer relationship in *Genesis B* enables the poet to show that Satan's pride is illegitimate. His rebellion is based on two mistakes: firstly that he *mæg swa fela wundra gewyrcean* [is able to perform as many miracles][32] as God, which is an error of fact; and secondly that, even if he could, he would therefore be equal with God, a proposition of which the comparison with *Beowulf* exposes the falseness and absurdity.

This distinction between legitimate and illegitimate pride may be further illustrated by a comparison with the *Battle of Maldon*. The epithet *ofermod* is used of both Satan and Byrhtnoþ, but whereas this excessive pride in Satan is the greatest of sins, in Byrhtnoþ it is shown as a 'last infirmity of noble mind'. The reason for this is again that Satan's pride violates the natural order, being therefore at once evil and preposterous:

ne meahte he æt his hige findan
þæt he gode wolde geongerdome
þeodne þeowian.[33]

How different is this from Byrhtnoþ, whose allegiance to King Æþelred is twice mentioned, once when Byrhtnoþ refers to Æþelred as his *ealdor* [lord], and the other time when the phrase *Æþelredes þegn* is used as a synonym for him. The result of Byrhtnoþ's pride is therefore neither evil nor unreasonable, but a splendid and generous

[32] *Genesis B*, 279 f.

[33] Ibid. 266 ff. 'he could not find it in his heart to serve the Lord with good allegiance.'

gesture, though, from the point of view of practical strategy, misguided. His granting of permission to the Vikings to cross the ford is of the same kind as Beowulf's refusal to fight Grendel with weapons: they both spring from an unwillingness to profit from an advantage over the enemy gained by fortunate circumstances, not by personal achievement. That the outcome of Byrhtnoþ's decision was less happy than Beowulf's is, from the moral aspect, irrelevant.

It is ironical that Satan, in *Genesis B*, who had denied the proper *þegnscipe* to God, yet expects from his followers in hell the loyal service in return for previous generosity which it was the duty of men in the meadhall to give to their lord. This appeal to a code of behaviour does not, however, long survive the Fall. Despite Satan's optimistic promise to his messenger, in *Genesis B*, there is nothing of value in hell to be given, all that he can dispense is evil, and he therefore becomes *morþres brytta* [dispenser of torment], not the familiar *sinces brytta* [dispenser of treasure]. The miserable devil in *Juliana* is only slightly less terrified of his *fæder* in hell than he is of the saint himself. The clear implication is that punishment in hell is not restricted to men who have failed to satisfy God, but is also inflicted on devils who have failed to satisfy Satan. The leader of the devils had not acted in such a way that, after the passage of years, loyal companions would still voluntarily stand by him.

The devil by his own sin had put himself into the position of a faithless retainer, and his punishment is therefore that of a faithless retainer: the deprivation of a lord and a meadhall. He is by his own actions self-condemned to be eternally *hlafordleas* [lordless]. That is why the devil in Old English poetry, with the exception of Satan in *Genesis B*, who is still flushed with the exhilaration of defiance, is always miserable, skulking wretchedly round the outskirts of the world. *Fah ond freondleas* [marked and friendless], he is doomed perpetually to *wadan wræclastas* [tread the paths of exile]. The last lines of the fiend's lament in *Christ and Satan* sum up his position:

sceal nu wreclastas
settan sorhgcearig, siðas wide.[34]

Although the Wanderer never stoops to the whining self-pity of the devil in some Old English poetry, there is yet in the speeches of both the Wanderer and the devil the same weariness and abandonment of

[34] *Christ and Satan*, 187 f. 'I must now, sorrowful, lay down the paths of exile, wide journeys.'

hope, the same yearning for what has been lost for ever.[35] The resemblance is carried a step further by the frequent description of heaven in terms of the meadhall. There was, of course, some biblical authority for this conception and for the language used. The *beorhte burhweallas* [bright city walls],[36] for instance, might so well belong either to Heorot or the New Jerusalem. The idea of life in heaven as a banquet, the *symbel* of the *Dream of the Rood*, may owe something to the parable of the marriage of the king's son, whilst the traditional association of harps and singing with celestial rejoicing might easily recall the minstrelsy at great feasts. But such a phrase as *wloncra winsele* [wine hall of the proud][37] seems rather to suggest a Germanic hall, or even Valhǫll, where the *einherjar*, the chosen heroes of the dead, feasted until the time of their last fight in support of Oðin.

The symbolical portrayal of heaven as a meadhall, the place where the greatest of men received the best of entertainment, does not then require any explanation. But in view of the customary association of a hall with happiness and rejoicing, it is somewhat surprising to find that this idea is also sometimes applied to hell. Apart from passages in such poems as the *Phoenix*, strongly influenced by Latin thought, heaven is never clearly described in religious terms. The description of hell, however, is usually orthodox: it is a place of darkness (this primitive, mythological, and biblical equation of light = goodness, darkness = evil is very pronounced in Old English poetry) and of flames, which, in the same tradition as Milton was later to follow, are *sweart* [black] and do not illuminate the blackness around; heat and cold alternate to increase the torment of the damned, and the place is infested with *wurmas*, sometimes used to mean snakes and sometimes worms, either the undying worm of Isaiah, or from contemporary graveyards, for such poems as the *Soul and Body* show that the Old English poets were as much horrified by the idea of bodily corruption as Donne or Webster. In contrast to this type of description, the customs of the meadhall are twice used with reference to hell: once in *Genesis B*, where its ironic force has already been noted, and once in *Juliana*,[38] where after the statement of the fact that Heliseus and his

[35] Despite the poet's comment on the Wanderer's attitude in the first line of the poem, and also, perhaps, in the concluding lines, there is nothing in the Wanderer's monologue to suggest that he hoped for or expected any relief from his distress through the benevolence of God.

[36] *Christ and Satan*, 294.

[37] Ibid. 93.

[38] ll. 683 ff.

followers were drowned and went to hell, the poet adds the curious comment that there, on the benches of the winehall, the men would have no need to look for gold rings from their lord: a typical example of Old English litotes, but unexpected and grimly incongruous in its place.

There is yet one aspect of the relationship between Satan and man, interpreted in the light of Germanic thought, which is so far unmentioned, because the evidence for it is by no means as certain and widespread as it is for the others. It is the aspect in which the devil is seen as the bringer of evil, one which is emphasized, for instance, in the confession of the devil to Juliana, in which he enumerates to the saint all the disasters which he has brought about—in particular, deaths by drowning, burning, and crucifixion;[39] and these were not caused by the incitement of human beings to wrong-doing, but by direct supernatural intervention. The precise theological doctrine behind this is not made clear, but it might be suggested that it sprang from a belief in a divine permission to the devil to afflict the good, such as was granted to Satan when he tormented Job, and in a divine commission of the evil into the hands of Satan. But although this may be logically deduced, from the literary point of view Satan is simply one who has power to bring misfortune to mankind. This is probably the reason for the surprising identification, found twice, of the devil with *wyrd*. So startling at first sight does it seem, that, were it not that this identification is incontrovertible in *Solomon and Saturn*,[40] and that good sense and the laws of syntax undoubtedly demand it in the *Andreas*,[41] its acceptance might still be disputed.

But *wyrd* in Old English poetry is also shown as the bringer of disaster; not with any regularity, for it was naturally in conflict with the philosophical reconciliation, which had been made between the new theological system and the old pagan concept of fate, whereby *wyrd* was defined as the active, pre-ordaining will of God. Such a formulation is given by Alfred in his translation of the *De Consolatione Philosophiae* of Boethius:

[39] *Juliana*, 468 ff.

[40] 434 ff.

[41]
Deofles larum
hæleð hynfuse hyrdon to georne,
wraðum wærlogan. Hie seo wyrd beswac,
forleolc ond forlærde. (611 ff.)

Mr Timmer in his article '*Wyrd* in Anglo-Saxon Prose and Poetry', *Neophilologus*, xxvi (1941), by only quoting the second half of the passage, ignores the necessary relationship of the whole.

Ac ðæt ðætte we hatað Godes foreðonc ond his foresceawung, þæt bið þa hwile þe hit ðær mid him bið on his mode, ærðæm þe hit gefremed weorðe. þa hwile ðe hit geþoht bið; ac siððan hit fullfremed bið, þonne hatað we hit wyrd[42]

and an identification is sometimes found in poetry; in the *Andreas* itself, for example in a passage which appears to be a deliberate reminiscence of the now famous lines in *Beowulf*,[43] the poet, using *god* instead of *wyrd*, as the author of the former poem had done, writes:

Forþan ic eow to soðe secgan wille,
þæt næfre forlæteð lifgende god
eorl on eorðan, gif his ellen deah.[44]

This logical compromise, however, was comparatively rare. Because of the poetical fluctuations between Christian belief and the heathen, heroic ways of thought, *wyrd*, which in Norse mythology had brought about the downfall and death of the gods, more often in Old English poetry was still shown as a power which afflicted the world. In *Beowulf*, for example, it is *wyrd* who has swept off so many of Hroðgar's band into Grendel's power, *wyrd* who carried off Hygelac when he fought the Frisians, *wyrd* who had deprived Beowulf of his kinsmen. The philosophical inconsistency, however, and the erratic treatment of *wyrd* make this adoption of the devil yet farther into the pre-Christian Germanic system far less happy than the other methods already noticed. It is deserving of interest but not of praise.

For the ease with which the devil was fitted into already existing tradition there remains one final, but important, reason, which is of a different kind from these identifications based on fundamental resemblances. This reason may provide the solution to the question of why *Genesis B* is a remarkable exception to the almost general mediocre standard of extant religious poetry in Old English.[45] The weakness in this verse seems to spring from the fact that the Germanic

[42] 'But we call that God's foresight and his providence while it is there with him in his mind, before it is brought to pass; as long as it is thought. But after it has been accomplished, then we call it *wyrd*.' Ch. xxxix. The Latin reads: 'Qui modus cum in ipsa divinae intellegentiae puritate conspicitur, providentia nominatur; cum vero ad ea, quae movet atque disponit, refertur, fatum a veteribus appellatum est.'

[43] ll. 572 f.

[44] *Andreas*, 458 ff. 'And so I will tell you truly, that the living God will never forsake a man on earth, if his courage is good.'

[45] This generalization does not, of course, apply to the *Dream of the Rood*. But the devotional tone and the absence of explicit heroic formulae exclude its consideration from the scope of this essay.

inspiration was essentially tragic, whilst Christianity left little room for tragedy: there could be no final sadness, as Professor Una Ellis-Fermor has pointed out with reference to later drama,[46] in a scheme of things where tribulation was restricted to this world, and was not worthy to be compared with the joys of the next: in other words, there was no longer room for the great type figure of the hero defiant in defeat, defeat that was eternal and absolute. But there yet remained one exception: the devil could still be the first and greatest tragic figure, not for the simple medieval reason which makes his story head the Monk's list of tragedies, but because for him, as well of course as for the damned, there could be no remission of unhappiness. He could be viewed against the background of eternity as well as of time and yet arouse that sense of pity which is an essential element of tragedy: a sense of pity, which is not theologically justified, but which human sensibility stirred by great art cannot withhold from Dr Faustus, Macbeth, and others who share the plight of Satan.

Therefore, whilst bearing in mind the simple possibility that *Genesis B* is better than the works of the Cædmonian and Cynewulfian schools because his author[47] was a greater poet than Cynewulf and these other nameless writers, one may still suggest that part of the explanation may plausibly be that the subject was more manageable. Satan, of course, degenerated, passed into the second phase defined by Gregory, and could no longer be a powerful central figure. But, immediately after his fall his situation and behaviour, as recounted by the Fathers, gave scope for a typically Old English treatment, for his situation was hopeless, but his courage remained. This situation was exploited in *Genesis B*, not to the full, of course—it remained for Milton to express, though no doubt unconsciously, the old heroic position from the mouth of Satan, with his 'unconquerable will' and 'courage never to submit or yield'—but, considering the apparent lack of precedent for this new blending, with extraordinary skill.

By the above approach it may be possible to discover subtleties undreamed of by the poet. Frequently, it may be argued, some heroic

[46] *The Frontiers of Drama* (London, 1946), pp. 146 f. Professor Ellis-Fermor does not, however, recognize characters such as Dr Faustus as tragic heroes.

[47] Whether the merit is to be ascribed to the Old Saxon or Old English poet is irrelevant to this point. It would be difficult to prove that the exploitation of this situation in *Genesis B* is of a specifically Old Saxon character. The use of the lord–retainer relationship is found, though not so fully developed, elsewhere, e.g. *Elene*, 766, *he þinum wiðsoc aldordome*.

phrase may be used of the devil because it was a familiar fragment of the common poetic stock, or some heroic word may be used because it was convenient for the alliteration. But this does not affect the general proposition that the heroic formulae, when applied to Christ and his apostles and saints, always remained separate from the fundamental conception, whereas, when applied to the devil, they became fused with the Christian idea and produced a deeper meaning. That this felicitous method may have been used by a conventional habit and not by deliberate poetic purpose need in no way invalidate an appreciation of its result.

II

THE FALL OF MAN IN *GENESIS B* AND THE *MYSTÈRE D'ADAM*

THERE can be no doubt that for his description of the temptation of Adam and Eve the Old Saxon author of *Genesis B* used a source. Short of the discovery of this source any remarks about the author's treatment of his subject necessarily remain tentative and inconclusive, but it may be possible to examine the problem and its implications more clearly than has hitherto been done. The most obvious and startling point about the work is that the author approaches his subject from the pyschological rather than from the dogmatic point of view. He does not present his material with a literal fidelity to the biblical narrative, nor does he use a dogmatic emphasis which would recall either of the two traditional theological antitheses, that between Eve and the Blessed Virgin[1] or that between the nature of Eve's temptation and that of Christ in the wilderness.[2] He is on the contrary chiefly interested in the realistic question of how it came about that Adam and Eve were persuaded to break the commandment of God. This concern with psychological realism not only divides the author's attitude from that of the Fathers in their exegesis, but also distinguishes his style of characterization from that of Old English poets—whatever their subject—from that of the Old Saxon writer of the *Heliand*, and from nearly all who composed literary treatments of the Fall, including the Hexaemeral poets[3] and the authors of the mediaeval mystery plays.

To the last item of this vast generalization there is, however, one exception—the twelfth century Anglo-Norman play the *Mystère*

[1] For quotations illustrating this see T. Livius, *The Blessed Virgin in the Fathers of the First Six Centuries* (London, 1893), pp. 35–39.

[2] This patristic idea has been examined with reference to Milton by E. M. Pope, *Paradise Regained and the Tradition of the Poem* (Baltimore, 1947).

[3] The most independent treatment of the Fall is that of Avitus in the *De originali peccato* (*Monumenta Germaniae Historica*, VI, Pt. 2, Berlin, 1883, 212–223), which Sievers postulated as a source. In this there is a fairly elaborate treatment of the Fall, in which Eve is praised for her beauty and nobility. The content, however, is inextricable from the dignity of the epic, Virgilian style, which makes it far more probably a source for *Paradise Lost* rather than for *Genesis B*.

d'Adam,[4] which is quite as startling for its own period as is *Genesis B*, for it shares with the earlier work both its psychological preoccupation and also the most curious features of its plot. The works in fact have in common the two most striking deviations from the Book of Genesis, namely, that Adam is tempted first and resists, and that the devil is not in the form of a serpent, but either in his own shape or disguised as an angel of light; both of these, as we shall see, are closely related to the pyschological development of the story. It is, however, inconceivable that either writer would have invented these points, which bear the mark of the apocryphal imagination of the East, and therefore it would seem that both are indebted to a common source, unless one would prefer to hold that the Anglo-Norman author had read *Genesis B*. The latter is by no means so wild a theory as it may at first sound, for the *Mystère d'Adam* is assigned by French scholars precisely to the few decades in the twelfth century in which there surely lived some English-born monks who wrote in French but could still understand Anglo-Saxon. But without any certainty of where the Cædmon Manuscript was in the twelfth century, though it may well have been at Winchester or Canterbury,[5] and without any knowledge of the identity of the author of the *Mystère d'Adam*, there is too much evidence missing for any conjecture to be made, and the general impression made by the works is that they are related by a common source rather than by the direct influence of one on the other. Whilst the question of direct influence is a fascinating one from the historical point of view, in terms of literary criticism it, in fact, makes little difference whether the works are immediately related or only indebted to a common source, for the interesting point here is how the apocryphal legend stimulated both writers to produce a work quite out of keeping with the literary style of their respective periods.

Unfortunately the psychological subtlety of the author of *Genesis B* has been obscured by the common assumption of modern critics that Eve in this poem was unfairly deceived and utterly blameless. This view is epitomized by Gurteen's description of Eve as 'the prototype of true Womanhood, selfless and self-sacrificing,'[6] but

[4] The edition referred to is that of P. Studer (Manchester, 1949). Most scholars agree that the play is the work of an Anglo-Norman poet, and there seems to be no reason for insisting that the Anglo-Norman forms are due to a scribe, other than a reluctance to admit its English origin. The work, however, would be equally exceptional whether it was written in France or England.

[5] On this see *The Cædmon Manuscript*, with an introduction by Israel Gollancz (London, 1927), pp. xxxvi–xxxvii.

[6] S. H. Gurteen, *The Epic of the Fall of Man* (New York and London, 1896), p. 216.

Ker's view that Adam and Eve were deceived[7] and Sievers' belief that Eve acted entirely out of loyalty to Adam,[8] are in a sense only cooler versions of this Victorian judgment. The fallacy behind such opinions is perhaps clearest in Ker's comment which largely begs the question, for no theologian would have denied that Eve believed the devil's words, but from this he would move on to investigate the motives which led to this clouding of her reason. A passage from Hugh of St. Victor's *De Sacramentis* can be used to clarify the nature of the problem: he is answering the question 'Quare diabolus in forma aliena venit' [Why did the devil not come in his own shape?]:

> Ne autem fraus illius omnino nulla esset, si nimis manifestaretur, in propria forma venire non debuit, ne manifeste cognosceretur, et nullatenus reciperetur. Iterum ne nimis violenta esset ejus fraus si prorsus occultaretur et homo simul (si Deus eum tali fraude quæ caveri non posset decipi permitteret) injuriam pati videretur, in aliena quidem forma venire permissus est, sed tali in qua ejus malitia prorsus non celaretur.[9]

Hugh of St. Victor was of course writing several centuries later than the author of *Genesis B*, and he is here concerned only with the question of the propriety of Satan's assumption of a serpent form, but his analysis pinpoints the problem of *Genesis B*, namely whether or not the devil's disguise was impenetrable. In a discussion of this there are three relevant points: the devil's disguise as an angel of light, his approach to Adam first, and the content of his tempting speeches. In all of these there are analogies between *Genesis B* and the *Mystère d'Adam*, and reference to the latter—in which the question of Eve's innocence does not arise—can serve to illuminate the treatment of the Fall in the Anglo-Saxon poem.

Both works demand that the main diabolical speeches should not be spoken through the mouth of the serpent: in *Genesis B* the devil is explicitly said to be disguised as an angel of light, whilst in the *Mystère d'Adam* he must be in some form which prevents immediate

[7] W. P. Ker, *The Dark Ages* (London, 1955), p. 259.

[8] E. Sievers, *Der Heliand und die angelsächsische Genesis* (Halle, 1875), p. 22. This view has been repeated by the mos recent editor of the poem, B. J. Timmer, *The Later Genesis* (Oxford, 1948), p. 58.

[9] *De Sacramentis*, VII, c. 2; *P.L.*, CLXXVI, col. 287. 'But lest his deception should be completely wrecked by his appearing too openly, he must not come in his own shape, lest he should be clearly recognized and not admitted at all. On the other hand, lest his deception were too thorough, if he were completely disguised, so that man would seem to suffer an injustice (if God allowed him to be deceived by a fraud of a kind against which he could not guard himself), the devil was allowed to come in a shape not his own, but such that his malice would not be entirely concealed.'

recognition of him. In both works, however, there is some inconsistency of treatment, as though the respective authors were uneasy at so startling a contradiction of biblical authority.[10] In *Genesis B*, when he first arrived in Paradise, the devil 'Wearp hine þa on wyrmes lice' [changed himself into the shape of a serpent], but the speech (addressed to Adam) which follows could not aptly be spoken by a serpent, for the devil claims that he is God's angel come from afar and that only recently he had been seated by God's throne. Adam's reply, in which he exclaims at the climax, 'þu gelic ne bist / ænegum his engla þe ic ær geseah' [you are not like any of his angels I have seen before], must be interpreted in the light of the devil's report to Eve in which he says that Adam denied that he was *godes engel*, adding later in self-defence, 'Ne eom ic deofle gelic' [I am not like the devil]. Throughout the speeches the issue is whether or not the tempter is angel or devil, there is no possibility of his being a serpent. But after the main temptation scene is over, there is a description in third person narrative of Eve's reactions and here she is said to be moved by the *wyrmes geþeaht* [serpent's advice]. Finally Eve in her persuasive speech to Adam refers to the devil as 'þes boda sciene, godes engel god' [this bright messenger, God's good angel]. It is obvious from this simple summary that the poet in his commentary imagines the devil in the orthodox way, but that in the actual dramatic speeches he follows a source which requires that the tempter be disguised as an angel of light. It may be noted in addition that this was how the eleventh century illuminator understood the work. In his first illustration of the Fall (f. 20v), a serpent is shown wound about the tree, whilst Eve holds her head in an attitude of listening close to his open mouth. On ff. 24v, 28v, and 31r, however, the tempter has become a handsome figure with magnificent wings, and clothed in drapery with the jagged fluttering edges typical of the Canterbury school, and on 24v he even wears a crown. On his return to hell (31r and 36v), however, the devil's hair has become serpentine and the dignified drapery has gone. The treatment in these illustrations of the

[10] It may be noted that the same kind of confusion occurs in the *Apocalypsis Mosis* (ed. C. Tischendorf, *Apocalypses Apocryphæ* [Leipzig, 1866], pp. 1–23), where Satan first turns himself into an angel of light (ὁ σατανᾶς ἐγένετο ἐν εἴδει ἄγγελου) but later answers Eve out of the mouth of the serpent (διὰ στόματος τοῦ ὄφεως). The *Apocalypsis* is obviously at least a remote analogue to the lost source, and it is therefore likely that the authors of *Genesis B* and the *Mystère* failed to remove the inconsistency rather than that they themselves invented it. Apocryphal texts have been discussed in their relationship to *Genesis B* by F. N. Robinson, 'A Note on the Sources of the Old Saxon *Genesis*', *M.P.*, IV (1907), 389–396.

angel of light and the returning devil is exactly paralleled by that on f. 3r of Satan and his followers, first of all as angels in heaven and then as devils entering the jaws of hell.

In the *Mystère d'Adam* there is the same inconsistency. In this the devil does not become a snake until the temptation is over, when a 'serpens artificiose compositus' [an ingeniously shaped serpent] appears in the tree, and Eve first places her ear to its mouth, then takes the apple. Despite its ample stage directions, the *Mystère d'Adam* unfortunately gives no instructions about the devil's appearance; the devil apparently comes straight from Hell to Eden without the assuming of any disguise, though he approaches Eve *leto vultu blandiens* [charming her with a friendly face]. But the interchange between him and Adam makes it clear that he is not recognizable as the devil; Adam at first listens to him courteously,[11] and when he at last dismisses him with 'Fui tei de ci! tu es sathan' [flee away from here, you are Satan], this recognition obviously comes as a climax to the dialogue, in which Adam has been made suspicious, not by the devil's appearance, but by his words. There is a close parallel in timing between the French Adam's 'Fui tei de ci' and the Anglo-Saxon's 'þu gelic ne biþ.' If the actor playing the devil's part did not assume any disguise before speaking to Adam, it can only have been—rather surprisingly—because the conventions of the stage allowed the hero not to be forewarned by his evil appearance.

There can be no doubt that behind both works lies an apocryphal account of the Fall, in which the devil tempted, disguised as an angel of light. The orthodox source for this idea was of course II Cor. 11:14, 'Ipse enim Satanas transfigurat se in angelum lucis' [For even he, Satan, transfigures himself into an angel of light], a text in which modern commentators see a reference to some earlier Rabbinic legend concerning the Fall. The most interesting extant analogue to this lost account of the Fall is the *Vita Adæ et Evæ*,[12] in which, after the Fall, Adam and Eve resolve to do penance by immersing themselves for thirty days, he in the Jordan and she in the Euphrates. After eighteen days, the devil disguised as an angel of light approaches Eve, claiming to be a messenger from God, bringing the

[11] E.g., line 132, 'Diabolus: Creras me tu? Adam: Oïl, mult bien.'

[12] Ed. W. Meyer in *Abhandlungen der philosophisch-philologischen Classe der königlich bayerischen Akademie der Wissenschaften, XIV (1878). R. H. Charles, The Apocrypha and Pseudepigrapha of the Old Testament*, II (Oxford, 1913), 122–133, gives a translation of the *Vita* with a Slavonic analogue and also of the relevant section from the *Apocalypsis Mosis*, and prefaces these with an introductory account.

divine instruction that she may leave the water, and that she may be given some of the fruit of paradise for which she had previously longed. This apocryphal work not only gives some idea of the character of the source postulated for *Genesis B* and the *Mystère d'Adam* but is also useful in its implicit demonstration that the disguise of an angel of light should not by definition be impenetrable. The devil's message is so exactly related to the two desires which one would expect Eve to feel (to escape the hardship of the penance and to recover part of what she had lost), that the meaning of the disguise of an angel of light becomes plain, that is, that it is an allegorical figure for the kind of self-deception by which a person may deceive himself that an action, wrong but much desired, is right. Eve's willing acceptance of the devil's message in the *Vita* may be contrasted, for instance, with Juliana's rejection of it in the Anglo-Saxon poem and its Latin sources. The devil's message to Juliana that God does not demand her constancy and wishes her to do sacrifice to heathen idols in order to save her life, has obviously the same psychological bearing as the message in the *Vita*. It may be emphasized that in both these stories the devil explicitly claims to have come from God, as he does in *Genesis B*, though not in the *Mystère d'Adam*, and it follows therefore that this detail was probably in the source, and certainly that it does not in itself excuse the victim's trust in the message.

That the interpretation of the disguise of the angel of light in terms of moral allegory does not spring merely from modern subjectivism is clear from many passages in the *Moralia* of Gregory the Great. A commentary upon the Book of Job was obviously a suitable place for observations upon the manner of the devil's tempting, and therefore over and over again Gregory allegorizes a text in order to show the deceptiveness of the devil and the way in which he conceals his evil intention beneath a superficial covering of good. Though St. Paul in II Cor. 11:14, explicitly at least intended only a warning against false preachers, Gregory applies the text also to the devil's tempting,[13] and in many other passages he sets out elaborate examples of how the devil adapts the content of his temptation to the disposition of his victim. Whilst admittedly in these passages Gregory is thinking of internal temptation, and obviously the temptation of the devil disguised was external, there was no traditional distinction between these, in that they were considered alike in kind and different in only

[13] E.g., *Moralia*, IV, c. iii B. Job, and XXXIII, c. xl B. Job; *P.L.*, LXXV, col. 641, and LXXVI, cols. 701–702.

in the extent to which they showed the devil's dominion over his victim.[14] It would of course be impossible to prove that the author of *Genesis B* had read the *Moralia*, but it is in itself quite likely that an Old Saxon monk would have read such an authoritative work. The hypothesis therefore that he found an apocryphal account of the Fall acceptable through an understanding of temptation learnt from the *Moralia* is not at all unreasonable.

From all this evidence it is clear that in the tradition of the Church the devil was thought sometimes to appear as an angel of light, and also that, even when he explicitly claimed to bring a divine message, this did not make his victim's lack of resistance blameless. Indeed it is clear from the *Moralia* and from many saints' lives that, whilst the devil might appear to the wicked in his own hideous shape, to the well-intentioned he would always appear disguised, and his instigation to evil would always be masked by an apparent suggestion of good. Therefore, whilst the poet's use of an apocryphal source in *Genesis B* necessarily led him to depart from the actual biblical story, it did not necessarily divert him from the basic truth of the Fall, that Eve sinfully heeded the devil's tempting. This is not a point which needs emphasizing with reference to the *Mystère d'Adam* for, though, as we shall see the most subtle part of its temptation speeches is close to *Genesis B*, nevertheless they contain also the biblical temptation, *eritis sicut dii* [you will be as gods], and therefore even without the standard set by Adam's rejecting of the devil and the fact that he even warns Eve not to heed him, no one would argue that Eve had been unfairly deceived. But in *Genesis B* there is no such open suggestion that it would be profitable to break God's commandment. Though there is no reason to doubt the intelligent orthodoxy of both poets, it may well be that there was greater intellectual pressure on a writer in the twelfth century than in the ninth, and that therefore a slightly inconsistent compromise was forced upon the author of the *Mystère d'Adam*, from which the earlier author was free. It still therefore remains to examine whether the content of the devil's speeches in *Genesis B* should have been sufficient to reveal his identity.

It is self-evident that when the devil appears disguised as an angel of light, he can only be recognized by a clear moral understanding of the nature of his speech. In the examples so far quoted he was thus recognized by Juliana and should have been recognized by Eve. But it

[14] A later summary of this distinction occurs in St. Thomas Aquinas, *Summa Theologica*, Pt. II, qu. 165, art. 2.

is possible to quote examples where this recognition is shown not to be possible. In *Paradise Lost*, for instance, Milton deliberately shows the angel Uriel deceived by Satan, because there is nothing in his words to contradict the outward righteousness of his appearance. Again, in a rather strange medieval story, a hermit is told by the devil, who is disguised as an angel of light, that the devil will appear to him next day in the shape of his father, and that he must instantly set upon him and kill him; the hermit obeys and thus kills his own father. This is a curious story, reflecting Greek irony rather than Christian morality, but it provides a most striking instance of the devil instigating to evil by a quite undetectable means. From such analogues it is clear that the question concerning *Genesis B* is whether or not the devil says something which anybody who did not respond with a stirring of sin would have understood as the counsel of the devil. In the first scene Adam recognizes the devil's lies by plain reason, almost perhaps by a philosophical understanding that God cannot contradict Himself, and therefore that a messenger who brings an instruction contrary to God's earlier command must be lying. But, though the devil repeats the same message to Eve, it might be argued that the traditional *wifes wac geþoht* [feeble mind of the woman], so much stressed by the poet, prevented her from taking the simple logical deduction so lucidly apparent to Adam. To prove the point therefore that Eve was to blame, it is necessary to show that her moral sense as well as her reason failed her.

In the *Mystère d'Adam*, Satan approaches Eve with flattery, complimenting her first in the poetic imagery of the romances, and then more insidiously:

> Tu es fieblette e tendre chose,
> E es plus fresche que n'est rose;
> Tu es plus blanche que cristal,
> Que neif que chiet sor glace en val;
> Mal cuple em fist li criator:
> Tu es trop tendre e il trop dur;
> Mais neporquant tu es plus sage,
> En grant sens as mis tun corrage.
> (Lines 227–234)[15]

[15] Studer, pp. 12–13.

> You are a fragile and tender thing,
> And fresher than a rose;
> You are whiter than crystal,
> Than snow which falls on ice in the valley;
> The Creator made a bad couple of you:

The point here which is strikingly paralleled in *Genesis B* is the comparison with Adam, and its climax in the words 'tu es plus sage.' Most of the temptation scene is in fact concerned with Satan's praise of Eve's superiority, and her gratification at this is suggested by her increasing willingness to listen to Satan, and her growing inclination to justify his praise by not dismissing him as Adam had done. Satan's final promise 'Al creator surez pareil' [you will be the equal of the creator] therefore does not come as the crucial point of the temptation, but rather to provide the rationalization for the devil's argument that by heeding him Eve will show superior wisdom. St. Thomas in his analysis of the temptation shows that pride did not precede the serpent's words, 'sed quia statim post suasionem serpentis invasit mentem eius elatio, ex qua consecutum est ut crederet verum esse quod dæmon dicebat.'[16] If we ask at what moment in the *Mystère d'Adam* Eve feels the first movements of pride in response to the devil's speech, the answer is clearly at the moment Satan praises her superior wisdom.

The same point is equally in the devil's speech of temptation in *Genesis B*. Like Satan in the *Mystère d'Adam* he does not conceal from Eve the revelatory information that Adam has refused to listen to him, but instead makes it the cornerstone of his temptation. Admittedly he does not openly say 'tu es plus sage,' but this comparison is implicit in his urging of Eve to save herself and Adam despite himself, and, if at this point the nature of the temptation is more insidiously concealed than in the *Mystère*, it is later made far more blatant by the promise 'Meaht þu Adame eft gestyran' [you can rule Adam afterwards]. That the first movements of pride in Eve should have been directed towards emulation and envy of Adam rather than of God was not a point made by theologians, since it had no foundation in the Bible, but to the literary and probing imagination it must have seemed extremely convincing. In *Paradise Lost*, for instance, though Milton does not show the inferior position of Eve as irksome to her before the Fall, yet he imagines it as an immediate consequence of it in that passage where Eve momentarily

You are too tender, and he is too hard;
But nevertheless you are wiser,
You are full of good sense.

[16] *Summa Theologica*, Pt. II, qu. 163, art. 1. 'But because immediately after the serpent's persuasive speech self-exaltation invaded her mind, the consequence of which was that she believed what the demon said to be true.'

enjoys the thought that she will not share the apple with Adam, in order that she may keep her acquisition of knowledge to herself:

> And render me more equal and perhaps—
> A thing not undesirable—sometime
> Superior.
>
> (Bk. IX, lines 823–25)

Before this point Milton had of course notably stressed Eve's subordination to Adam, and in the *Mystère d'Adam* the same idea had been expressed in the words of the *Figura* to Adam, 'El seit a tun comaundement' [may she be under your control], but in *Genesis B*, as it survives, this preliminary emphasis is missing. It is possible anyway that the structure of the poem prevented an extensive narrative of the Creation, which would normally provide a context for the statement, or alternatively, if two sections have been lost, then an account of the Creation was almost certainly contained in them.[17] But even if the poem did not make explicit the point that Eve was created inferior to Adam, this idea cannot have been unfamiliar to poet, translator, or audience. The tradition of the Church was quite plain, with its basis in the famous comment of St. Paul 'Mulieres viris suis subditæ sint sicut Domino' [women shall be subject to their men as to God] and in the influential image of the relationship of husband to wife as that of Christ to the Church. In a commentary on Genesis, St. Augustine extracted this Pauline didactic idea precisely from the situation of Adam and Eve, 'sicut vir debet feminam regere, nec eam permittere dominari in virum.'[18] Nor was there any element in Germanic society or literary conventions which could have made the Church's teaching strange or uncongenial or which could have led to the idea of female mastery losing its traditional unnaturalness. It is impossible to doubt that when *Genesis B* was read in monastery or hall, either audience easily recognized in the devil's speech an attempt to stir up pride. It follows therefore that the devil's disguise was not impenetrable, and that Eve listened with a wilful credulity springing from nascent vanity.

There remains one further point which has hitherto been misinterpreted, that is, the poet's gentle and apologetic comments upon Eve, for these should be taken to reveal his sympathy, not her

[17] On the gatherings of the manuscript, see Timmer, pp. 14–15.

[18] *De Genesi contra Manichaeos* II, xi; *P.L.*, XXXIV, cols. 204–205, 'just as the man shall rule the woman and not allow her to rule the man'. In the same chapter St. Augustine quotes another important biblical text, I Cor. 11.3, 'Caput enim viri Christus, et caput mulieris vir'.

innocence. The poet's attitude to Adam and Eve is partly determined by the structure of his work for in general Adam and Eve can be seen as hero or villain according to the point of contrast. If, as in the work of the Fathers, Adam is seen antithetically to Christ and Eve to the Blessed Virgin, their disobedience against His obedience, etc., then obviously in literary terms the villain's part is taken by Adam and Eve. But if, as in *Genesis B*, they are opposed to Satan, then their role is that of hero, and in this poem the devil continues in his role of villain and the poet's often interposed denunciations are reserved for him. The second relevant point about the poet's sympathetic comments on Eve is that, with one exception, they occur not in the account of the Fall, but in the scene in which she persuades Adam to eat the apple. In the exceptional occurrence, at the time when Eve is about to take the apple, the poet refers for the first time to her *wacra hyge* [weaker mind]; at this point it is obviously an extenuation of evil conduct rather than a denial of it, and is perhaps aimed partly at the devil, who, against the Germanic sense of honour, had chosen to fight an opponent on unequal terms. This passage would perhaps not have been taken to do more than express sympathy for Eve as the victim of the devil's cunning, had it not been misleadingly associated with the later comment, 'heo dyde hit þeah þurh holdne hyge' [yet she did it through a loyal spirit].

Genesis B, unlike the *Mystère d'Adam*, gives as much attention to Eve's temptation of Adam as to the devil's temptation of Eve. In the *Mystère* in fact there are only a few perfunctory lines between the two tastings, and the problem therefore of Eve's motives in urging Adam to eat does not arise. In this *Genesis B* can be compared with *Paradise Lost*, where Milton examines Eve's state of mind after the Fall at length, and shows her moved entirely by the basest self-interest.[19] The author of *Genesis B*, however, is strikingly concerned to show that Eve acted in good faith, being at that point entirely deceived by the illusory vision provided through the devil's power, and, lest anyone should nevertheless suspect Eve of acting with deliberate malice, he adds the comment, 'heo dyde hit þeah þurh holdne hyge.'[20]

[19] The point of comparison with *Paradise Lost* is of course only a general one and no implication is intended of a direct or indirect relationship. The treatment of the Fall cannot be used to support the argument that Milton knew *Genesis B*.

[20] This sentence and the other crucial one, 'Ac wende þæt heo hyldo heofoncyninges / worhte mid þam wordum' (lines 711–712), should not, with Timmer, p. 58, be referred back to the first temptation. As the conclusion of the second sentence shows ('þe heo þam were swelce / tacen oðiewde and treowe gehet'), they refer to her encouragement to Adam to eat. Krapp's punctuation of lines 708–717 makes the meaning quite plain. G. R. Krapp, *The Junius Manuscript* (New York, 1931).

This insistence upon Eve's *holdne hyge* was perhaps necessary to redress the balance of the actual description of Eve's persuasions. That Eve had used persuasion in order to induce Adam to eat the apple was a traditional idea; St. Augustine in his commentary on *Genesis* had speculated that Eve gave the apple to Adam, 'fortassis cum verbo suasorio, quod Scriptura tacens intelligendum relinquit.'[21] But in *Genesis B* the poet not only gives to Eve a long and fluent speech, but also adds 'hio spræc him þicce to and speon hine ealne dæg / on þa dimman dæd' [she spoke to him often, and all day tried to persuade him to [do] the dark act], whilst Adam is given no answer to make and the devil all the while stands silently by. In this powerfully ironic scene, Eve with her incessant persuasion—the unsual use of *þicce* is particularly evocative—lacks dignity, and might almost be said to anticipate the nagging wife of medieval literature. It is only the poet's apology which prevents an excessive diminishment of her.

It is self-evident from this short analysis that there is some discrepancy between content of dialogue and the poet's comments upon it, and that without this commentary Eve, until her contrition, might appear vain and silly, that in fact she acquires her stature through the poet's compassion. The failure of modern critics to distinguish Eve's culpability is unfortunate in that it leads to a misunderstanding of the poet's style of characterization. The poet's treatment of Eve cuts across the Anglo-Saxon—and presumably Old Saxon—kind of characterization according to ideals, the noble to be admired and the wicked abhorred, by presenting a character sinful but sympathetic; and in his guidance to a sympathy of Eve which her conduct alone would not have provoked, he comes nearer to the attitude to Chaucer in *Troilus and Criseyde* than does any writer in the intervening period.

This particular kind of treatment was obviously not possible in the *Mystère d'Adam*; to differentiate between the sin and the sinner in a play requires a degree of dramatic skill well beyond the range of medieval playwrights. From the literary point of view the important point of comparison between the two works is that both authors are alike in their concern, not with the theological implications of the Fall, but with the manner in which this almost unimaginable event might have taken place, a problem of course peculiar to the writer of

[21] *De Genesi ad litteram*, XI, c. 30, *P.L.*, XXXIV, col. 445. 'Maybe with a persuasive word, something which Scripture silently leaves to be understood.'

literature. The traditional doctrine that Adam and Eve wished to be as God is far richer and more subtle in its theological and moral implications, but the idea that Eve wished to be as Adam is from the literary and psychological point of view far more convincing. The wish to be as God probably requires considerable exposition before it can become recognizable in one's own experience, but the wish to be equal or superior to one's neighbour is no doubt familiar to all.

The justification for bringing together *Genesis B* and the *Mystère d'Adam*, despite the differences of date, language, form, and style, is threefold. Firstly, their juxtaposition gives strong support for a common source, whereas the respective critics and editors of both works have nearly all with some improbability inclined to the view of the authors' originality. But the outline plot of the devil disguising himself as an angel of light and tempting Adam first and then Eve through an incitement to emulation, is so clear in both of them, that the possibility of independent invention can be dismissed. Secondly, the authors of both works, contrary to the literary conventions of their respective periods, treated the Fall with psychological realism, and it is difficult to resist the inference that stimulus and assistance in this was provided by their common source. Finally, the *Mystère d'Adam* can be used as an aid to the correct interpretation of *Genesis B*, since the same plot occurs in it, but without the elements, such as the poet's sympathetic interventions, which have led to misunderstanding. As a result, the treatment of the Fall in *Genesis B* gains considerably in literary interest and subtlety, and, though so different in style, may perhaps be seen to be equal in power and quality to the section on the Fall of the Angels, which in modern studies has had a disproportionate share of the attention given to the poem.

APPENDIX

In the Cornish mystery plays and in the noncyclic Norwich play of the Creation and Fall similar action occurs.[22] They are not directly relevant to *Genesis B*, for the situation is treated so briefly that, far from illuminating the earlier tradition, they must themselves be interpreted in the light of it. The Cornish plays are so filled with apocryphal elements that in some ways it is not surprising to find that in them the devil disguises himself as an angel of light, though there is considerable inconsistency in that the stage direction says *diabolus tamquam serpens loquitur ad evam in arbore* [the devil

continued

[22] *The Ancient Cornish Drama*, ed. and trans. E. Norris (Oxford 1859), pp. 13–21; *Non-Cyclic Mystery Plays*, ed. O. Waterhouse, E.E.T.S., E.S., CIV (London, 1909), pp. 8–18.

in the shape of a serpent speaks to Eve from the tree] but the 'serpent' tells Eve 'From heaven I came now,' and Eve when tempting Adam refers several times to the 'angel.' The Norwich play is the more striking in that it provides interesting evidence of the survival of the tradition into the sixteenth century. The earlier text, that in use in 1533, like the Cornish play, exemplifies exactly the contradictions analyzed earlier in this article. As a *dramatis persona* the tempter is identified as *serpens*, but nevertheless he assures Eve 'Almighty God dyd me send,' and Eve describes to Adam how 'An angell cam from Godes grace / And gaffe me an apple of thys tre.' The historically curious point is that in the later version of 1565 (disingenuously described in the manuscript as being revised 'accordyng unto þe Skripture') clears up these inconsistencies by making the devil's disguise more explicit. The devil at the beginning announces, 'Unto this angell of lyght I shew myselfe to be,' and Eve's later reference to him as God's *angell* is therefore appropriate. There is no contradition until Eve's biblically based excuse, 'The Serpente diseayvyd me with that his fayer face' (obviously a female-headed serpent). Although here, as in the Cornish plays, the temptation is that of Genesis *erint sicut dii*, one may note the devil's approach to Eve with flattering words, 'O lady of felicite ...' It is just possible that the sixteenth century reviser pondered the peculiarities of the earlier text, and thus by chance arrived at a version closer to the original tradition, but one would have expected a Reformation redactor to have tidied the text by omission of such detail rather than by expansion. It is tempting to suppose that some work which amply embodied the tradition was known to him.

III

DOCTRINAL INFLUENCES ON THE *DREAM OF THE ROOD*

THE unique quality of the treatment of the Crucifixion in the *Dream of the Rood* has been long admired, and memorably commented upon.[1] It is unique, not only in Old English poetry—that would not be remarkable since so little survives—but in the whole range of English, and perhaps even western, literature. It is almost certain that this uniqueness of conception is the Anglo-Saxon poet's own, and that he did not have before him a source which he followed closely. There is a compactness and intensity in the poem that would be startling in an Anglo-Saxon translation or paraphrase; nor is its individuality more easily accounted for by the hypothesis that it was originally the work of a Roman rather than of an Anglo-Saxon Christian. Nevertheless all literary and historical probability is against the supposition that nothing but the poet's personal inspiration lies between the gospel narrative and the *Dream of the Rood.* But, whilst the poem is obviously not a Biblical paraphrase in conventional style, yet it is influenced hardly at all by Latin hymns,[2] nor by certain antiphons of the liturgy, such as lie behind the treatment of the Crucifixion in the *Crist.* The influences to be considered are in fact not of the kind that can be isolated in any specific text, but rather those of the religious thought of the poet's period, in particular its philosophic view of the person and nature of Christ and definition of the Redemption. The most remarkable achievement of the poem is its balance between the effects of triumph and suffering, and their paradoxical fusion in the Crucifixion is suggested first by the alternation between the jewelled radiant cross and the plain and blood-covered cross in the prelude,[3]

[1] The most notable comment is in W. P. Ker *The Dark Ages* (London 1904), p. 265.

[2] It is clear from H. R. Patch 'The Liturgical Influence in the *Dream of the Rood*', *P.M.L.A.* xxxiv (1919), 233–51 that the influence of Latin hymnody is confined to a few phrases.

[3] There is ample evidence for the symbolic meanings of both the gemmed cross and the red cross. The jewelled cross symbolizing triumph is particularly associated with Constantine and the well-known story of his conversion. At Constantine's command a most splendid cross was erected in the Holy Places of Jerusalem: this was reproduced in the late fourth century mosaic of the apse of S. Pudenziana in Rome: L. Bréhier, *L'art*

continued

and secondly and much more subtly and powerfully by the two figures of the heroic victorious warrior and the passive enduring cross. At the time when the poet wrote, the Church insisted on the co-existence of these two elements in Christ, divine supremacy and human suffering, with a vehemence and rigidity deriving from more than two centuries of heretical Christological dispute, and which abated only when the orthodox view was no longer questioned. In the soteriological doctrine of the time there also co-existed the two ideas of a divine victory and a sacrificial offering, though here not as the result of a carefully formulated orthodox dogma, but simply because as yet the nature of the Redemption had not become a central subject of theological speculation, and contradictory views were therefore stated not only by different writers but also often in different works of the same writer. The author of the *Dream of the Rood*, then, in emphasizing at once both triumph and suffering in a way that would have been inconceivable in the Middle Ages, reflected exactly the doctrinal pattern of thought of his time, though this fact, of course, by no means detracts from the brilliance with which this thought, so difficult of imaginative comprehension, is transmuted into a poetic form which brings home its meaning to the understanding in a way that is beyond the dry precision of philosophical language.

The stress that will be laid on the Crucifixion as a scene of triumph or a scene of suffering depends upon the stress that is laid on Christ as God or Christ as a man. These two possible emphases developed in the late fourth century in the theological schools of Alexandria and Antioch, and both led to Christological heresy. The Monophysites, whose philosophic definition of Christ sprang from the speculative mode of thought of Alexandria, correctly insisted on the unity of

Chrétien (Paris 1918), fig. 21. It is interesting to note that in this mosaic the gemmed cross appears to tower in the sky; cp. *Elene*, 88–92. According to Eusebius (*Vita Constantini*, III, 49) even upon the ceiling of the main chamber of the imperial palace there was represented a cross in gold and precious stones. The splendour of gold and jewels symbolized not only the triumph of Christ, but also His divinity. This is made clear by the formula for the consecration of a cross in the earliest known Pontifical, that of Egbert (consecrated Archbishop of York in 732): 'radiet hic Unigeniti Filii tui splendor divinitatis in auro, emicet gloria passionis in ligno, in cruore rutilet nostra mortis redemptio, in splendore cristalli nostræ vitæ purificatio' (Surtees Society xxvii, 112). The obvious point that a plain red cross symbolizes the redeeming blood of Christ is made as early as the fifth century by Paulinus of Nola, who, in his church dedicated to St. Felix had inscribed on either side of two red crosses: 'Ardua floriferæ crux cingitur orbe coronæ, / Et Domini fuso tincta cruore rubet' (*P.L.* lxi 337; this is referred to by J. Wilpert, *Die römischen Mosaiken und Malereien* (Freiburg im Breisgau 1918), p. 45). In the time of the author of the *Dream of the Rood* such symbolic associations may well have been commonplaces to the educated.

Christ's person, but at the cost of a tendency to confuse His two natures: the result was that they overstressed His divinity, for in this confusion His humanity, unsafeguarded by an essential distinctiveness, might seem to be absorbed as a drop of water by the ocean. The undesirable but logically inevitable conclusion of such a philosophic view was either that the Godhead must be thought of as passible—as the Eutychians of the fifth century were accused of maintaining—or Christ must be said to have been immune from the ordinary human experience of suffering, and in the sixth century some of the more extreme Monophysites scarcely avoided this Docetic belief. The heresy of the school of Antioch takes its name from Nestorius, although modern scholarship has shown him to have been at least partly maligned. The Nestorians had the moral and literal way of thought which characterized all Antiochene studies. They, unlike the Monophysites, correctly distinguished between the two natures of Christ, but at the cost of almost denying the unity of His person, and hence of overstressing Christ's humanity. The Nestorians were notorious for their rejection of the term *Theotokos* (God-bearer) as a descriptive title of the Virgin, and in their most obviously extreme statements held that the indwelling of God in Christ was not different in kind, although of course in degree, from His indwelling in the prophets. To stress that Christ was subject to all the natural pains of human nature was therefore particularly characteristic of the Nestorians. This summary has stressed what is extreme and exaggerated in the Christology of the two heretical schools, for it was this that was remembered and feared by the orthodox. The difference between the moderate and unfanatical thinkers of both sides was more a matter of emphasis than of deep dogmatic division, and each side when speaking cautiously and charitably could reach agreement with the other, as they did at the time of Cyril's Formulary of Reunion (433), but the effect in the heat of hostile argument or in private eccentric speculation was that the Monophysites seemed to deny that Christ was fully man, and the Nestorians to deny that Christ was fully God.

The Church in Rome insisted on a middle way between these two extremes, and the dispute was first settled to the philosophic satisfaction of the west at the Council of Chalcedon (449).[4] There the Council accepted a number of documents as orthodox, besides

[4] A detailed account may be found in R. V. Sellers, *The Council of Chalcedon* (London 1953).

composing its own *Definitio Fidei.* Of these documents the one of most lasting importance was the *Tome* of Leo I.[5] In this the Pope established a razor-edge position between Alexandria and Antioch, maintaining the true western tradition that there was in Christ one person and two natures, the person undivided and the natures unconfused. He also defined the correct manner of speaking of Christ's life on earth, so that this bare definition might be expressed in terms of narrative or exegesis. From Antioch he borrowed the principal of 'recognizing the difference', that is of dividing, as the Nestorians had commonly done in their scriptural commentaries, all the acts of Christ's life into those which appertained to His humanity and those which appertained to His divinity. In His humanity, for instance, He hungered, thirsted, felt fatigue, and suffered: in His divinity He healed, forgave, and accomplished all His miracles—or, to quote a popular and pointed example, in His humanity Christ wept for the death of Lazarus, but in His divinity He raised him.[6] This method preserved admirably the doctrine of the two natures without confusion, but for full orthodoxy it required the corrective and corollary of the principle of *communicatio idiomatum* [communion of properties], which Leo adopted from Alexandria. The philosophic basis of this principle was that, since Christ's person was a unity, the properties of both natures could be ascribed to it, provided, of course, that the word used for Christ's person was a concrete not an abstract noun (e.g. God, not Godhead). The method was therefore to attribute to Christ under a divine title one of the limitations of humanity: authority for this could be found in the works of St. Paul himself, who had written in a much quoted text, 'If they had known it they would not have crucified the Lord of Glory' (I Cor. ii. 8). The unity of Christ's person was thus emphasized in a manner which from a literary point of view produced a startlingly paradoxical effect.

Although Leo's *Tome* established for centuries the orthodox way of describing Christ's life, it did not at the time put an end to Christological dispute, but rather stimulated further dissension. With the doctrinal issue aggravated by motives of imperial policy, Rome and Byzantium remained opposed until the Oecumenical Council of 682, when the Monophysite and Nestorian controversy was finally

[5] A good translation of the *Tome* and also of other important documents in the dispute can be found in E. R. Hardy, *Christology of the Later Latin Fathers*, 346–85, *Library of the Christian Classics*, vol. III (London 1954).

[6] E.g. Paulinus of Nola, *Carmen* xxxv 119–20, 'Tanquam homo, defuncto lacrymas impendit amico / Quem mox ipse Deus suscitat e tumulo' (*P.L.* lxi, 678).

determined, though only at the cost of the schism of the churches of Egypt and Asia Minor. Even in the west Christological orthodoxy did not then remain undisturbed, for in the eighth century the Adoptionist heresy (the view that Christ was Son of God by adoption only) became strong in Spain and France, and Alcuin was one of those who defended western orthodoxy against it.[7]

Theological disputation may at first sight seem remote from Anglo-Saxon England of the late seventh century. But whilst the fact that the Anglo-Saxon ecclesiastics of this period came of a people only comparatively recently converted, and without any tradition of philosophical thinking, no doubt led to their accepting western orthodoxy unquestioningly, it did not necessarily mean that they accepted it ignorantly. It was not the policy of the Pope to keep them innocently unaware of heretical dangers, but rather to instruct the Anglo-Saxon church against them; nor could they have read the works of any of the great Fathers and remained ignorant of the eastern heresies. The Anglo-Saxons were in fact in an ideal position for upholding the western tradition. On the one hand it is clear that they had sufficient grasp of theological teaching to understand the issues involved, but on the other hand they had neither the fanaticism of spirit nor the confidence of a long tradition of independent scholarship, which might lead them into disagreement with Rome.

In the year 679, the Christological heresies were particularly brought to the attention of the Anglo-Saxon Church. The Pope, in preparation for the Oecumenical Council, wished to assure himself of the invariable orthodoxy of all the countries in the west. In accordance with this wish, Theodore of Tarsus, Archbishop of Canterbury, in 679 summoned the Synod of Hatfield,[8] and in the presence of the papal legate inquired diligently of the bishops and doctors there assembled what doctrine they held, and found that they were all of the Catholic faith. This Council condemned the great heretics, including Nestorius and Eutyches, and read and accepted the documents of the Lateran Council of 649, which, of course, included Leo's *Tome*.[9] Theodore also set down the declaration of faith of the Council in a Synodical letter 'for the instruction and faith

[7] A. Harnack, *History of Dogma*, trans. J. Millar (London 1898), V, 289.

[8] An account of the Synod of Hatfield is given by Bede, *Historia Ecclesiastica*, IV, xv [xvii], ed. C. Plummer, *Venerabilis Baedae Opera Historica* (Oxford 1896), I, 238–40.

[9] A. W. Haddan and W. Stubbs, *Councils and Ecclesiastical Documents relating to Great Britain and Ireland* (Oxford 1871), III, 145–51, give the canons of the Lateran Council as an appendix to Bede's account of the Synod of Hatfield.

of aftercomers', and a copy of this was given to the legate to take back to Rome. At the Oecumenical Council itself the faith of the Anglo-Saxon Church was attested by Wilfrid,[10] on the first occasion when the Anglo-Saxons were represented at such a Council.[11] The papal legate at Hatfield had been John, the arch-chanter or precentor of St. Peter's, who had spent the previous year under the guidance of Benedict Biscop in the monastery at Wearmouth, instructing the monks in the Roman manner of singing the monastic office, and during that time a copy of the documents of the Lateran Council, which he had brought with him, was made at Wearmouth.[12] It is inconceivable that during this time he left unheeded the other half of his commission from the Pope, and failed to discuss and instruct in western Christology. Similar guidance and instruction must have been given by Theodore and his colleague Hadrian of Naples, both of whom are known to have made extensive journeys through England. Theodore himself had been brought up in the geographical centre of the dispute, and was so learned and skilled in the Monophysite controversy that the previous Pope had wished him to lead the Roman legation to Constantinople.

It was not, however, solely from the teaching of such men as Theodore and Hadrian, or from the assembly at Hatfield, or from the documents of the Councils deposited in England, that knowledge of the heretical doctrines of the person and nature of Christ would reach the Anglo-Saxon Church, but also from the works of the great Fathers, Ambrose, Jerome, Augustine and Gregory the Great. In separate tracts and in their exegesis of the New Testament the later Fathers constantly refuted the Nestorian and Monophysite heresies, and various key texts in the gospels became conventional starting points for an attack on the wicked Nestorius or the madness of Eutyches. These anti-heretical arguments based on scriptural texts are repeated by Bede, whose own commentaries on the four gospels were written in the first quarter of the eighth century.[13] There is little in Bede's commentaries that is original, but neither are they simply translations, and Bede must be supposed to have selected from the works of his authoritative predecessors those arguments and explanations which he thought most relevant and important, and all his four commentaries are extraordinarily full of refutations of the

[10] F. M. Stenton, *Anglo-Saxon England* (Oxford 1947), p. 137.
[11] *Christology of the Later Latin Fathers*, p. 382.
[12] Bede IV xvi [xviii], Plummer, I, 240–2.
[13] *P.L.* xcii.

earlier heretics.[14] From the combined evidence of the historical information and of Bede's commentaries it is clear that the heresies of Nestorius and Eutyches were a living issue in England for at least the fifty years from about 675–725. Since the identity of the author of the *Dream of the Rood* is not known, it cannot be conclusively proved from evidence outside the poem that he knew of the Christological controversy. But the burden of proof is undoubtedly on anyone who would maintain that an educated man of this period could remain unaware at the very least that the greatest theological care and precision was required in any statements about Christ's life, and in particular about His Crucifixion, and that an equal stress must be laid on Christ's divinity (against Nestorius) and Christ's humanity (against Eutyches).

The tension between divinity and triumph on the one hand and humanity and suffering on the other might also arise from the doctrine of the Redemption as it was taught at this period. No comprehensive and consistent soteriological theory was evolved until that of Anselm in the eleventh century, and this point—no doubt because it had not been associated with heresy—was not treated with the same philosophic depth and perception with which the Fathers had analysed the person of Christ, and on it they were often ambiguous and self-contradictory. Apart from the typically eastern idea of humanity being cleansed and immortalized through its assumption by the divinity, which though important is not relevant here, two other main ideas can be clearly distinguished. The earlier is that which was commonly held by the eastern church, and it was dualistic, though of course not Manichaean. According to it, the nature of the Redemption was that God, by His Incarnation and Passion, released or redeemed mankind from the devil, who, by the Fall had acquired a just claim to man. Christ's death was seen either as a bait or an offering, and through his acceptance of it the devil was outwitted and overcome. The issue was therefore between God and the devil, and the result was God's defeat of the devil. Although this idea was of eastern origin, it was repeated by the great western Fathers, Leo, Augustine and Gregory I.[15] They, however, following the New Testament, and in particular the Epistle of the Hebrews, also

[14] A valuable discussion of Bede's Commentaries will be found in A. Hamilton Thompson, *Bede, His Life, Times, and Writings* (Oxford 1935), pp. 152–200.

[15] The works of these Fathers, including those in which this doctrine is stated, were of course known to the Anglo-Saxons. See J. D. Ogilvy, *Books known to Anglo-Latin Writers from Aldhelm to Alcuin* (Camb., Mass. 1936).

stressed the Crucifixion as an offering or sacrifice made on behalf of man by Christ as man, the spotless for the guilty. The emphasis in the New Testament on man being redeemed by the blood of Christ could scarcely be ignored, and a recognition of this was aided by the growing devotion to the Eucharist. Gregory I contributed much to the Catholic doctrine of the mass, and in self-contradiction stated both theories of the Redemption, developing a theory of Christ's suffering and death as a sacrificial offering, which is Anselm's view in rudimentary form; though elsewhere he also speaks of the Crucifixion in terms of conflict and triumph, repeating Gregory of Nyssa's grotesque image of Christ's humanity being a bait swallowed by Leviathan.[16] These two theories were not normally combined, but if they were associated in thought a tension and paradox would be inevitable. In the one view the stress is on Christ's divinity: God enters the world to free man from the devil, and the moment of His triumph is the Crucifixion; in the other view the stress is on Christ's humanity: God becomes man that as man He may offer to God the due sacrifice which man is unable to offer for himself, and the Crucifixion is the supreme moment of pain and abasement. It must, however, be added that these two views were not entirely mutually exclusive, but rather what was central in one became secondary in the other.[17] Thus in the theory of the 'devil's rights' it was not forgotten that the result of the defeat of the devil was the restoration of the former relationship between God and man, and in the 'satisfaction' theory it was remembered that the further result of God being reconciled to man was that the devil lost his former possession of the whole human race. For this reason it was not ridiculous that both ideas should be implied or stated within one passage or poem.

The *Dream of the Rood* then was written at a time when both Christology and soteriology laid this double stress on the Crucifixion as a scene of both triumph and suffering, and the author has succeeded in fulfilling what might seem to be an artistically impossible demand. Without such a brilliant conception as that of the poet's, the two aspects would inevitably have become separated, as

[16] Gregory of Nyssa, *Oratio Catechetica Magna*, xxiv, *P.G.* xlv, 66; Gregory I, *Moralia* xxxiii, 9, *P.L.* xxvi, 682–3. The source of the image is Job xl, 20, the text upon which Gregory is commenting.

[17] This point is made by Gustav Aulén, *Christus Victor* (London 1953), p. 72. This work is an interesting but tendentious study of the doctrine of the Redemption. A more detailed and objective account can be found in the works of Jean Rivière, particularly in *Le Dogme de la Rédemption au début du Moyen Age* (Paris 1934).

they were usually in the Middle Ages. The Crucifixion in both mediaeval art and medieval literature is usually a scene of utmost agony: in accordance with the doctrine of 'satisfaction', Christ as man offers His suffering to its farthest limit, until the body hangs painfully from the Cross without blood or life. The note of triumph is necessarily reserved until the Harrowing of Hell, when Christ, approaching as the King of Glory, conquers the devil, often using His Resurrection cross as a weapon of war and plunging it into the mouth of the defeated Leviathan.[18] The timing of this, of course, exactly expresses the pattern of the medieval doctrine of the Redemption, the sacrifice being primary, the defeat of the devil secondary.

The image of the Crucifixion as a conflict and Christ as a warrior is very appropriate to the dualistic theory of the Redemption, for the essence of this image is that there should be an opponent to be overcome, and that the hero should be triumphant; as a symbol of the 'satisfaction' theory it would lose its force and appear crude and irrelevant. In the Middle Ages, therefore, the image of Christ as a feudal knight is rarely used, and, when it is, is normally accompanied by a statement of the theory of the 'devil's rights'.[19] A clear example of this may be seen in *Piers Plowman* (*Passus* xviii, B Text), where Christ is represented as contestor and victor in a tournament, and releases man justly from the devil's power since 'gyle is bigyled' (l. 358) and Christ's soul given in ransom (ll. 325, 337–42), the ideas of the bait and the offering being here combined. We might conjecture that the image of the Crucifixion as a battle would otherwise have almost died out, had it not been given a new force by the association of courtly love with chivalry, so that Christ becomes the lover-knight, loving his lady (mankind) to the point of death, and deserving thereby to win her love in return. The *exemplum* of the lover-knight, of which the most moving form is in the section on love in the *Ancren Riwle* and Henryson's *Bloody Serk*, makes this much-stressed point of Christ's

[18] This detail is found in English art as early as the eleventh century, when it was strikingly carved on the Bristol stone. It is an interpretation of '... posuitque dominus crucem suam in medio inferni, quæ est signum victoriæ', *Evangelium Nicodemi*, B, x, ed. C. Tischendorf *Evangelia apocrypha* (Leipsig 1876), p. 430.

[19] The theory of the 'devil's rights' was not forgotten in the Middle Ages, and its inclusion in the third book of the *Sentences* of Petrus Lombardus must have made it known to every trained theologian. That it is the doctrinal basis of the *Ludus Coventriae* has been pointed out by Timothy Fry, 'The Unity of the *Ludus Coventriae*', *Studies in Philology*, xlviii (1951), 527–70. Its occurrence in Langland, however, has not been commented upon.

love for man with beauty and clarity.[20]

The presentation of Christ in the *Dream of the Rood* as a young warrior advancing to battle has been much commented upon as an example of the common Anglo-Saxon convention of treating Christian subject matter in heroic terms. The conception of Christ as a warrior is, however, not peculiar to the Anglo-Saxon imagination. In visual art, for instance, it was a common Mediterranean theme, of which one of the most striking extant examples is a mosaic in the Chapel of the Palace of the Archbishop at Ravenna. There Christ, dressed in Roman military style, stands strongly, the symbolical animals subdued beneath His feet, and a cross of the Resurrection style swung over His shoulder as though it were a weapon.[21] The effect is of a triumphant hero. The armour of Christ probably derives from the description of the divine warrior-redeemer in Isaiah lix. 17, whilst the animals beneath His feet are an illustration of Psalm xci. 13. Whilst it is not improbable that the Anglo-Saxons knew the *Christus Miles* theme, it cannot be proved that they did, for, although there is a Christ standing over the animals on both the Ruthwell and Bewcastle Crosses, the original was probably in the hieratic style, in which Christ, dressed in a long mantle, seems to stand as a ruler with serenity and power over the prostrate animals.[22] The concept of the Crucifixion as a battle, however, was not restricted to the visual arts. The idea of a military conflict had been common in the patristic statements of the theory of the 'devil's rights', and became, no doubt therefrom, a commonplace of early Latin Christian poets and hymn-writers, and with it was associated the idea of kingly victory. This derived supposedly from Psalm xcvi. 10, which in the *Psalterium Romanum* read: 'Dicite in gentibus quia dominus regnavit a ligno'

[20] The concept of Christ as a knight has been discussed by W. Gaffney, 'The Allegory of the Christ-Knight in *Piers Plowman*', *P.M.L.A.*, xlvi (1931), 155–68, and by Sister Marie de Lourdes le May, *The Allegory of the Christ-Knight in English Literature* (Washington 1932). Although both works are useful and interesting, neither writer relates the image to theological doctrine, and therefore they do not emphatically distinguish between the feudal knight and the lover-knight.

[21] According to E. H. Kantorowicz, *The King's two Bodies* (Princeton 1957), p. 72, Christ has here the golden armour and shoulder fibula of a Roman emperor, and therefore the idea expressed here is not simply of victory but of a royal victory. On pp. 61–78 Kantorowicz gives an interesting account of the theme of the royalty of Christ in early thought and art. The Ravenna mosaic is reproduced by J. Wilpert, *Die römischen Mosaiken und Malereien*, III, pl. 89, and commented upon in I, p. 47. For the reference to Kantorowicz and for other helpful references and comments I am indebted to Mr J. A. W. Bennett.

[22] See F. Sax, 'The Ruthwell Cross', *Journal of the Warburg and Courtauld Institutes*, vi (1943), 1–19.

[say among nations that the Lord ruled from the wood]. Versions in which *a ligno* did not appear were dismissed by the early church as malicious alterations of the Jews, so admirably did this reading express their doctrine of the Crucifixion. The idea that Christ reigned from the tree was given popularity by the famous hymn of Venantius Fortunatus, *Vexilla Regis Prodeunt*, a hymn undoubtedly used by the Anglo-Saxon Church,[23] and was given iconographical expression in the earliest crucifixes and representations of the Crucifixion. In these Christ, a young man of noble appearance, stands firmly on the Cross, His feet supported by a *suppedaneum* [footrest], and on His upright head a halo or royal crown.[24] All these are but illustrations of a common imaginative theme of the early church, which must have been known to the Anglo-Saxons, and which presents such striking affinities to both conception and tone of the *geong hæleð* [young warrior] in the *Dream of the Rood*, that it would be perverse to prefer the theory of coincidence to that of influence.

In the *Dream of the Rood* the heroic quality of Christ is suggested by the three actions ascribed to Him: He advances to the Cross with bold speed, strips Himself, and ascends it. All these emphasize the confidence of divine victory and the voluntariness of Christ's undertaking the Crucifixion. They are therefore absolutely consonant with the teaching of the early church, and in intense contrast to the medieval treatment of the Crucifixion[25] The medieval picture of Christ exhausted and stooping beneath the weight of the Cross is so well-known and so moving that it is easy to forget nowadays that this is not a literal illustration of the gospel narrative, but a medieval interpretation which, though the Christian

[23] This hymn with an Anglo-Saxon Gloss will be found in *Latin Hymns known to the Anglo-Saxon Church*, Surtees Society, xxiii (1851). These hymns are mainly collected from an eleventh-century manuscript, but it is reasonable to suppose that most of them were known at an early date.

[24] No crucifixes of the date of the *Dream of the Rood* survive in England. There is, however, a reference to a *crux antiquissima* with crown in a story of William of Malmesbury. It is quoted by D. Rock, *The Church of our Fathers* (London 1849), I, 306–7, note 8. Cf. also the *Peterborough Chronicle* s.a. 1070, where the raiders on the monastery are said to seize a gold crown from the head of a figure of Christ. Many triumphant crucifixes of a later date also survive. An interesting example is the eleventh-century Aaby Crucifix from Denmark, which is reproduced by R. W. Southern, *The Making of the Middle Ages* (London 1953), pl. 2.

[25] It was not that the Middle Ages did not lay stress on the idea that Christ suffered the Passion *quia ipse voluit*: on the contrary this point was emphasized over and over again. But, in order to drive home to the imagination the measure of what Christ was willing to suffer, they ceased in art and literature to express this willingness in the actual Passion scene symbolically.

may well believe it to be true, is at most faintly implicit in the gospels themselves. There is a discrepancy in the gospel accounts of the carrying of the Cross. In the first three gospels the Cross is said to have been borne by Simon of Cyrene, whilst in St. John Christ carries it Himself. According to the orthodox exegesis, which Bede follows, the discordant statements are reconciled by the view that the Cross was first carried by Christ and later by Simon. But it is interesting to notice that Bede, again following an authoritative tradition, makes only an abstract and moral deduction from this: Simon is allegorically a Christian obeying Christ's command to take up his cross and follow Him, and literally a gentile in order to signify the gathering in of the whole world into Christ's Church.[26] The naturalistic deduction that Christ was too exhausted to carry it farther Himself, which accorded so well with the medieval doctrine of the Crucifixion, was not made until later. It was therefore not a wilful divergence from the gospel narrative to represent Christ advancing without the Cross (although that the Cross is already in position and watches Christ advancing to it seems to be the poet's own variation). In the mosaics of San Apollinare Nuovo at Ravenna, for instance, Christ Himself advances with His hands outstretched in a gesture of sacrificial self-offering. The poet has taken advantage of this tradition to heighten the heroic and voluntary nature of the Crucifixion.

The stripping of Christ is not described in any of the gospels. The soldiers divide His garments amongst themselves, but their actual removal is not given as an essential detail of the narrative. The Middle Ages, of course, imagined that Christ's robes were torn from Him by the soldiers, as a further stage in their grotesque brutality, and the manner in which this caused the wounds of His flagellation to reopen was often gruesomely described. Since Matthew and Mark a few verses before the description of the Crucifixion tell of the previous stripping of Christ, when the purple robe was placed upon Him, it is plausible to imagine the scene preparatory to the Crucifixion analogously. But the author of the *Dream of the Rood* was following a patristic tradition, to be found, for instance, in Ambrose's commentary on Luke, of Christ as kingly victor removing His clothes: 'Pulchre ascensurus crucem regalia vestimenta deposuit'.[27]

[26] *P.L.* xcii 286. The alternative harmonization in which the Cross was carried by Christ and Simon of Cyrene together, although it occurs in Ambrose (*P.L.* xv 1923), was rare until the later Middle Ages, when it became popular in both art and exegesis.

[27] *Expositionis in Lucam Libri x, P.L.* xv 1923. 'Very fitting when about to ascend the Cross, He laid down His royal vestments.'

Though to this is added an Old Testament parallel, that as Adam defeated sought clothing, so Christ conquering laid down His clothing. In the *Dream of the Rood* Christ is very clearly a hero stripping Himself for battle in a description which has been compared with an analogous scene in the *Aeneid* (V. 241 ff.),[28] where Entellus strips himself, and stands imposing of appearance, ready for his encounter with Dares: a resemblance, of course, of heroic description to heroic description, not of derivative to source. Christ's stripping of Himself, then, is voluntary and heroic, and so also therefore is His nudity. In the Syrian tradition of Christian art, in which nakedness was considered shameful, Christ on the Cross for the sake of reverence and decorum was dressed, with hieratic effect, in the long *collobium* [sleeveless tunic]. But Hellenic Christian art retained the idea of the nudity of the hero, and therefore represented Christ as naked, or almost naked, upon the Cross, without this in any way conflicting with the idea of the Crucifixion as a royal and heroic triumph; and it is this conception which also lies behind the phrase *ongyrede hine* [he stripped himself] in the *Dream of the Rood.*[29] It is interesting to notice that in the Middle Ages writers and artists adhered in this point to the gospel account and to the outward form of Hellenic art, but saw the enforced nakedness of Christ as a humiliation added to torment, and it was sometimes imagined that the Virgin intervened to save her Son from such shame by covering Him with her veil.

Christ's mounting the Cross is the climax and end of the description of the Crucifixion in heroic terms. Again in the gospels the method of attaching Christ to the Cross is not described, and exegesis, as in Bede, normally only expounds the allegorical significance of the Crucifixion, and is not primarily concerned with turning the gospel story into a continuous naturalistic narrative. Of the great Fathers, only Ambrose in the passage referred to above describes Christ ascending the Cross as victor. In Latin hymnody there were two conventional expressions, *in crucem ascendere* [to ascend the cross] and *in crucis stipite levatur* [is raised up by the tree of the Cross]. The poet, perhaps following Ambrose, and certainly with

[28] *Dream of the Rood*, ed. A. S. Cook (Oxford 1905), p. 24.

[29] By the sixth century, however, western Christians did not always retain the idea without uneasiness, as is shown by the story of Gregory of Tours (*Libri Miraculorum* I, *Societé de l'histoire de France*, cliii (1857), 62), who relates how there appeared to a priest at Narbonne a terrible and angry Christ, who demanded that His painted representation should be given a complete covering instead of merely the loincloth which it had.

the same intention in mind, makes use of the Old English equivalent of *crucem ascendere*: *gealgan gestigan*. This is the consummation of his theme, and Christ ascends the Cross of His own will, in contrast to the later mediaeval representations in art and mystery plays, where the body of Christ is nailed to the Cross as it lies on the ground, and the thrusting of its base into the socket is an additional agony for Christ. The young hero's advance, and ascent of the Cross, is thus at once painless and heroic, and is therefore a most admirable symbol of the divine nature of Christ and the earlier definition of the Redemption.

In any narrative stressing the divinity of Christ, the greatest difficulty lies in the description of Christ's death, a difficulty which is not only literary but theological. To this the poet's image of Christ resting and asleep after His great struggle is a most brilliant poetic solution: 'Aledon hie ðær limwerigne ... ond he hine ðær hwile reste, meðe æfter ðam miclan gewinne'* (ll. 63–5). It had been a fairly common view that at the moment of Christ's death, the Godhead forsook the body, and that the obviously anguished cry of *Eli, Eli, lamma sabacthani*, was the lament of the human body as it felt the divinity depart. Such a conclusion was dangerously near to the Apollinarian heresy (that in Christ the place of the rational soul was taken by the Divinity), but the alternative, which seemed to involve the theologically impossible statement that God could die, and that it was the dead body of God which was removed from the Cross, was not immediately acceptable, and it is little wonder that Christian writers faltered before a so apparently incomprehensible paradox. At the same time there was an insistence on the voluntary nature of Christ's death—that, unlike the thieves and all other human beings, He had died at the exact moment that He chose. That Christ inclined His head before death, not after, was thought to demonstrate this, as also the comparatively short duration of His agony. The text of John X. 18 was orthodoxly associated with this, as can be seen from Bede's commentaries on Mark and John. This theological uneasiness over the death of Christ is negatively reflected in early representations of the Crucifixion, in all of which Christ is shown alive; in the west it is not until the Middle Ages that Christ is shown hanging dead upon the Cross.[30] The author of the *Dream of the Rood* similarly does not

* 'They laid him down there limb-weary... and he rested himself there for a time, exhausted after the great struggle'.

[30] This point is well made and discussed by L. H. Grondijs, *L'Iconographie Byzantine du Crucifié mort sur la Croix* (Utrecht 1947). The conclusions of Grondijs concerning the date at which the dead Christ appears in art have been disputed. That

speak of Christ's death: the climax of the poem is simply, *Crist wæs on rode* [Christ was on the Cross], and His death is thereafter described as a sleep, in terms which with cathartic effect suggest exhaustion, release and temporary rest.[31] In describing Christ's death as a sleep the poet was probably not original. The image had already been used of Christ; for instance, by Augustine in his commentary on St. John, and by Bede in imitation.[32] Both intend by it to emphasize the voluntary nature of Christ's death: just as He slept when He wished, so He died when He wished, though Augustine also draws a further allegorical point, that just as Eve was born from the side of Adam as he slept, so the Church was born from the side of Christ in His flowing sacramental blood as He slept on the Cross.[33]

But, though the poet may have borrowed the image, the use he makes of it in suggesting a body still potentially instinct with life is his own. Modern usage may have reduced the image of death as a sleep to a sentimental euphemism—a danger perhaps inherent in the Homeric and late classical usage—but in its earliest Christian form, in Christ's words to Jairus, its point is not to evade the terror and finality of the word death, but to assert the power of God to bring the dead to life, and therefore its use in the *Dream of the Rood* is sublimely appropriate.

Whilst the effect of the poet's treatment of Christ the warrior is indeed fine, it is not here that his brilliance of invention lies, but rather in his emphasis on Christ's human nature, which is found in his treatment of the Cross. Wonder at the mere device of making the

the dead Christ is represented by the middle of the ninth century in Byzantine art as an artistic assertion of orthodox theology has been argued by J. R. Martin, 'The dead Christ on the Cross in Byzantine Art', *Late Classical and Mediæval Studies in honor of Matthias Friend Jr.*, ed. K. Weitzman (Princeton 1955), pp. 189–96. Most recently A. Grillmeier in *Der Logos am Kreuz* (Munich 1956) has interestingly maintained that the sixth century Syrian Crucifixion of Rabulas represents Christ dead, the eyes being open to signify His divinity. In support of his view, Grillmeier cites the *Physiologus* legend of the lion sleeping with its eyes open, with which was associated the Song of Songs v, 2, 'Ergo dormio, et cor meum vigilat'. Certainly, however, there was no naturalistic representation of Christ dead as such an early date.

[31] He does, however, emphasize that the body is God's, with a deliberate startlingness of effect, which we shall analyse later.

[32] *P.L.* xcii, 915.

[33] *In Joannis Evangelium tractatus* cxxiv *P.L.* xxxv 1952. Bede also makes this point in his hymn on the six days of the creation and six ages of the world, F. J. Mone *Lateinische Hymnen des Mittelalters* (Freiburg im Breisgau 1853) I, 1. The image of death as a sleep was also often associated by the Fathers with the Resurrection of the dead, and various passages in the Psalms were thus interpreted. On the latter point see M. B. Ogle 'The Sleep of Death' *Memoirs of the American Academy in Rome* x (1932) 81–117. This article is an interesting and learned study of the image of death as a sleep in classical and Christian writings.

Cross speak has perhaps been exaggerated, for, as scholars have sufficiently shown, there are adequate parallels in the Anglo-Saxon Riddles and in Latin literature to the convention of ascribing speech to an inanimate object, and to this can be added the point that in at least one dramatic passage in the Fathers in a Pseudo-Augustinian sermon, the Cross itself is actually imagined as speaking.[34] It is the use made by the poet of this device that rather deserves admiring praise: his identification, in part, of the Cross with Christ.

In reaction from the forms of Monophysitism, which so stressed the divinity of Christ that he was thought to be naturally free in both body and consciousness of all human experience of discomfort and pain, orthodox commentators stressed that like other men He hungered and thirsted. He must therefore also have felt the pain of the Crucifixion, though of course in His humanity, not in His impassible Godhead. The sufferings of Christ in His human nature the poet suggests most movingly by the sufferings of the Cross. The Cross shares in all the sufferings of Christ, so that it seems to endure a compassion, in the sense in which that word was used in the Middle Ages to describe the Virgin's identification of her feelings with those of her Son in His Passion. The real emotional intensity of Christ's agony is thus communicated without the reasonable and insoluble bewilderment arising of how impassiblity and passibility could co-exist in one consciousness.

The Cross not only experiences the extremities of pain but, having within itself the power to escape them, endures with a reluctance heroically subdued. This reluctance must primarily be referred to the other aspect of the Cross, that of the loyal retainer, and its steadfastness then gains an impressive force, since by a tremendous and ironic reversal of the values of the heroic code, it has to acquiesce in and even assist in the death of its lord, forbidden either to protect Him or avenge Him. To see the Cross's reiterated statements of obedience solely as another reflection of Christ's human nature would undoubtedly be to narrow and misinterpret the range of emotion expressed, much of which consists of the anguish of being the cause of death to another, particularly since the other is by

[34] On the device of making the Cross speak see Margaret Schlauch, '*The Dream of the Rood* as Prosopopoeia', *Essays and Studies in Honor of Carleton Brown* (New York 1940), pp. 23–34. The most probable direct source, however, is one of those dramatic passages in the works of the Fathers, whose influence on literature has yet to be thoroughly examined. The passage from the Pseudo-Augustinian sermon (*P.L.* xlvii, 1155) is probably not unique of its kind, and it or some analogue may well have been known to the author of the *Dream of the Rood.*

implication its lord, to whom it feels that mixture of love and loyal duty, which was the proper feeling of a retainer. It is, moreover, theologically undesirable to over-emphasize the reluctance of the Cross as being also a feeling of Christ. The Church, in opposition to Monothelitism, had defined the coexistence of two wills in Christ, but had added that there was no conflict between them, since the human will conformed itself voluntarily to the divine. There was also a view, which sprang from a sense of decorum rather than from philosophic reasoning, that even if moderate fear were not in itself evil, it would nevertheless be unfitting that Christ should in any way experience it and recoil from the Crucifixion, thus detracting from the voluntariness of the act. Nevertheless there was one notable passage in the gospels, the account of the Agony in the Garden, which in its literal sense precisely ascribed to Christ that revulsion from pain and death which is an inherent element in human nature. There is a sense of strain in Bede's commentaries on this scene in all three gospels. On the one hand, following Ambrose and Jerome, he does not interpret the cup, as it was commonly interpreted in the Middle Ages, as the cup of Christ's sufferings, but refers it to the Jews, who having the law and the prophets can have no excuse for crucifying one whom they should have recognized. On the other hand the passage interpreted literally provided the strongest evidence against the Gnostics and Phantasiasts who had denied the reality of Christ's human body—a point which Bede makes in exclamatory style—whilst the actual texts, 'The spirit is willing but the flesh is weak'[35] and 'Not my will but thine be done' had similarly become *loci classici* for the refutation of the Monothelites; and in his commentary on the first of these in Matthew and Mark, Bede, following a common tradition, allows that Christ in His human nature shrank back from death:

> Facit hic locus et adversus Eutychianos, qui dicunt unam in mediatore Dei et hominum Domino ac Salvatore nostro operationem, unam fuisse voluntatem. Cum enim dicit *Spiritus quidem promptus est, caro autem infirma*, duas voluntates ostendit: humanam, videlicet, quae est carnis, et divinam, quae est deitatis. Ubi humana quidem propter infirmitatem carnis recusat passionem, Divina autem ejus est promptissima.[36]

[35] It was not until later that it was denied that the first of these texts could be applied to Christ Himself.

[36] *P.L.* xcii, 277. 'This passage also works against the Eutychians who maintain that there is only one action and one will in the mediator between God and men, our Lord and Saviour ... For when he says that "the spirit is willing but the flesh is weak", he expresses two wills, viz. the human which is of flesh, and the divine which belongs to His Godhead. For where the human because of the weakness of the flesh draws back from the passion, His divine will is most ready for it.'

Whilst, therefore, the parallel must not be pressed too far, nor in any way exclusively, it is difficult not to see a correspondence between the antithesis of the divine and human wills in this passage from Bede and the contrast in the poem between the hero who hastens to his death and the Cross enduring only with reluctance.

It might at this point be urged that the reflection in the *Dream of the Rood* of the divine and the human in the young hero and the Cross has been overstated, and that the figure of the warrior might symbolize no more than Christ's glorious humanity. But it was precisely this element in Christ which had been ignored in Leo's *Tome* and by subsequent commentators. All actions had been assigned to the two categories of divine and human, and the possibility of a third category—actions possible to a sinless humanity—had not been mentioned. It is therefore certain that anybody who understood the Christological doctrine at all would think in terms of this rigid distinction, which may appear unfamiliar and exaggerated to the modern reader.

The treatment of the young hero and the Cross has so far been seen to fulfil the principle of 'recognizing the difference', but the distinction between divinity and humanity, triumph and suffering, is reunited by the stylistic form of the *communicatio idiomatum*. It is interesting to compare the style of the *Dream of the Rood* with that of the description of the Crucifixion in the *Crist*. Since the latter is a complaint, the main point is the contrast between man's sin and Christ's goodness, man's ingratitude and Christ's love. The characteristic of the style is therefore a series of antitheses, which are stylistically pointed by the alliteration:

Ic wæs on worulde wædla, þæt þu wurde welig on heofonum,
earm wæs ic on eðle þinum, þæt þu wurde eadig on minum.
(1495–6)[37]

This, of course, is not native to Anglo-Saxon style, but derives from the Easter liturgy, particularly the *Improperia* of Good Friday, conceivably with the stimulus of a sermon intermediary. The effect of the *communicatio idiomatum* is likewise not native to Anglo-Saxon style, for it provides the shock and astonishment of violent paradox. The strangeness of both these styles to Anglo-Saxon literature is immediately evident if we think of them as characteristics of metaphysical poetry: the antitheses being found in their most polished and pointed form in Herbert's 'The Sacrifice', and the

[37] 'I was a poor man in the world, that you might be rich in heaven; I was wretched in your native land, that you might be blessed in mine.'

potentialities of the *communicatio idiomatum* most fully exploited in such an objectively meditative sequence as Donne's *La Corona.* But although the Anglo-Saxons lack the stylistic poise of the Metaphysicals, it might well be maintained that they managed these stylistic forms with greater assurance than did the writers of the mediaeval lyric.

In the thirty lines of dramatic description of the Crucifixion in the *Dream of the Rood* there are ten examples of the *communicatio idiomatum*, and each one stimulates a shock at the paradox, a shock which grows in intensity as the peom progresses. Those towards the end are particularly striking: 'Genamon hie þær ælmihtigne god' [They seized there Almighty God] (60), 'Aledon hie limwerigne ... beheoldon hie ðær heofones dryhten' [They laid him down, limb weary ... they gazed there on the Lord of Heaven] (63–64), 'gesetton hie ðæron sigora Wealdend' [They placed therein the Lord of Victories] (67). The habit of variation in Anglo-Saxon poetic style and the richness of synonym in Anglo-Saxon poetic diction, assist the poet in each instance to use a fresh word or phrase to emphasize some attribute of God, His rule, majesty, omnipotence; and at the early date of the *Dream of the Rood* there can be no question of such periphrases having become so conventional as to be weakened in meaning. The theological point that the Christ who endured the Crucifixion is fully God and fully man is thus perfectly made, and with it the imaginative effect which is the natural result of the *communicatio idiomatum* is attained, the astonishment at the great paradox of Christianity that God should endure such things.

There is a further and related point of contrast to be made between the description of the Crucifixion in the *Crist* and in the *Dream of the Rood.* Since the first takes its form from the antiphons of the liturgy, it anticipates the medieval lyrics and mystery plays, in which the audience or readers are made to feel participants in the action, by Christ's direct address to them, and the making of their actions and feelings one half of the stylized antitheses. The didactic and devotional intention of this is plain, but it also serves another useful literary purpose, though probably unintentionally: it removes the difficulty of the customary instinctive reaction of the audience—which is, to identify themselves with the character in the play or poem with whom they sympathize. There can be no danger of them unconsciously identifying themselves with Christ in His torment because they feel themselves present in their own person. Their own feelings and situation are dramatically relevant to what is being said or done in the literary work. Now this is not so in the *Dream of the Rood*, where the dreamer, with his consciousness of the tragic and terrifying contrast between his own sinfulness and the glory of the Cross, is forgotten once the Cross begins to speak. However, particularly in the Anglo-Saxon period, a treatment of the Crucifixion in which the hearer was led by his intense sympathy for Christ's pain to identify himself with Christ in the poem, would obviously be unfortunate, since it would carry with it the implication that Christ's consciousness was solely human and therefore comprehensible to fellow human beings. But to imagine Christ's consciousness as the Crucifixion in terms of human experience would be to revert, though no doubt unsuspectingly, to the Gnostic heresy which was even more obviously un-Christian than the extremes of Nestorianism and Monophysitism, that before the Passion began Christ's divinity left Him. By the semi-identification of the Cross with Christ, the poet enables his hearers to share in an imaginative recreation of Christ's sufferings, whilst the problem which bewilders the mind—the nature of Christ's consciousness—is evaded.

The general feeling and vocabulary of the *Dream of the Rood* suggest affinities with the school of Cynewulf rather than of Cædmon. But it is evident from the early date of the Ruthwell Cross, on which modern archaeologists and art historians are agreed, that the *Dream of the Rood* must have been an offshoot of the school of Biblical poetry begun by Cædmon.[38] Yet, when Bede speaks of Christ's Passion as on of Cædmon's subjects, one inevitably thinks of the style of the section of the *Heliand* which describes the Crucifixion (5534–715), rather than of the *Dream of the Rood.* But the poem must have been written round about the year 700, and that the poet did not simply write a Biblical paraphrase in native style must surely be accounted for by the fact that he was steeped in the doctrine of the Church, and thus gave to his treatment of the Crucifixion the full richness and subtlety of its theological significance. The exigencies of a complex and rigid doctrine, far from hampering the poetic imagination, have here provoked a magnificent response: a profound and dramatic meditation that could never have been inspired by unchartered freedom. It is, in fact, this poetic transformation of the philosophic and theological views of the Crucifixion that gives to the poem its unique quality, and adds depths below depths of meaning under the apparently lucid surface.

[38] On the other hand that part of the poem which follows the description of the Crucifixion must surely be a later addition by a writer of the school of Cynewulf.

IV

THE EFFECT OF TYPOLOGY ON THE ENGLISH MEDIEVAL PLAYS OF ABRAHAM AND ISAAC

THE story of Abraham and Isaac, of which there survive in England seven medieval plays,[1] including one Cornish, is the most consistently well told tale of all those in the Corpus Christi cycles. These plays might also be called the most successful, in that, although others such as the famous *Secunda Pastorum* or the Towneley Play of Noah may be more lively, they are less integrated: they are diverting in both the modern and original meaning of the word, for they interest and amuse by characterization and action which have no relevance to the religious meaning of the story. By contrast, in the plays of Abraham and Isaac there is no development of character and no incidental action which is irrelevant to the story, though this relevance must be measured, not by the relation of the plays to the twenty-second chapter of Genesis but by their relation to the traditional interpretation given to it by the Fathers of the Church. There is a radical distinction between these two. In the Biblical account Abraham is the only important figure—Isaac is mentioned only as an object of sacrifice—and the sole point of the narrative is the testing of Abraham's obedience. He therefore seems to be on the very threshold of becoming a tragic figure, and the stress of the story, both dramatic and moral, seems to fall naturally upon the feelings of Abraham towards the immense demand made of him. In any expansion of the story he might at least be expected to hesitate, as he does in the best sixteenth-century plays on the subject, such as the Protestant classical tragedy of Theodore Béza, *Abraham Sacrifiant*, in which Abraham, in a long scene immediately before the sacrifice, is stirred by but rejects the evil arguments prompted by the devil,[2] or the

[1] The editions used are as follows: *The Chester Plays*, ed. Deimling and Matthews, E.E.T.S., E.S., LXII, 62–83; *Ludus Coventriæ*, ed. K. S. Block, E.E.T.S., E.S., CXX, 43–51; *The Towneley Plays*, ed. England and Pollard, E.E.T.S., E.S., LXXI, 40–49; *York Mystery Plays*, ed. L. Toulmin Smith (1885), pp. 56–67; *The Non-Cycle Mystery Plays*, ed. O. Waterhouse, E.E.T.S., E.S., CIV, Dublin and Brome Plays 26–53; *The Ancient Cornish Drama*, trans. E. Norris, I, 96–108.

[2] *Abraham Sacrifiant*, sixteenth-century translation by Arthur Golding, ed. M. W. Wallace (1906), pp. 31–36.

Italian-influenced Cretan play, *'Η Θυσία τοῦ 'Αβραάμ*,[3] where Abraham's immediate reply to the angel's message is a moving speech of protest and resistance. In the medieval plays, however, this potentiality is ignored, and Abraham accepts the will of God with what at first sight may seem an unsympathetic and implausible swiftness. But Abraham in these is not the central figure, and his speech of submission to God's command is no more than a necessary preliminary to the main action of the play, which takes place on the mountain in the 'land of vision.' Isaac is the hero. It is he whose feelings are emphasized, and it is his confession of obedience to his father and to his death, which is the dramatic peak in all but one of the plays.[4] The explanation of this transference of roles lies in the common recognition in the Middle Ages of Abraham's sacrifice as a type of the Crucifixion, and it is this figurative meaning of the story which modifies character and action, and at the same time deepens them by adding such an august allegorical signification.

Although Abraham's sacrifice was not one of the earliest types, since it was not one of those established by Christ Himself, nor of those recorded by St. Paul, it very quickly became one of the most popular. It is mentioned in the works of the great Fathers, both Latin and Greek, Ambrose,[5] Augustine,[6] Origen,[7] Tertullian,[8] and many

[3] The play has been translated into English verse in F. H. Marshall and John Mavrogordato, *Three Cretan Plays* (1929), and into French prose by M. Valsa in *Le Sacrifice d'Abraham, mistère grec du xvie siècle* (1924); the latter is stylistically preferable. It is interesting to notice that in *Lo Isach* by Luigi Grotto, from which *'Η Θυσία* probably derives, Abraham is given two sections to his speech, in the first of which as *huomo spirital* he rejoices in the angel's message, seeing in Isaac's sacrifice a figure of the Crucifixion, whilst in the second, speaking as *huom carnale*, he laments over it and wishes for some means of lessening his distress. The other well-known Italian treatment of the subject, *La rappresantazione d'Abraam e d'Isaac suo figliuolo* (A. d'Ancona, *Sacre rappresantazione dei secoli xiv, xv e xvi* (1872), I, 41–59) is far more mediaeval in that Abraham is completely unhesitant, and no additional action detracts from the effect of Isaac's childish fear resolving itself into obedience to God's will. In the other plays mentioned Isaac is also obedient, but his consent is either obscured by too much action throughout the play irrelevant to this point, or else, as in *Abraham Sacrifiant*, it is made subordinate and complementary to Abraham's consent.

[4] The exception is the Towneley Play, in which the issue is obscured since Isaac is never told that the sacrifice has been commanded by God. This play is dramatically inferior in that the sentiment, though incidentally touching, is not directed to a climax. The moral strength of the story, which is also its dramatic backbone, is sacrificed to a slightly sentimental naturalism.

[5] *De Abraham*, J. P. Migne, *Patrologia Latina*, XIV, 445–449.

[6] *De Civitate Dei*, xvi, 32, *P.L.*, XLIV, 511.

[7] *In Genesim*, ix, *P.G.*, XII, 208.

[8] *Adversus Judaeos*, x, *P.L.*, II, 626; the passage is repeated in *Adversus Marcionem, P.L.*, II, 346.

others,[9] who not only expound it in their exegesis of the Book of Genesis, but also use it in their defence of the religious value of the Old Testament against the Manichaeans and in their arguments designed for the confutation of the Jews. It was almost equally common in early Christian art,[10] where it probably served the purpose of signifying the Crucifixion at a time when an actual representation of this subject was considered indecorous. Augustine, when urging the propriety and moral worth of the story of Abraham to the Manichaean Faustus, testified to its popularity: '... nisi forte non ei veniret in mentem factum ita nobile, ut non lectum, nec quæsitum animo occurreret, ut denique tot linguis contatum, tot locis pictum, et aures et oculos dissimulantis feriret.'[11]

In the Middle Ages it would have been even more difficult for the story of Abraham's sacrifice to escape the eyes and ears of anybody, however uninterested he might be in it. The comments of the Fathers were quoted in every kind of religious work from the Biblical commentaries to manuals of popular instruction and devotion, whilst the tradition of visual representation also continued and multiplied itself in stained glass, carving, wall painting, manuscript illumination, and in the great compendiums of typology, such as the *Biblia Pauperum* and the *Speculum Humanæ Salvationis*. In all the written works the typological significance of the story was expounded, often as in the *Glossa Ordinaria*,[12] with the most minute allegorisation. In visual art, however, the significance had to be indicated by some other means. Sometimes this was achieved solely by the choice of episode: thus the typological intention is quite clear in any representation of Isaac bearing the wood of his sacrifice, since this detail is comparatively unimportant in the Biblical narrative, but extremely significant as a striking prefiguration of Christ carrying the Cross. Again this significance could be indicated by the context in which the

[9] Other references may be found in Vol. CCIX of the *Patrologia Latina* in the Index of Old Testament Figures, col. 245.

[10] On the early representation of the subject see A. M. Smith, 'The Sacrifice of Isaac in Early Christian Art', *American Journal of Archaeology*, XXVI, 159–173, and J. Wilpert, 'Das Opfer Abrahams', *Romanische Quartalschrift*, I, 126–160.

[11] *Contra Faustum*, xxii, 73, *P.L.*, XLII, 446. This passage is quoted by Wilpert, *loc. cit.*, p. 130, and by Jean Daniélou, *Sacramentum Futuri*, p. 110, a work which also contans a valuable study of this type, 97–111. 'Unless perhaps this deed did not come to mind, <a deed> so renowned, that even without reading about it, or looking for it, it would come to mind, <a deed> narrated in so many languages, represented in pictures in so many localities, that it would hit the eyes and ears even of an inattentive person.'

[12] *P.L.*, CXIII, 139.

representation was set. In the *Biblia Pauperum*, for instance, Christ carrying the Cross is bounded on one side by Isaac bearing his faggots and on the other by the Widow of Sarepta gathering sticks.[13] The typological resemblance, however, is most often pointed by some iconographical peculiarity. Thus, the bundles of faggots or pieces of wood may be arranged on Isaac's back (or on the altar) in the shape of a cross, as for example in the windows at Canterbury, Bourges, and Chartres, or in the scene of the sacrifice Isaac may lie or kneel, quiet and obedient, upon the altar, with his hands tied, as those of Christ were said to be according to the Gospel of Nicodemus, or else folded in prayer: there is no suggestion of reluctance or struggle.

Abraham's sacrifice was thus commonly known as a type of the Crucifixion, but, being with Abel's offering of the lamb and Melchisedek's offering of bread and wine one of the three great typological sacrifices *ante legem*, it was also a prefiguration of the sacrifice of Christ in the Eucharist. The association was made plain in the liturgy itself, in which the priest with hands outstretched crosswise over the sacraments prayed: 'Supra que propicio ac sereno vultu respicere digneris, et accepta habere sicuti accepta habere dignatus es munera pueri iusti abel. et sacrificium patriarche nostri abrahe ....'[14] On this passage the great medieval expositor of the liturgy, Durandus, writes: '... quia illi eorum sacramenta, specialius cæteris, hoc sacramentum præsignaverant.'[15] The connection is driven home farther by the illuminations of medieval sacramentaries.[16] The latter have very few illuminations, but of these the most common subject is the Crucifixion, and the next most common subject is the sacrifice of Abraham. The latter is most frequently an illumination of the initial T of the *Te igitur*, the first words of the canon of the mass. This letter T was very important allegorically, and, according to Durandus, it was by the grace of God that the canon (the most solemn part of the mass) so began.[17] For this T was not only the Tau of Ezekiel and hence associated with the blood

[13] *Biblia Pauperum*, ed. Johan Henrik Cornell, Stockholm, 1925, pl. 10.

[14] *Sarum Missal*, ed. Wickham Legge, 223. 'Deign to look upon these with a favourable and glad countenance, and to accept them as you were pleased to accept the gifts of the just youth Abel, and the sacrifice of Abraham, our patriarch.'

[15] *Rationale Divinorum Officiorum*, IV, xliii, 13, ed. Naples 1859, p. 278. 'Because their sacraments had prefigured this sacrament, more particularly than others.'

[16] The following account of this subject is based on the description of manuscripts in Abbe V. Leroquais, *Les Sacramentaires et Missels manuscrits des bibliotheques publiques de France* (1924).

[17] *Rationale*, IV, XXXV, ll, *ed. cit.*, p. 239.

of the Paschal lamb[18] but also, and more importantly, a Tau Cross,[19] and upon it illuminators sometimes placed the figure of the crucified Christ, thus pointing the matter visually.[20] It is, of course, only a T of Roman style that can have this significance. But the rounded T of the Carolingian style, which was also used, had this advantage, that it could conveniently contain a small scene, and very often it was thus enabled to acquire the same allegorical significance as the Roman T by enclosing within itself a scene of the sacrifice of Abraham. Therefore, to the innumerable verbal and visual illustrations of the sacrifice of Abraham as a type of the Crucifixion can be added a considerable number of references—notably in the mass itself—to the sacrifice of Abraham as a prefiguration of the Eucharistic sacrifice; and this secondary significance must have added greatly to its effectiveness as a type and given it a particular daily relevance. It would, indeed, be fair to conclude that in an age when the typological interpretation of the Old Testament was everywhere well known and accepted, there was no type which was so popular, so familiar, and so recurrent.

The medieval plays of Abraham and Isaac cannot be disassociated from this background of typological interpretation. Indeed if the Old Testament plays developed from the *lectiones* and *responsaria* of the breviary for the period of Septuagesima and Lent—which is the more probable theory of their origin[21]—then in its very beginnings the story was accompanied by its allegorical interpretation, for it is told and commented upon in *lectiones* v and vi for Quinquagesima Sunday, which are drawn from the *de fide Abrahæ* of St. John Chrysostom, and the play would have formed part of a

[18] The Tau Cross is the typical cross of the Old Testament. It is mentioned in Ezekiel, ix, as the sign to be inscribed on the foreheads of the innocent whom God wishes to spare. From the influence of this it was commonly assumed that, on the night of the slaying of the Egyptian first-born, the Jews marked their doors, not simply with the blood of the lamb, but with the blood in the shape of a Tau cross; this mark thus became even more closely a prefiguration of the Passion.

[19] This point is made not only by Durandus, but by other scholars such as Honorius Augustodunensis, *Gemma Animæ*, I, ciii, *P.L.*, CLXXII, 577, and Joannes Belethus, *Rationale Divinorum Officiorum*, xlvi, *P.L.*, CCII, 54.

[20] Examples of this may be seen in Leroquais, Vol. IV, pl. xv, and H. Swarzenski, *Monuments of Romanesque Art* (1954), pl. 94.

[21] Cf. Hardin Craig, 'The Origin of the Old Testament Plays', *Modern Philology*, x, 473–483. The earlier view of M. Sepet, *Les Prophètes du Christ* (1878), that the Old Testament Plays developed from dramatic expansions within the *Ordo Prophetarum*, whilst less probable, would be equally relevant to our argument if it were true, since then Abraham's sacrifice would have grown in a framework of the foreseeing and foreshadowing of the New Testament in the Old Testament.

Passion series, as opposed to a Nativity sequence, until the two groups were combined and arranged in chronological order. Moreover, the authors of these plays, who were learned men and often in religious orders, must inevitably have been so accustomed to the traditional significance of the story, that it would have seemed to them the obvious and natural way of approaching it. Admittedly the English are not so explicit about the typological meaning of their subject matter as are the authors of the French and German mystery plays. The Chester cycle is alone in having an expositor who comments on the prefigurative sense at the end of each play, and the only other actual statement of an Old Testament type is in the Cain and Abel of the *Ludus Coventriae*, in which Abel sees in his lamb a prefiguration of Christ. In contrast, the continental writers are often extremely explicit. In the *Mistère du Vieil Testament*, for instance, the story of Abraham and Isaac (as of the other Old Testament subjects) is set within the framework of the common mediaeval theme of a debate between the four daughters of God, and therefore God and Justice and Mercy are able throughout the play to interpose comments which interpret it allegorically, and the action is seen continuously under its prophetic aspect.[22] In German drama the play of Abraham and Isaac in the *Sündenfall* is followed by a Play of the Prophets, in which Melchisedek comments upon the spiritual meaning of the preceding play,[23] whilst in the *Freiburger Passionspiel* the Proclamator announces it in advance in his Prologue.[24] The most striking example of all, however, is the *Heidelberger Passionspiel*, of which the main section consists of a series of pairs of types and antitypes (Play xxxiii consists of Abraham and Isaac followed by Christ carrying the Cross[25]). It has been called 'an acted *Biblia Pauperum*,' and cannot but be associated with the popular interest in typology which must have both preceded, and resulted from, the publication of the *Biblia Pauperum* and the *Speculum Humanæ Salvationis* as block books.

In all these plays English, French, and German, whether the allegorical meaning is stated or not, the treatment from the typological point of view is largely identical. It would, therefore,

[22] *Mistère du Vieil Testament*, ed. J. de Rothschild, II, 1–79.

[23] Arnold Immessen, *Der Sündenfall*, ed. Friedrich Krage, 1896, ll. 2128 ff., p. 158.

[24] 'Freiburger Passionspiel des XVI Jahrhunderts', ed. Ernst Martin, *Zeitschrift der Gesellschaft für Beförderung der Geschichtkunde zu Freiburg im Breisgau*, III, 4, ll. 25–28.

[25] *Heidelberger Passionspiel*, ed. Gustav Milchsack (1880), pp. 231–232.

perhaps be unwise to deduce from this comparison that the English were less interested in or less conscious of the typological significance than their continental counterparts. Certainly there is no evidence outside the plays that the English were comparatively indifferent to typology. For instance, as M. R. James has shown,[26] there were vast and elaborate typological cycles in wall painting and stained glass at the cathedrals of Peterborough, Canterbury, and Worcester, at a time when in France there only existed isolated typological scenes. And again England seems to have made its contribution to the typological compendiums by the unusually large collection made by 'Pictor in Carmine.'[27] It might even, therefore, be argued that the English writers of the mystery plays did not usually explain their typological point because it was sufficiently well known, and that such undisguised didacticism would have been hampering and unneccesary, since the audience would understand the symmetrical pattern within the chronological arrangement, and mentally always supply antitype to type. It is certainly difficult to believe that the author of the *Ludus Coventriae*, who is clearly theologically minded and steeped in medieval religious tradition, would not have pointed out the typological meaning of Abraham's sacrifice, as he did incidentally and casually of Abel's lamb, had he supposed that most of his audience would otherwise be ignorant of it.[28]

Some further evidence of the unlettered layman's knowledge of typology may be derived from the medieval carols. It is worth making a connection between these and the plays, for both forms seem to have been written by the learned for the benefit of the unlearned, and both contain thought of a serious or doctrinal kind expressed in a style unsophisticated almost to the point of naïveté. But the carols instruct in, and expect a considerable understanding of, medieval typology. They range from reference to common types such as Gideon's fleece or the burning bush to the more abtruse address of Christ as King Ahasuerus;[29] without such knowledge

[26] 'Pictor in Carmine', *Archaeologia*, XCIV, 146.

[27] *Archaeologia*, XCIV, 140–166.

[28] There is a possibility that the audience may sometimes have been reminded of the typological meaning by some device in the production. Isaac, for instance, may have carried his wood in the form of a cross, as he so often does in visual art. The acknowledged resemblance between representation on the stage and in art makes this not at all unlikely, but unfortunately there is no definite evidence. In the alabasters, for example, where an undoubted connection has been proved (*Archaeologia*, XCIII, 51–101), there are no Old Testament scenes.

[29] Examples of these and others may be found in R. L. Greene, *The Early English Carols* (1935), Nos. 66, 189, 193, 203, etc.

quite a number of the carols cannot be understood and a large number cannot be appreciated. The demands which the dramatists seem to have made on their audience are very modest by comparison.

A possible source of instruction in the typological interpretation of the Old Testament is the medieval sermon. But, although the *Artes Prædicandi* recommend the use of all three levels of allegory as a method of *dilatio*,[30] it is evident from the English popular vernacular sermons themselves that, of the three, only the tropological was consistently used, it being the moral and practical as opposed to the devotional and intellectual.[31] Nevertheless, the other levels of allegory were not ignored, and scattered through the sermons we find mention of common prefigurations such as the brazen serpent as a type of the Crucifixion[32] or the manna in the wilderness as a type of the Eucharist.[33] The sacrifice of Abraham is expounded in some detail in the sermon for Quinquagesima Sunday in Mirk's *Festial*:

> Then by Abraham ȝe schull undyrstonde þe Fadyr of Heven, and by Isaac his sonne Ihesu Crist. þe wheche he sparyd not for no love þat he had to hym; but he suffered þe Iewes to lay þe wode apon hym, þat was þe crosse apon hys schuldres, and ladden hym to þe mount of Calvary,[34] and þer dydyn him on þe autre of wode, þat was þe crosse.[35]

The fact that this exposition occurs in the *Festial*—and not in a private collection of sermons—gives it added weight as evidence of homiletic typology, for these sermons were designed as models for parish priests who 'for defaute of bokis and also by simpleness of connyng' were unable to compose effective sermons themselves, and Mirk would have selected with care the additions which he made to his self-acknowledged source the *Legenda Aurea*. Moreover, Mirk's intention was manifestly successful, since the *Festial* was copied in numerous manuscripts and printed by both Caxton and Winkyn de Worde. It would clearly be perverse to consider this passage either an

[30] On this see H. Caplan, 'The Four Senses of Scriptural Interpretation and the Mediaeval Theory of Preaching', *Speculum*, IV, 282–290.

[31] Hardin Craig (*op. cit.*, p. 485) maintains that the typological exposition of the Old Testament was common in sermons of the Middle Ages, but refers only to Ælfric's. It is evident that such an exposition was less likely to occur in sermons preached on a text drawn from the epistle or gospel for the day, and more likely to occur in sermons suited to the season; thus in both Ælfric and Mirk the references to Abraham's sacrifice are contained in the sermons designed for Quinquagesima.

[32] *Twelfth Century Homilies*, ed. A. O. Balfour, E.E.T.S., CXXXVII, 11.

[33] *Old English Homilies*, ed. R. Morris, E.E.T.S., LIII, 99.

[34] The Mount of Calvary was identified with Mount Moriah (and, incidentally, with the burial place of Adam).

[35] E.E.T.S., E.S., XCVI, 77.

innovation or unique; therefore we have evidence of the typological significance of Abraham's sacrifice reaching the common people by means of direct homiletic instruction.

It was, however, probably from the visual representation of types in stained glass and carving—which we have already discussed—that medieval people became most familiar with them, for the comparative scarcity of types in sermons is here compensated for by an abundance. The reason for this may well have been that typology lent itself better to visual representation, for a resemblance, which when didactically expounded might sound laboured and unenlightening, could be immediately perceived and appreciated when presented to the eye. The eye anyway is always a more effective channel of communication to the unlearned than the ear, and it was no doubt an awareness of this which led to such plentiful visual art in every form in the Middle Ages, and which underlay the theory of long-standing authority that religious art was *muta prædicatio* or *libri laicorum.*[36] This moral-aesthetic theory links illustrations of Biblical history, not only with preaching on the one hand but with mystery plays on the other, for, as we can deduce from the famous Lollard sermon attacking the playing of mysteries, this doctrine was also used apologetically for the drama, except that it was enlarged by the claim of the superiority of the miracle plays over the visual arts, since 'this is a deed bok, the tother a quick.'[37] Whilst the whole passage from which this quotation comes is interesting proof of the didactic value attached to mystery plays—even the Lollard polemicist cannot deny that men have been converted by them—this particular argument of superiority is undoubtedly specious, in that, whilst there is the traditional mixture of profit and delight in both plays and art, the element of entertainment is far greater in the former. At any rate to the exposition of typology the fact that the plays were 'a quick bok' was at least potentially a ruinous disadvantage.

From the aesthetic typological point of view the essential difference between a dead book and a living is this, that in visual art, as also in a gloss on a text, a single moment in time can be isolated, so that only

[36] A useful collection of texts illustrating this point from the Fathers and Medieval authorities has been made by L. Gougaud, 'Muta Prædicatio', *Revue Bénédictine*, XLIII, 168–171.

[37] Thomas Wright and J. O. Halliwell, *Reliquiæ Antiquiæ*, London, 1841, II, 46. In his reply to this argument the author shows even more plainly that he has in mind the doctrine of *libri laicorum*, for he says that painting is 'as nakyd lettris to a clerk to riden the treuthe', whilst plays are 'more to deliten men bodily than to ben bokis to lewid men'.

the exact point of comparison is presented, whereas in a play one action cannot be detached from its context. But the singleness of the moment is essential in very many of the types, since the context is often at best irrelevant and at worst unedifying. In a slightly anxious discussion of the frequent lack of moral concord in the typological interpretation of the Old Testament, the author of the *Speculum Humanæ Salvationis* quotes as an example the story of Samson carrying off the gates of Gaza,[38] which was a common prefiguration of Christ rising from the dead. The lack of concord is striking here, since the reason that Samson found the gates of Gaza closed against him was that he had remained there during the night with his mistress. The point of resemblance therefore lies in the single action, not in character or situation, and it is this one action, without regard to moral concord, upon which typology usually seizes. A clear example of the disastrous literary effect of this is the early Latin liturgical drama of Isaac and Rebecca.[39] The progress of the plot of this play is interrupted by the singing of an allegory, which explains that Isaac represents God, and Rebecca His grace, by which Jacob (the Church) is brought to supersede Esau (the Synagogue). But in the literal meaning of the story Esau is deprived of his birthright, which he in no way deserved to forfeit, by an unjust and deceitful trick, devised by Rebecca and assented to by Jacob. It is Esau who is the faithful and honest son, and this is pointed not only by the plot but by its dramatic treatment, and particularly in the speech of willing and affectionate obedience, with which he replies to the message that Isaac desires to see him:

> Letus ad patrem ambulo;
> eius me fovet visio,
> et mutua colloquia;[40]

There is therefore no literary relationship between the literal meaning of the play and its allegorical significance. The latter, if it does not ruin the play completely, is an unhelpful encumbrance, without which the play—if we can judge it in its extant imperfect form—would be modestly satisfactory.

The plays of Abraham and Isaac are a magnificent exception, for in them the allegorical interpretation does not run contrary to the

[38] *Speculum Humanæ Salvationis*, ed. P. Perdrizet, Mulhouse, 1907, *Prologus*, I, 3.

[39] Karl Young, *The Drama of the Medieval Church*, Oxford, 1933, II, 259–264.

[40] ll. 45–48, p. 260. 'Gladly I walk to my father / the sight of him is warming to me / and my conversation with him.'

feeling of the story. We are not required to perform the mental acrobatic trick of sympathizing with and admiring on one level what we must disapprove of on the other.[41] Literal and allegorical senses move forward smoothly side by side, and the typological meaning in fact contributes, without any improper distortion, to the development of character and action. The allegorical meaning is therefore also clear, even though it is usually only implicit and, when it is actually stated, as in the Chester cycle, it is a natural culmination of the play, and not an irritating and irrelevant appendage.[42]

In the medieval plays of Abraham's sacrifice, as we observed at the beginning, it is Isaac who is the hero rather than Abraham. Therefore, although according to the literal narrative the point of the sacrifice is the testing of Abraham's faith, the dramatic structure of the plays instead directs our interest and attention to Isaac's consent.[43] In a discussion of the motives and manner of this voluntary act of immolation, Isaac's age must first be considered. In the Middle Ages (and up to the seventeenth century), two traditions of Isaac's age at the time of the sacrifice existed side by side.[44] The first, according to which Isaac was only a child, appears in the earliest visual representations of the subject and in the Middle Ages was defended strongly by Nicholas de Lyra. The second tradition, that he was twenty-five or thirty years of age, was, however, by far the more common in exegesis; it seems to derive ultimately from Josephus, although it probably became widely familiar in the Middle Ages through the more well-known *Historia Scholastica* of Petrus Comestor, who refers to Josephus as his authority for this point. In

[41] This lack of moral correlation was particularly frequent, in that an allegorical meaning had been all the more urgently sought for in those passages in the Old Testament where the literal meaning was unedifying.

[42] It should be noted that the play of Abraham and Isaac is the only one which is typologically ideal, and it is perhaps, therefore, the result of deliberate literary design that the Chester Expositor comments only on it and one other play, that of Melchisedek. In the latter there is also no strain between literal and allegorical levels, but the ordinary meaning of the story is comparatively dull and unimportant.

[43] In the Brome Play, however, and in an unprinted German play described by T. Weber, *Die Præfigurationen im geistlichen Drama Deutschlands* (Marburg thesis, 1919), Abraham's obedience is commented upon didactically. In the Brome play the doctor's remarks at the end about mothers who are not resigned when their children die suggests a topical allusion in its preciseness, although this may also have been a traditional moral of the story, since it is drawn by St Jerome in a letter to Paula (Epistle xxxix, *P.L.*, XXII, 472).

[44] See Minnie E. Wells, 'The Age of Isaac at the time of the Sacrifice', *Modern Language Notes*, LIV, 579–582. There seems to be no reason for supposing with her that the Isaac of the *Ludus Coventriæ* is adult.

the miracle plays this tradition of Isaac as a man of mature years is alone followed by the author of the York cycle. On first consideration it might seem that Christ could more appropriately be prefigured by an adult than by a child, for, besides love and obedience, an adult could also demonstrate the fullness of resignation and self-sacrifice of which only maturity is capable. Such a representation has at least been achieved in art, as in the carving of Abraham's sacrifice on the right of the west door of the church of Souillac. But the York play is evidence that this is not so in drama. Here the author has lost the pathos of the situation and gained nothing in power and amplitude. Perhaps such a conception demanded a strength of imagination and a dignity of expression, which the inevitable naïveté of technique in the early drama was itself sufficient to prevent.

There was also a particular disadvantage typologically to the prefiguration of Christ as an adult in any work in which there is an extension of time: he could not be sinless; and therefore in the York Play Isaac suitably confesses to Abraham that he has sinned, and asks and received forgiveness from him. But in the other plays Isaac's sinlessness is emphasized: in Brome Abraham blesses the 'ȝowng innosent' and exclaims that Isaac has never once grieved him,[45] whilst in Towneley Abraham, in words which perhaps deliberately echo those of Pilate, says, 'Bot no defawt I faund hym in.' The phrase 'young innocent' sums up Isaac's character, and relates it to a semi-theological and imaginative conception of childhood common in the Middle Ages, which made the figure of a child particularly suitable as a type of Christ.[46] The doctrinal view is epitomized in the comment of

[45] The version of this in the Chester Play, where Abraham says that Isaac has once grieved him, and for that he grants him forgiveness, must surely, as J. B. Severs maintains ('The Brome and Chester *Abraham and Isaac*', *Modern Philology*, XLII, 145–146), represent the mechanical reproduction of a corrupt form of the Brome line '... thow grevyd me never onys'. This article also contains very strong evidence for supposing that the Chester Abraham and Isaac is an inferior form of the Brome Play, in which case it cannot, according to the old view recently revived by Hardin Craig (*English Religious Drama*, Oxford, 1955, pp. 171 ff.), be based on an earlier version of the play in the *Mistère du Vieil Testament*. The argument of the present article does not depend upon any theory of these relationships. It is clear that western Europe shared a common dramatic tradition, and it is possible to find coincidences in various combinations of English, French, German, and Italian plays, but, on account of the quantity now lost, it would be quite profitless to attempt to construct a stemma of these relationships.

[46] In exegesis an insistence on the youth of Isaac springs from a literal comment on the text. Nicholas de Lyra in the *Additio*, ii, and *Replica* for Genesis, xxii, argues that if Isaac had been an adult he would have been stronger than Abraham, and therefore his consent and obedience would also have been required. But, he says, Isaac *ex defectu ætatis* did not have freedom of will, and therefore, the Bible describes the reward as

the *Glossa Ordinaria* on Matthew, xviii, 4 ('Suffer the little children to come unto me'):

> Invitat discipulos suos, et omnes alios Dominus, ut quod puer habet per naturam, id est innocentiam et humilitatem, hoc habeant discipuli et omnes alii per virtutem .... Innocens erit sicut iste parvulus, qui non perseverat in ira: Jesus non meminit: visam mulierem non cupit.[47]

The important point here is that Christ like a child, and unlike all other adults, possessed innocence, not *per virtutem*, but *per naturam*.

In literature this physical and spiritual innocence showed itself especially in the face of hardship, danger and death. The boy-martyr of the Prioress's Tale is a famous example of this, as are also the little sons of Hugolino in the Monk's Tale.[48] But this conception is not confined to Chaucer, although it found its most masterly and moving expression in his works. Mirk, for instance, imitating a patristic tradition, describes the babies in the massacre of the innocents smiling with love into their slayers' faces,[49] whilst another instance may be seen in the *exemplum* of the repentant adulteress in the *Gesta Romanorum*, which tells of the innocent sweetness and simplicity of the little boy born in prison.[50] In all these children there is no

being only to Abraham: '... Abraham accepit mandatum a deo et obedivit non ysaac, ideo fit memoria de merito illius non istius'. Nicholas repeatedly emphasises the point of the reward being to Abraham alone. It is therefore interesting to notice how, although in exegesis the idea of Isaac as a child was associated with a non-allegorical interpretation of the text, in art and literature it particularly served the purposes of typology.

[47] *P.L.*, CXIV, 116. 'The Lord invites his disciples and all others, that what the child has by nature, *viz.* innocence and humility, the disciples and all other men should have through virtue. Innocent like that little boy will be the man who does not persevere in his anger. Jesus did not remember <injury>, he did not desire the woman he looked on.' The physical innocence of childhood would have seemed a point of importance in the Middle Ages. For instance, Apoc. xiv, 4 ('Hi sunt qui cum mulieribus non sunt coinquinati, virgines enim sunt'), becomes emphasised as a refrain in the versicles and responds for Holy Innocents' Day.

[48] It is very interesting to compare Chaucer's treatment of this incident with Dante's in the *Purgatorio* (Canto xxxiii). Dante's stress is chiefly on grimness and horror, the tragedy of the father who must see his children die, one by one. But Chaucer, although he does not use Dante's one striking touch of pathos, the exclamation of the first child as it dies, 'Padre mio, che non m'aiuti?' (xxxiii, 69), adds much pathos of his own, particularly the stanza beginning at l. 3621, and over and over again he stresses the tender age of the children. Whilst Dante is stirred by the agony of the father, Chaucer is stirred by the pathetic innocence of the children.

[49] E.E.T.S., E.S. XCVI, 29. This is a traditional detail deriving from the Fathers. Tertullian, for instance, in a description of an imaginary slaughter, mentions infants smiling at the sword (*Apologeticus*, viii, *P.L.*, I, 364), and it occurs again in the third *lectio* taken from Severianus, for the Feast of the Holy Innocents: 'Arridebat igitur parvulus occisori: gladio adjocabatur infantulus.'

[50] E.E.T.S., E.S. XXXIII, 12.

rebellion and no fear, but only a tender and submissive resignation. Although these particular children do not show fear, fear itself is not necessarily antithetical to innocence, provided that it is not that kind of immoderate fear that by its own uncontrolled vehemence leads to sinful thought or conduct. The distinction between innocent and sinful fear is well made by Ludolphus Carthusiensis, who, in his description of the Agony in the Garden, contrasts Christ's natural fear of death, which, as He foresaw the Passion, led Him to pray that the cup might pass from Him if that were possible, with the 'timor rationem submergens et hominem contempto dei percepto in peccatum ducens,' which led St. Peter to deny Christ.[51] Christ's fear, however, was circumscribed by His own intention of voluntarily redeeming mankind, and His obedience to the Father. That Christ offered Himself voluntarily to save mankind, because nothing else could make satisfaction for man's sin, was a theological dogma, which became a commonplace of religious poetry and prose of the Middle Ages; that He was obedient to the Father derived from the Agony in the Garden ('Nevertheless not my will but thine be done'), and more especially from St. Paul's comment that Christ was 'obedient unto death, even unto the death of the Cross.' This obedience of Christ distinguished Him as the 'second Adam', for as man fell by Adam's disobedience, so was he restored and redeemed by Christ's obedience, and the latter was therefore stressed only slightly less frequently than his voluntary sacrifice.

In the Isaac of the English miracle plays we see precisely this natural fear of death, tempered by obedience to Abraham and an instinctive willingness to self-sacrifice. At first Isaac hopes for a remission, asks in what way he has sinned, and whether a beating will not suffice instead, hopes that some animal might serve in his place, and even childishly imagines that if Sarah were there she might save

[51] *Vita Cristi*, Pt. II, ch. 59 (Paris, 1517), fol. 203 v: 'Fear submerging reason and leading man into sin by disregard of God's precept.' The same general point had been made in the description of the Agony in the Garden in the *Meditatione* of Bonaventura (trans. Nicholas Love, ed. L. F. Powell (1908), 219–220), where 'thre manere of willes' are distinguished in Christ, the first of which was 'the wille of the flesche and the sensualite and that grucched and dredde and wolde nouȝt gladly duffre deth'. Indeed, that Christ experienced fear of death seems to have become a commonplace of medieval thought. The following verse, for instance, occurs in a *Timor Mortis* poem of the fifteenth century (Greene, no. 370):

> Jhesu Cryst, whanne he schuld dey,
> To hys Fader he gan say;
> 'Fader,' he seyd, 'in Trinyte,
> Timor Mortis conturbat me.'

him; but when he realizes that Abraham's decision is the will of God, his fear is transmuted into a willing, obedient, and loving resignation. The exact pattern of the Agony in the Garden is reproduced in the *Freiburger Passionspiel*, where Isaac touchingly reminds Abraham that he is his son, and asks, if it is Abraham's will, that a lamb may be offered instead of him, but concluding:

> Doch soll allczeit dein will vorgohn
> Und nicht wie ich gebëtten han.[52]

Whilst in the *Mistère du Vieil Testament* the words of St. Paul are echoed, combined with a direct statement of voluntary self-sacrifice:

> A cestefois mort souffriray;
> Devant mon père m'offriray,
> Jusque a la mort obedient.[53]

Although the extant English plays do not thus verbally recall the Gospel scene, they are no less explicit in showing an obedient and voluntary self-sacrifice: in the Brome Play, when Isaac understands that his death is required by God, he exclaims:

> Now, fader, aȝens my Lordes wyll,
> I will never groche, lowd nor styll.[54]

Complete self-commitment is perhaps even clearer in the Dublin Play, where Isaac says 'With al my hert I assent þerto,' whilst in the *Ludus Coventriae* willing obedience extends even to urging his father to the deed:

> Al-myghty god of his grett mercye
> Fful hertyly I thanke þe sertayne
> At goddys byddyng here for to dye
> I obeye me here for to be sclayne
> I pray ȝow fadyr be glad and fayne
> trewly to werke goddys wyll
> take good comforte to ȝow agayne
> and have no dowte ȝour childe to kyll.[55]

The only play in which Isaac's deliberate self-offering is not emphasized, either by a long speech or in the form of a recurrent motif, is the Towneley Play, and, apart from some moving lines, this

[52] ll. 233–234. 'Yet your will must always prevail, / and not what I have pleaded.'
[53] ll. 10190–93. 'Now I will suffer death / I will offer myself before my father / Obedient unto death.'
[54] ll. 190–191.
[55] ll. 145–152.

play is in every way inferior to the others.

It is interesting to notice how in Isaac's obedience the tropological and typological levels of the allegory merge, for Isaac's submission to Abraham also has an obvious moral value as an example of how children should behave. In the Coventry Play Isaac agrees to accompany Abraham, rather pointedly making the moral statement, that to his father 'it ovyth þe childe evyr buxom to be,' while in the *Freiburger Passionspiel*, Isaac, addressing the audience at the end, sets himself up as an edifying example to children:

> Diss beyspill merckhet alle khindt,
> Dass sy den eltern gehorsam seindt.[56]

A connection with the sermons, as Professor Owst supposes, is probably to be seen in this approach, although he undoubtedly exaggerates their influence on the plays of Abraham and Isaac in his reducing of these to 'a dramatisation of current pulpit themes setting forth the right and dutiful relations between parent and child.'[57] The passage, however, which he quotes from Caxton's translation of *Le Livre de Bonnes Moeurs* of Jacques Legrand is worth quotation for a second time as a commentary upon this aspect of the plays:

> And chyldern also owen to theyr parentes, to fader and moder and to theyr maysters, to obeye in folowynge Ysaac, the whiche obeyed in suche wyse to his fader that he was all redy to receyve the deth at his commaundement ... and yet he was at that time of the age of xxxii yere.[58]

This quotation, incidentally, illustrates well the advantage of Isaac being imagined as a child, for though absolute filial obedience may be more morally striking at the age of thirty, from the literary point of view it is more instantly touching and sympathetic in a child, and it must especially so have been in the Middle Ages, when the author could draw on reserves of association, for, though the sermons make it clear that in every day life children were 'rebelle and unbuxom,' literature had established this idealization of children as instinctively obedient and innocent. The plays then had this moral significance, but of course the more Isaac's obedience was emphasized in moral terms, the more typologically appropriate his treatment became, and indeed the wheel can be brought full circle by the following comment

[56] ll. 297–298. 'Let all children take note of this example, / That they be obedient to their parents.'

[57] G. R. Owst, *Literature and the Pulpit in Medieval England*, Oxford, 1961, p. 493.

[58] Bk. IV, ch. 2; Owst, p. 493.

of St. Jerome, quoted by Ludolphus: 'Usque ad finem non cessat [Jesus] docere nos patribus obedire et voluntatem eorum voluntati nostrum preponere.'[59] It was this voluntary obedience which was invariably stressed from the earliest patristic times until the beginning of the Renaissance, when doctrine could be forgotten for humanistic realism, and Ghiberti, for instance, represents on his baptistery door a struggling Isaac, with a body strong and curved in protest. But it should be emphasized that it is not that medieval dramatists do not appear to have asked the essential dramatic question of how would a child behave in these circumstances, but that they answered it in literary rather than realistic terms, with a result that touchingly combines idealism and realism. The author of the Brome Play, in particular, has conceived an Isaac who behaves with a naturalistic childishness, culminating in a supreme effect of pathos; yet at the same time restraining this pathos from degenerating into an excess of sentimentality, but also heightening it, there is this emphasis on Isaac's deliberate obedience: and both the childishness and the obedience have their point typologically.

But although Isaac has become the hero and most interesting character, Abraham on the allegorical level of the narrative—as also on the ordinary—is only slightly less important, for he pre-figured God the Father, whose charity in giving the Son was constantly emphasised in the Middle Ages. Like the doctrine of the obedience of the Son, it has firm foundation in the New Testament, firstly in John iii, 15 ('God so loved the world, that He gave His only begotten Son ...'), and secondly in Romans, viii, 32, ('He that hath not spared His own Son ...'), and these two texts were frequently quoted together, notably in the writings of the mystics about the love of God. St. Bernard, for instance, cites them in the first chapter of his famous treatise, *De diligendo Deo*,[60] as the measure of God's love for man, a love immense and pure, because utterly without selfish aim; and we can observe that it was this kind of love of which Abraham had demonstrated the possibility, when he was willing to offer his son 'pour faire d'autry la plaisance.'[61] The second of these New

[59] Pt. II, 59; fol. 204 r. 'To the end Jesus does not cease to instruct us to obey our fathers and put their will before ours.'

[60] Ch. 2, *P.L.*, CLXXXII, 975. Other examples may be found in many of the mystical writers, both English and continental. The same thought is stated in English sermons, e.g. *Old English Homilies*, E.E.T.S., XXIX, 119: 'And we sculan þonkian him þere muchele mildheortnesse þe he dude on us þa he na sparede ne ihesu crist his aȝene sune ac salde hine to deðe for moncunne ...'

[61] *Mistère*, l. 9486: 'to do another's pleasure'.

Testament texts in fact so closely resembles Genesis, xxii, 16, that it has been conjectured that St. Paul deliberately echoed this passage, and must therefore have been familiar with the typological significance of Abraham's sacrifice. The connection at least was often pointed in the Middle Ages. An interesting example of this is the passage which we have already quoted from Mirk's *Festial*, where the two stories are so fused together that the 'He' of the second sentence could equally well refer to God or Abraham. Another valuable illustration of this is a passage from Durandus, which ingeniously conjoins a third text, in order to intensify farther the parallelism between God giving Christ and Abraham giving his only and beloved son:

> Quid per sacrificium Abrahæ dilectum et unigenitum filium offerentis, nisi Christi passio designatur? de quo dicit Apostolus. Proprio filio suo non pepercit Deus: sed pro nobis omnibus tradidit illum. Hic est (inquit) filius meus dilectus in quo mihi complacui.[62]

The participation of God in the Crucifixion was also shown visually: sometimes by typological means, as when in the *Biblia Pauperum* the Sacrifice of Abraham accompanies the actual Crucifixion,[63] and the fact that the stress is on the Father rather than the Son is not only stated in the explanatory text but demonstrated, in that Abraham is an elongated and majestic figure, whilst Isaac is disproportionately small; whilst sometimes it was shown non-allegorically as in those paintings or sculpture in which the figure of God the Father holds a Crucifix against His breast:[64] the significance of this, that the Father gives, whilst the Son obeys and suffers, seems plain.

There is one further small point of similarity, which would automatically be made clear in the mystery plays, and that is the

[62] IV, xliii, 13; *ed. cit.*, p. 278: 'What else is signified by Abraham's sacrifice of his beloved and only son but the passion of Christ? As the Apostle says: "God did not spare his very own son, but surrendered him for all of us. This is, he said, my beloved son in whom I am well pleased."'

[63] Cornell, pl. 10.

[64] Emile Mâle in *L'Art relgieux du xiie siècle en France*, Paris, 1922, p. 182, attributes the original conception of this iconographical theme to the Abbé Suger of St-Denis. In England it is found, for instance, on roof bosses; see C. J. P. Cave, *Roof Bosses in Medieval Churches*, Cambridge, 1948, pls. 71 (Chester) and 118 (Lichfield). In the first of these the Dove is clearly visible, and, although in the second it cannot be seen, the boss is so much worn than it may have disappeared. But the Dove, which is present in all later representations of this theme, only slightly modifies the iconographic meaning.

physical resemblance between God the Father[65] and Abraham. For a long time the figure of the Father was rarely represented pictorially, except sometimes by a hand outstretched to bless or command; and when He did appear, as in pictures of the Trinity, He was physically identical with Christ, for the reason that he who had seen Christ had seen the Father. But when, in the thirteenth century, God the Father began to be commonly represented, partly because he was 'the ancient of days' and partly for the naturalistic reason that He should seem older than the Son, He was imagined as a white-bearded, aged man. But Abraham had always been represented as old and bearded. Thus fortuitously the connection between Abraham and the Father must have been driven home in a quite strikingly visual way.

Whereas the typological interpretation led to an effective amplifying of the character of Isaac, it had on the contrary a straitening effect on the character of Abraham, for to the question of how Abraham would feel in this situation there was no conceivable answer which would not have been typologically inappropriate. The most modest realism—even ordinary sensitivity—demanded that Abraham should hesitate, that he should at least have one moment of rebellion when he would feel that his child's life must be preserved, no matter what the cost.[66] But, since Abraham prefigured the Father, he could not even momentarily show himself irresolute over offering his son as a sacrifice. The difficulty of conceiving the action of a father giving his son to death as morally desirable exists equally on the theological level, and might even be thought to be aggravated there. Anselm, for instance, answering the arguments of his imaginary hostile questioner, in the *Cur Deus Homo*[67] reasons with skill and subtlety to prove that those Biblical texts, which we have already quoted, are not unfitting and unreasonable, but he reaches his solution only weakening their meaning to that of the Father acquiescing in the will of the Son. This answer, however, serves only

[65] On the pictorial representation of God the Father see M. Didron, *Iconographie Chrétienne (Histoire de Dieu)* (Paris, 1843), pp. 172–239.

[66] The apparent need for Abraham to rebel is so evident to the modern critic that he may even read a spirit of rebelliousness into the plays, in despite of the text. Thus, in a pleasant article, '*The Sacrifice of Isaac* e il *miracle play*' (*English Miscellany*, IV, 1–43), which, however, completely ignores the typological meaning, Agostino Lombardo writes of the Brome Abraham, 'Abramo accetta di compiere il sacrificio, ma non senza una continua, tormenta ribellione': 'Abraham consents to carry out the sacrifice, but not without a continuous agonized rebellion.' This comment fails to distinguish between anguished obedience and anguished rebelliousness.

[67] Chs. ix and x, *P.L.*, CLVIII, 370–376.

to illustrate farther how perplexing the idea is, whether with reference to God or man.

The medieval dramatists therefore deserve praise for the manner in which they preserved typological consistency in the character of Abraham, without at the same time turning him into a callous and unconvincing figure. They achieve this by balancing Abraham's unfaltering willingness to sacrifice Isaac with his love and distress. Although in all the plays Abraham accepts God's command with instant willingness and with no more than a brief expression of regret, this is counteracted by his overwhelming sorrow at the time of the sacrifice. In the Towneley Play, for instance, Abraham has to pause, blinded by his tears; in the Brome Play, he exclaims how gladly he would die in Isaac's place, and indeed his weeping is so great that it grieves Isaac's heart as much as his own death; and by this sweet distress of Isaac over Abraham's position, we are brought to share in his sympathy. It might therefore be said that the writers made a virtue of necessity, for from Abraham's single-minded determination to sacrifice his son, combined with his deep love and great grief, there arises a simple moral grandeur. To have shown Abraham tormented by the terrible alternative of disobeying God or slaying his son might have made a play more dramatically tense and exciting, but it would also have been a play less quietly moving. The pathos of the story, which is so much admired nowadays, undoubtedly springs from the imposition of the typological pattern upon the basic sequence of the story.

In the Dublin Play, Sarah, the mother of Isaac, is introduced as a third character, and, although she does not appear in person in any of the other English mystery plays, in both Brome and Chester she is an important character off stage, since she is in the thoughts and speech of both Abraham and Isaac. On the Continent she appears in the *Mistère du Vieil Testament*, and, as in Brome and Chester, should be accounted a character in the *Freiburger Passionspiel*. Sarah, of course, has no proper place in the typological exposition of the story, since she does not occur in the Biblical narrative. She did, however, have a connection with the Virgin outside the story of the Sacrifice, in that she when aged and barren bore a child in consequence of a promise to God, a miraculous conception, which, according to St. Ambrose, for example, forshadowed that God would later cause a virgin to conceive.[68] The marvel of Isaac's birth was also sometimes

[68] *De Isaac et de Anima* I, *P.L.*, XIV, 527.

brought into a symmetrical parallelism with the strangeness of his supposedly approaching death,[69] since they were both ordained by God outside the natural course of events. But we cannot therefore maintain, when discussing the sacrifice of Abraham, that Sarah prefigures the Virgin in the sense that Isaac prefigures Christ; nor can we ignore that there was a strong Jewish tradition in the Middle Ages, which also, in spite of the Biblical silence, associated Sarah with the story of the sacrifice: a tradition which may well have influenced the part of Sarah in the sixteenth-century plays, where it grew to overwhelming proportions. This tradition may also well explain the presence of Sarah in the Cornish Play and the *Mistère*, but it can in no way completely explain the treatment of her in these, nor account for the allusions to her in the other plays. In the Talmud, for instance, Sarah dies of an excess of emotion, after first hearing that Isaac is dead and then that his life has been spared; again, according to a tradition summarized by Beer,[70] Isaac when thinking of Sarah and his death takes consolation in the thought that she will grieve for him, instead of this thought increasing his distress as in the mystery plays. These are but two examples of a radical difference in both historical action and moral and literary tone. Whilst the presence of Sarah therefore may well have arisen from a common Judaic-Christian tradition, her treatment draws attention to the obvious analogy with the Virgin, and must surely at least in part be explained by the fact that the maternal and filial relationship between Christ and His mother was so constantly meditated upon and analyzed in the Middle Ages, that Christ in His life on earth could scarcely be thought of without reference to it. Christ's love and consideration for the Virgin, the Virgin's love and consideration for Christ: to many mediaeval Christians it must have seemed that their salvation depended upon that polarity of affection.

The evidence from the gospels of Christ's consideration of the Virgin lies in the word from the Cross entrusting her to St. John; and here the Middle Ages saw more than natural filial duty, for they interpreted Christ's seemingly brusque address to the Virgin as 'woman' as a tender and sensitive avoidance of the word 'mother,' lest this title should increase the Virgin's sorrow.[71] Furthermore they insisted that Christ's own agony was intensified by the sight of that of

[69] This idea, deriving from Josephus, was popularized in the *Historia Scholastica* of Petrus Comestor, *P.L.*, CXCVIII, 1104.

[70] B. Beer, *Leben Abrahams nach Auffassung der jüdischen Sage* (Leipzig, 1859).

[71] *Meditations*, p. 241.

His mother as He prayed that her sufferings might be lessened, and in their imaginative reconstructions of the scene of the Crucifixion, they invented many comforting words which might fittingly have been spoken by Christ. They also believed, not as a devotional imagining but as a fact, that Christ's first Resurrection appearance was to His mother.[72] This loving concern for the Virgin is recalled particularly in those plays where Sarah does not appear: in the Brome Play, for instance, in Isaac's distress at the grief which he knows Sarah will feel for him, his anxiety that the truth should be hidden from her, and in his message of blessing and farewell. In fact Isaac's dying thoughts here are his concern for Abraham and Sarah. The same thoughtfulness is shown in the *Freiburger Passionspiel*[73] in Isaac's request that, when the fire has consumed him, Abraham should tell Sarah that before he died he blessed and commended her to God.

Now it may be argued that Isaac's tender concern for Sarah is no more than the expression of the proper affection of the idealized child for his parents: we see similar emotion in the children of Hugolino and in the little boy of the *exemplum*. Similarly, Isaac's prayer in the Brome Play 'Lord, reseyve me into Thy hand' could be either a deliberate repetition of the penultimate Word from the Cross, or only an example of the correct dying prayer of the Christian. But this last example shows the unreality of the distinction, for these words were considered the proper dying words of the Christian because they were first the dying words of Christ, and, when spoken by Isaac, they can be disassociated from neither the moral nor the typological levels of the allegory. By analogy, therefore, we may see in Isaac's concern for Sarah one point of a triangle, of which the other two are Christ's concern for Mary and a dutiful child's concern for his mother, all of them related to one another and inter-connected with one another.

It is far less straightforward to connect the actual treatment of Sarah herself in the Dublin Play, and to a lesser extent in the *Mistère du Vieil Testament*, with the Virgin, because it touches on a mysterious ambiguity and paradoxical quality in the feelings of the Virgin herself, as conceived in the Middle Ages. On the one hand, Mary was almost exalted to the role of co-redemptrix, and was therefore imagined to have consented voluntarily to the Crucifixion and her own identification with her Son in His sufferings. There is obviously no parallel whatsoever between the Virgin thus imagined

[72] *ibid.*, pp. 263–264.
[73] ll. 245–248.

and Sarah, for the latter is always expressly excluded from any association with the sacrifice, lest she should try to prevent it.[74] Even the Sarah of the *Mistère*, who is otherwise a model of the submissive and devoted wife, says forthrightly at the end that, had she known of the intended sacrifice, she would never have agreed to it, and in the more sharply colloquial tone of the Dublin Play she exclaims to Abraham when she has heard what has happened, 'Alas, where was your mynde?' On the other hand, since the Virgin was thought to have been the most loving and devoted of all mothers, it was difficult to imagine how she could have acquiesced so single-mindedly in the death of her Son. Here we see the same apparent clash between logic and natural sentiment as underlies the embarrassment over the point of God not sparing His son, only the theological problem appears in human terms. The solution in works designed for the imagination rather than for cool logic lay in showing the Virgin, not as outrightly rebellious, but as intensely anxious to protect her Son. Thus, in the famous *Meditations* of St Bonaventura, the Virgin pleads with Christ that He should not go up to Jerusalem and there be at His enemies' mercy;[75] and later, when she hears of the arrest, she prays that the Redemption may be accomplished by some other means, so that her Son may be returned to her.[76] In Arnould Gréban's passion-play Mary's feelings are even more heightened, as she beseeches Christ with all maternal care that He should not go to Jerusalem, lest He die of hunger or be betrayed to His enemies,[77] and not only are her wishes there clearly opposed to the will of Christ, but also her final submission is one of necessity rather than voluntary acquiescence. Now Mary's anxiety that Christ should not go to Jerusalem for fear of the various dangers He might meet with forms a parallel with Sarah's reluctance in the Dublin Play that Isaac should accompany Abraham on his expedition of sacrifice, and her fears that his horse may be wild or stumble by the wayside. In this speech we see Sarah's

[74] That Abraham concealed God's command from Sarah, lest she should try to prevent the execution of it, is a tradition that goes back to Josephus, and is repeated by the Fathers. The unanimous judgement on Sarah is expressed with admirable brevity by St Basil Seleucienis: φιλόθεος ἡ γυνὴ ἀλλὰ μήτηρ ἐστί ('the woman is God-fearing, but she is a mother'), *P.G.*, LXXXV, 107.

[75] *ibid.*, 189. Although the author of the *Meditationes* is commonly referred to as 'the pseudo-Bonaventura', I have not used this description here, since the Passion section, which is the only part I refer to, is almost certainly by Bonaventura himself. On this see P. Columban Fischer, O.F.M., 'Die "Meditationes Vitæ Christi"', *Archivum Franciscanum Historicum*, XXV, 449–483.

[76] *ibid.*, p. 227.

[77] *Mistère de la Passion*, ed Gaston Paris, Paris, 1878, pp. 213–215.

loving concern for Isaac, and if there is also a note of sharpness in it, it is probably no more than a touch of realism, for anxiety and irritation are closely allied.[78] It must be admitted, however, that when Abraham says tartly to Isaac, 'þi modre may not have hir wille all way,' the relevant background seems to be the shrewish wife of the *fabliaux* rather than the Virgin, though this hint is not corroborated by Sarah's own speeches. We might almost conjecture, however, that had it not been for her semi-typological associations, Sarah might well have gone the way of Noah's wife.

The contrast with Noah's wife is indeed a particularly interesting and relevant one for pointing the unexpectedness of the writer's treatment of Sarah. It may be stated as a broad but by no means misleading generalization that women in medieval literature (until Chaucer's realistic characterization of Creseide) are either idealized as reflections of the Virgin or denigrated as reflections of Eve. In other words, they are either dutiful and devoted wives or temptresses and betrayers of their husbands.[79] In this sense, then, Noah's wife is not simply a *fabliau* character who has strayed inappropriately into the miracle plays, but has significance within a Christian religious pattern. The resemblance to Eve is made quite clear in the Newcastle Noah's Ark, where Noah's wife tempts her husband at the prompting of the devil,[80] and in all the plays, except for that of the *Ludus Coventriae*, she represents Eve in that she is stupidly and stubbornly opposed to the decision of her husband, who himself has a clear understanding of the will of God.

It is clear that in this radical division, Sarah belongs to the side of the Virgin, and this is remarkable, for according to the natural pattern of the story she should surely, like Noah's wife, have been the obstinate short-sighted woman, who in contrast to her husband has no deep sense of obedience to God. But this obvious development of her character is almost completely ignored, and instead she is very clearly presented as a loving mother. Therefore, whilst it might be far-fetched to argue that Sarah has the same kind of typological associations as the other characters, there can be little doubt that in this broad sense she follows the pattern of the Virgin. The reason for

[78] Such a touch of psychological realism would, of course, not be out of keeping with the style of the mystery plays.

[79] Otherwise they are the great ladies of courtly love, who in another way reflect the dignity of the Virgin, being set high above man, as causes of virtue and sources of mercy.

[80] E.E.T.S., E.S., CIV, 19–25.

this is equally certain: Isaac was so clearly a type of Christ that he could not be shown as the son of a self-willed rebellious woman; he must be the son of a mother who reflected, not Eve, but the Virgin.

There is a fourth figure in the drama, which must finally be mentioned, the ram: a figure which is very important typologically, since, in succession to Isaac, it prefigures Christ. It is, of course, an animal of sacrifice, and in the drama is sometimes described simply as a lamb, thus being associated with Abel's sacrifice, the lamb of the Passover, and Christ who was led as a lamb to the slaughter, and was Himself the Lamb of God.[81] In early art it was represented without horns, that it might more clearly appear the traditional *hostia* [sacrifice].[82] The horns, however, were put to allegorical service by the Fathers: in themselves they represented the arms of the Cross, and by them the ram was entangled in the thornbush, which signified the crown of thorns. The substitution of the ram for Isaac was interpreted in two different ways by the Fathers. According to one tradition, that followed by Ælfric[83] for instance, it signified that Christ suffered only in His manhood and not in His divinity; according to the other, which is that of the *lectio* for Quinquagesima Sunday, Isaac was spared 'quia perfecta sacrificii hostia Christo Domino servabatur.'[84] These explanations of the substitution obviously could not be given satisfactory literary expression in the plays of Abraham and Isaac, and indeed the release of Isaac with the sacrifice of the ram is normally represented in a markedly perfunctory manner, and without the emotional emphasis which on the ordinary level of the story it would seem to deserve. It would therefore be sufficient to note here the breakdown of a typological meaning capable of transference into literary terms, with a consequent brevity in the corresponding part of the plays, were it not that some attention is directed to the ram in the Brome Play, where Isaac shows a touching attention, mingled plausibly with relief, that the ram must die in his place:

> Thow þou be never so jentyll and good,
> Gyt had I lever thow schedyst þi blood,
> Iwisse, scheppe, than I.[85]

[81] In the Towneley play of John the Baptist, Christ actually gives a lamb (the *Agnus Dei* according to the stage direction) to John the Baptist as a symbol of Himself (*ed. cit.*, p. 201).

[82] *Romanische Quartalschrift*, I, 140–141.

[83] *The Homilies of the Anglo-Saxon Church*, ed. B. Thorpe, London, 1844, II, 62.

[84] *Breviarum ad usum insignis ecclesiæ Sarum*, Fasc. 1, ed. F. Procter and C. Wordsworth, London, 1878, p. dxlvii. 'Because to be the perfect sacrificial victim was being reserved for Christ the Lord.'

[85] ll. 364–366.

This may be no more than a part of the common sympathy with animals shown in the Middle Ages, of which St Francis was the great exemplar, and in particular of the decorous sentimentality over animals shown frequently in medieval literature: not in the well-known example of the Prioress's indulgence of her lapdogs, which, as no doubt Chaucer intended, is a debasement of this emotion, but, for instance, in the descriptions of the dog in the bestiaries, where moving stories are told of a dog's devotion to his master,[86] or in the story in the *Gesta Romanorum* of the faithful greyhound.[87] The same kind of sentiment is seen also in medieval art, of which an interesting example is those representations of the Nativity, where the Christ Child strokes the nose of the ass, which, incidentally, is but a complement to the common medieval idea that the animals in the stable kept the Christ Child warm with their breath. Nevertheless, this attitude towards animals may not be the sole explanation of this part of the Brome Play, and it is worth considering for a moment that, if we remember when reading the play that the ram prefigures Christ, then Isaac's speech acquires a touch of melancholy irony in its mixture of consideration and relief. If this irony had occurred in any but the Brome Play, it would certainly have been too subtle to have been intended by the author, but, since the Brome writer is much more delicate and accomplished in his work than any of the other dramatists, we would hesitate to deny it to him outright. At any rate this speech of Isaac's undoubtedly brings the dramatic emphasis of the literal meaning of the play into line with its full allegorical exposition, for, instead of there being only a perfunctory reference to the ram, it is turned into an object of affectionate pity and consideration.

The effect of this discussion may at first sight appear to be the sinking of medieval drama beneath a weight of allegorical commentary and exposition, which the plays themselves in their simplicity are not strong enough to sustain, so that their charm and vigor may seem to be squeezed out beneath this load. But this is perhaps only because the argument and explanation of the religious background and interpretation has had to be supported by burdensome references to religious and theological works which

[86] A good example of this may be found in the Latin bestiary translated by T. E. White in *A Book of Beasts*. The theme, however, was a common one, and may be found in most standard commentaries on animals, such as Hugo of St Victor, *De Bestiis et aliis rebus*, *P.L.*, CLXXVII, 65 and 86.

[87] E.E.T.S., E.S., XXXIII, 98 f.

exemplify the various points. In the Middle Ages the typological significance of Abraham's sacrifice would not have been a recondite gloss or an intellectual ingenuity of the scholar; it was part of the small stock of knowledge which the common people might be expected to have received, and certainly the background of accepted ideas about the parts played in the Crucifixion by God the Father, Christ, and the Virgin would have been commonplaces of the faith of the average Christian. When reading the plays nowadays, therefore, we should discard the scaffolding of reference and remember only the main points of background and interpretation, so that the allegorical meaning may flicker through the story, not dulling it, but on the contrary adding here and there an illumination of meaning, which adds subtlety and power to the narrative.

V

CHAUCER AS A SATIRIST IN THE GENERAL PROLOGUE TO THE *CANTERBURY TALES*

MANY people nowadays acquire an early and excessive familiarity with the *General Prologue* to the *Canterbury Tales*, which later blunts their sharpness of perception. Since the *Prologue* is read at school, necessarily out of its literary-historical context, its methods of satire seem to have an inevitability and rightness which preclude either surprise or analysis. This natural tendency to remain uncritically appreciative of the *Prologue* has been partly confirmed by various works of criticism, which, though admirable in many ways, effusively reiterate that 'here is God's plenty': they thus awaken an enthusiastic response to the vitality and variety of the characterisation in the *Prologue*, at the cost of making the exact manner and tone of Chaucer's satire quite indistinct. Despite the bulk of Chaucerian criticism, there is still need for a detailed and disciplined examination of Chaucer's style and methods of satire, which would include a careful consideration of Chaucer's work against the background of classical and medieval satire. Such a study would be of considerable scholarship and length: it is the purpose of this short article only to make a few general points about Chaucer's methods of satire.

It is sometimes taken for granted that the satirist speaks in his own voice, and that any reference to his opinions and feelings are a literal record of his experience. This assumption perhaps requires testing and reconsideration with reference to any satirist, but it is never more dangerous than when it is accepted without limitation about Chaucer. Chaucer was writing at a time when there was no tradition of personal poetry in a later Romantic sense: a poet never made his individual emotions the subject-matter of his poetry. Though the personal pronoun 'I' is used frequently in medieval narrative and lyric poetry, it is usually a dramatic 'I', that is the 'I' is a character in the poem, bearing no different relation to the poet from that of the other characters, or it expresses moral judgments or proper emotions which belong, or should belong, to everybody. Chaucer's use of an 'I' character in his early poems belongs to the tradition of such characters in dream visions, but, with an ingenious variation that the character appears naive, well-meaning, and obtuse, and the joke thus depends on the discrepancy between this figure in the poetry and the poet of wit and intelligence who wrote the whole. Thus this treatment of the 'I' character is new in that it pre-supposes the poet in a way that the other characters do not.

It is well-known that this character re-appears strikingly in the links of the *Canterbury Tales*, when he is rebuked for telling a dull story, but his presence in the *Prologue* has not been particularly stressed, yet it is through this character that both the apparently vivid individuality of the pilgrims and the satiric aim are achieved. Though there are various departures from consistency (to be noticed later), it is through the eyes of Chaucer the pilgrim, not Chaucer the poet, that the characters in the *Prologue* are chiefly presented. Obviously the choice of detail shows the sharp selectiveness of the satirist, but the friendly, enthusiastic, unsophisticated, unjudging tone is that of Chaucer the pilgrim.

From this invention there result two important advantages. Firstly by his fiction of having been a close companion of his characters, Chaucer suggests their reality and individuality, an individuality which is largely an illusion brought about by poetic skill. Chaucer makes us feel that we know them as individuals, though often, apart from physical description, they are simply representative portraits of various groups in society—friars, monks, summoners, nuns, etc. The same details of their tastes and behaviour can be found in any medieval moral denunciation of these people. Secondly, in his satiric character-sketches, Chaucer achieves a twofold irony. He implies that most of the information which he gives us derives, not from a narrative-writer's omniscience, but from the characters' own conversation. In other words Chaucer unobtrusively uses a pointed satirical method, by which the characters are shown to have erred so far from the true moral order, that they are not ashamed to talk naturally and with self-satisfaction about their own inversion of a just and religiously-ordered way of life. At the same time Chaucer makes his response to this that of a man who accepts and repeats with enthusiasm, and without critisicm, whatever he is told. It has been observed before how often Chaucer implies or states explicitly that each of his characters is an outstanding person (although a distinction should be made here between the statement when made of a virtuous character, such as the parson, when it comes as the climax of a well-ordered enumeration of his virtues, and when it appears as a random remark in the sketches of the satirised characters). This has been explained as part of Chaucer's genial enthusiastic appreciation of all kinds of people or, in a manner less wildly wrong, as part of a literary convention of magnifying each character (Kemp Malone, *Chapters on Chaucer*, p. 167). But it is surely Chaucer the easily-impressed pilgrim who so indiscriminately praises the characters, sharing with them through an obtuse innocence the immoral premises from which they speak.

Chaucer the poet, for instance, must have shared the common knowledge and opinion in the late 14th century, that the friars, instead of serving all classes of men indifferently, though with a special tenderness for the poor who reflected the poverty of Christ, instead chiefly sought out the rich and those from whom they could make profit, and took the opportunity given by the privacy of the personal interview and confession for exploitation and unchastity. All this Chaucer could not have failed to have known to be an abuse, evil and widespread, of what had originally been a holy and noble conception. But Chaucer the character relates these details of his fellow pilgrims as though they were both inoffensive and idiosyncratic, and in this way both the satiric point and the illusion of individuality are achieved. Similarly it was a common accusation that daughters of aristocratic households, who entered a convent, often did not discard their former manners and affectations. Genteel table-manners, careful attention to dress, and a narrowly sentimental affection for pet-animals, might possibly in a noble household appear signs of a refined sensiblity, but in a convent their worldliness would be plain. But of the distinction between the lady of the house and a nun Chaucer the pilgrim is ignorant, so he records all the details sweetly, as though there were no matter here for blame.

The clearest example, however, of this method is the account of the monk. Just as in the description of the friar Chaucer shows clearly by a sudden change to colloquial rhythms that he is ostensibly repeating the friar's own arguments for not caring for the poor, 'It is nat honest, it may nat avaunce ...', so in the account of the monk Chaucer repeats the monk's arguments, and then even adds a reply, 'And I seyde his opinion was good', supporting this by two foolish rhetorical questions and a blustering retort 'Lat Austyn have his swynk to hym reserved'. That Chaucer the poet would reject the authority of St Augustine is as manifestly untrue as that he had not the skill to tell an entertaining story. His protested sympathy with the monk is of the same kind as Juvenal's stated agreement ('you have just cause for bitterness') with the utterly debased and contemptible Naevolus in the ninth satire. To suppose that Chaucer's attitude here is ambivalent is to be deceived by the sweet blandness of Chaucer's mask, just as to search for historical prototypes of the characters is to be deceived by the brilliant accuracy of Chaucer's sleight of hand, whereby he suggests an individuality which is not there.

Amongst many other examples of the simplicity of Chaucer the pilgrim may be noticed the frequent device of giving a false explanation of a statement—the physician loved gold because it was of use in medicine—and the making of absurd judgments: the remark that the wives of the guildsmen would be to blame if they did not support and approve their husbands in their smug prosperity, or the query of whether it was not 'by full fair grace' that the maunciple was able to cheat and outwit his learned employers. It is in passages such as the latter that the ironic tone of Chaucer the satirist can be most clearly heard behind the blank wall of obtuseness of Chaucer the pilgrim. Illustrations of the naivete of Chaucer the character could be multiplied to the point of tediousness, and so too there could be laboured at length the demonstration that the substance of the description of each character consists solely of common medieval observation about the group to which he belongs. It should be added, however, that the appearance of individuality is not achieved by the intimate tone of Chaucer the character alone: at least equally important is the style. The near grace of Chaucer's lines often deceptively suggests that he had made a sharp and lucid observation, when in fact it is but a commonplace, and the precision lies, not in its thought, but in the style. Thus his method of pretending that the generalisation about a group is the idiosyncracy of an individual is given persuasive force by his exact use of words and the shapeliness of his couplets. There is an interesting contrast to this in the undisguisedly generalised attack of Langland, the generality of which is driven home by his swift but sometimes indiscriminate use of forceful words, and his form of the alliterative metre, which has within the line a great strength and impressive rhythm, but no larger pattern, so that there seems to be no metrical reason why one line should not succeed another without end.

The question to what extent we are aware of Chaucer the poet in the *Prologue* is not easy to determine. Sometimes an example of obtrusive poetic skill draws attention to him: it is Chaucer the pilgrim who observes mildly of the unhealthy sore on the cook's leg that it was a pity, but the placing of this one line in the middle of the account of the fine dishes made by the cook exceeds the licence of poetic cleverness which may by convention be allowed to a dull character in poetry. Similarly the image which implies censure or ridicule is self-evidently the satirist's: the monk's bridle jingling like a chapel bell, the squire's coat so embroidered with flowers that it was like a meadow, the snow-storm of food and drink in the franklin's house, the fiery-red cherubym's face of the summoner, all undisguisedly spring from the imagination of a satiric poet. Occasionally Chaucer even speaks outright in his own voice, making a pointed exposure of affection or self deception, which is in a quite different style of satire, and provides an exception to the general truth that the characters are not the result of actual observation. A well-known example is the comment about the lawyer:

> Nowher so bisy a man as he ther nas,
> And yet he semed bisier than he was.

This kind of remark shows the same mocking penetration into the ridiculous complexities of human feeling and behaviour, as Chaucer had already displayed in *Troilus and Creseide*, from which one striking example may be quoted: it was a commonplace in medieval descriptions of a lover that by pining he grew pale and thin; but in Chaucer's more subtle description, Troilus in the humourless self-absorption of his love *imagines* that he has grown so pale and thin that everybody notices and comments upon it. At first sight Chaucer seems to be an exception to the general rule of the classical period and 18th century that the satirist is to be feared. His disguise of Chaucer the pilgrim and elsewhere a sustained friendliness and moderation of tone imply that no man could be less alarming to those who knew him. But, whilst undoubtedly he was the less to be feared in that he did not make individual contemporaries the objects of his satire, as a century later Skelton was to do, yet only people free from all excesses of emotion and affectation could be sure that they would not be the source of some detail shrewdly observed in Chaucer's work.

Chaucer also speaks in his own voice in his occasional denunciation of evil in the descriptions of the Miller and the Pardoner, and, most effectively in his descriptions of the virtuous characters, one drawn from each order of society with the addition of the Clerk. In these Chaucer establishes the true moral standard by which the topsy-turvyness of the rest may be measured. It was a tradition of satire to provide an ideal standard: some earlier medieval Latin satirists made use of the classical fable of the Golden Age, identifying it uneasily with the Garden of Eden: an example is the famous *de Contemptu Mundi* of Bernard of Cluny; Langland in a more complex and magnificent scheme makes his standard the pure charity of the Redemption of man by Christ. But Chaucer, lacking Langland's sublimity of imagination, but with a shrewd, clear thoughtfulness, gives a positive analysis of representative types of a well-ordered society, religious and secular. The detailed justice of these descriptions prevents the actual satire from seeming too mild or perhaps too pessimistic. Without them Chaucer's satire might seem to have too much detachment, too much ironic acquiescence. In Langland's angry denunciatory satire there is by implication a hope of reform; but in Chaucer's one feels the tone of a man, who, aware of the incongruity between the gravity of the abuse and his own inability to help, is moved to an ironic and superficially good-humoured laughter. The virtuous characters, however, by their very presence imply a censure of the rest, which dispels any impression of over-sophisticated aloofness. The idea that Chaucer loved his satirised characters despite or including their faults is of course false, and springs from an imprecise consideration of Chaucer's methods of satire.

To what extent Chaucer was influenced by classical and medieval traditions of satire remains the final difficult but fascinating question. There is no incontrovertible evidence about his knowledge of classical satirists: Juvenal he quotes from and mentions by name, but the quotations he could very easily have gained at second hand; Horace he does not mention at all, but since, as other critics have pointed out, he does not mention Boccaccio either, this negative evidence is worthless. Juvenal had attacked with moral horror the widespread vices of his own time under the satiric disguise of describing historical personages of a previous age. This device was not imitated by the Fathers or the medieval satirists who were influenced by him, and the writers of the Middle Ages with their preoccupation with what was common to all men rather than with what makes one man different from another, were not concerned to give any appearance of particularity to their satire. The result was either the blackened generalised picture of all men as totally corrupt, found in the *de Contemptu Mundi*, or the combination of allegory with satire, ingeniously used, though not invented, by Langland. But though the aim of Chaucer's satire is, like Langland's, the distinctive vices of people in various orders and occupations throughout society, he does not generalise but, like Juvenal, reduces the generalisation to a description of particular characters. This, however, seems to be

Chaucer's only resemblance to Juvenal, since self-evidently there could not be a greater difference of tone than there is between Juvenal's savage vehemence and Chaucer's specious mildness.

The resemblances between Chaucer and Horace are more subtle and more specific. The object of Horace's satire had been different from Juvenal's, in that Horace was chiefly concerned with those who disrupted the social harmony of life, the fool, the bore, the miser, and these he portrayed with a minute and particular observation of habit and conversation, which gives the impression that his description is of an individual, though by definition not unique, personality. His account, for instance, of the host who makes dinner intolerable for his guests by a tedious analysis of the sources and method of cooking of each dish, suggests a recognisable personality, not a moral generalisation about excessive eating and drinking. The tone of Horace's satire is not designed to arouse horror or anger, but amused contempt for something worthless. It is obvious that this satiric manner required a sophistication not usually possessed in the Middle Ages, and a point of view less easily identifiable with the Christian than that of Juvenal. For, though evil was seen as a fit object for laughter in the Middle Ages, it was a strong laughter at the ugly and grotesque—the devils in the mystery plays, for example—rather than the slight ironic smile of the civilised man at those who deviate from reason and intelligence.

Chaucer shares some characteristics with Horace, though there is no certainty whether by influence, or by coincidence and some affinity of temper. He has in common with Horace the easy tone of a man talking to friends who share his assumptions and sympathies, though usually with a deceptive twist: for when Horace meets the characters in his satires, he expects his audience to sympathise with his misery, whereas Chaucer, as we have already seen, pretends that the situation was delightful and the characters to be admired. He shares with Horace too some other characteristics already noticed, such as the use of comic images, and, above all, the quick observation of human affectation, and the suggestion of a recognisable personality as in the lines quoted about the lawyer. Chaucer, however, extends Horatian ridicule to the kind of objects satirised in the Juvenalian tradition, and modifies it by the tone of pretended naivete, not found in Horace's style, but almost certainly learnt, at least in part, from Ovid, whose works Chaucer had undoubtedly read and who might indeed be called Chaucer's master.

The fact that it is relevant to ask the question, was Chaucer influenced by classical satirists, is in itself interesting, and throws light on Chaucer's distinctiveness. Though it cannot be answered definitely, his indebtedness to classical writers in general is indisputable, and is most interestingly noticeable in the fact that he thought of himself as a poet in a way that earlier medieval writers seem not to have done. He is the first English medieval poet explicitly to accept the permanent value of his work, and hence to care about the unsettled state of the language and its dialectal variety, the first to see himself as of the same kind as the classical poets. The writers of medieval lyrics, romances, plays, etc., almost certainly had a workaday conception of themselves, and did not think of a poet as a man of particular perception and judgment, but as a man who wrote verse in a craftsmanlike way for specific use. But Chaucer sees himself as a poet in the classical tradition, and it is for this reason that, despite the fact that the substance of his satiric portraits are medieval commonplaces, and despite his usual disguise of Chaucer the pilgrim, behind this disguise, and sometimes heard openly, is the truly personal tone of the satirist, which is quite un-medieval.

VI

SOME NON-MEDIEVAL QUALITIES OF *PIERS PLOWMAN*

Piers Plowman is most frequently discussed as a poem entirely typical of its period. But, whilst many of the ideas and arguments expressed in it are rooted in fourteenth century thought, as a poem it has a number of qualities which are startlingly new, and which indeed are far more 'modern' than anything to be found in the fifteenth century. The way in which Piers Plowman is untypical of medieval literature can be most clearly seen in the handling of the allegory, and in particular in the treatment of the figure of Piers and of the dreamer himself. It has over and over again been said or implied that the allegory of *Piers Plowman* can be illuminated by reference to earlier traditions of medieval allegory, but this is only self-evidently true, when all that is meant by it is that individual episodes can be shown to have sources. The well-known, rather brusque and grotesque passage, in which the procession is formed to take Lady Mede to London may seem slightly less odd and perfunctory if one recognises in it the kind of allegory which had been used by Nicolas Bozon in his Anglo-Norman poem, *Le Char d'Orgueil.*[1] Langland obviously borrowed some of his methods of allegory in a highly eclectic way, and probably more light could be thrown on individual passages by a further investigation of them. But, when by the assumption that *Piers Plowman* is dependent on earlier traditions of allegory, is intended the well-known view that *Piers Plowman* appears a clear and well-organised poem once one understands the medieval conception of allegory, and in particular the four levels of meaning, then this view can far less easily be substantiated.

One of the most obvious characteristics of the allegory of *Piers Plowman*, and that which often makes it so difficult to follow, is that the literal level of the allegory is so slight and poetically unimportant. The allegorisation of the Old Testament, however, had led to quite a different treatment, for every commentator began with the literal text which he normally held to be exactly true, and to be instinct with

[1] *Deux poèmes*, ed. Johan Vising, Gothenburg, 1919.

allegorical meaning. God was thought of as a master-allegorist, who had so guided the course of history, or so designed the natural world analysed in bestiaries and lapidaries, that in all of these man could discern allegories of the Redemption. The consequence of this view was that no writer had need to fear that he might disproportionately stress the literal level of his story, and a poetic emphasis upon it, as in the Old Testament mystery plays for instance, would be in no danger of detracting from the allegorical significance, for story and allegory were not arbitrarily joined, but formed, as it were, one organism. The particular medieval capacity to respond to allegory, which distinguishes it from later periods, was the readiness to see through a story or object, however complete or interesting they might seem in themselves, to some moral or typological allegory.

Piers Plowman departs from this traditional style of allegory by its lack of a sustained literal level. Indeed there can be few medieval poems in which the literal level is so tenuous and confused. The only approximate parallel, which comes easily to mind, is Jean de Meung's continuation of the *Roman de la Rose*, in which many of the figures exist chiefly as mouthpieces for argument, and in which the literal story of the lover's quest for the rose is treated in a perfunctory way. This continuation, however, seems to have been intended as a deliberate and satiric disruption of the clear and courtly allegory of Guillaume de Lorris, and it therefore cannot be considered a typical mode of allegory, though admittedly it might to Langland have seemed to set a precedent. This comparison between the allegorical methods of Jean de Meung and Langland is, however, an inadequate commentary upon *Piers Plowman*. Admittedly there can be seen in both works a body of thought which spills over from the meagre capacity of the literal level, but it is also clear from the figure of Piers Plowman himself that Langland was by design using allegory in a far more literary and subtle way than his predecessors had done.

The startling point about the figure of Piers Plowman is that it cannot be said clearly and indisputably what it is that he symbolises. It has been argued that Piers represents mankind, the Church, the Pope, St. Peter, Christ in His humanity and other allied subjects. It is obvious of course that Piers changes in significance as the poem develops, and most of the suggestions can be shown to be relevant to one or two references. There is, however, no rational combination of allegorical significances which provides a simple key to the interpretation of the text or to the weight which is given to Piers. Over and over again he is referred to in the poem, or makes a momentary appearance, but from the time that he tears up the Pardon his significance is uncertain: yet he is the central figure of the poem, as the title, almost certainly given by Langland himself, shows. The figure of Piers has in fact the peculiar force of something which is only half understood. This kind of romantic uncertainty, however, was quite alien to the earlier Middle Ages. Panowsky has ingeniously elaborated a likeness in the quality of explicitness between the great theological *Summae* of the Middle Ages and the style of architecture of Gothic cathedrals.[2] But this even lucidity, this unwillingness to leave any detail or idea, however small, unstated, which is, incidentally so apparent in medieval illumination, is perhaps also the most characteristic quality of the literature. Until the late fourteenth century there are never any shadows or half-light in medieval poetry: everything that the poet wishes to say is set out clearly, exactly, and in detail. There are no ambiguities in allegory or language. This explicitness is delightful to imagination and reason, but it lacks the emotional insidiousness of a more allusive manner, the unique power of the half-stated. This clarity in literature and art obviously reflected the thirteenth century as an age of reason: it was the only Christian century in which there was a serene, intellectual certainty that every kind of knowledge and revelation, everything on earth—and indeed everything in heaven and hell—could be examined and set out in the light of reason, without there remaining any residue of mystery. In the fourteenth century, with the dissociation of philosophy and theology, this harmonious confidence disappeared. The effect of this on the character of the dreamer in *Piers Plowman* is, as we shall see later, unmistakeable, but it surely also contributed to the imprecision of Piers, to the fact that he is the focal point of a sense of security in the poem, and yet cannot clearly be defined.

The combination in Piers of uncertain significance with deep emotional power is exactly the reverse of what is normally found in medieval allegory. The imaginative impact of an object or an episode in a typical medieval allegory was usually strictly bounded by limits imposed by the common lack of moral or aesthetic concordance between the literal level and the allegorical. Well-known examples of moral inconsistency are of course Noah drunk symbolising Christ, and Orpheus looking back at Eurydice representing man looking back with longing at his former sins. The lack of aesthetic consistency, however, can be equally disastrous to a literary use of

[2] *Gothic Architecture and Scholasticism*, London, 1957.

allegory: Christ could be typologically foreshadowed by David slaying Goliath or by Samson slaying the lion, but He could equally well be signified by the hydrus, a mythical little creature, which rolled itself in mud, and then slid down the throat of a crocodile to destroy it from within. In these examples, and in innummerable others, it is the pattern of the action rather than the dignity of the actor which is important. For this reason it is only rarely that an image is used in which there is any point of correspondence apart from that explicitly set out. The medieval method can perhaps be thrown into relief by a contrast with the Anglo-Saxon. In the elegiac poetry, for instance, the traditional Christian image of life as an exile is used technically for its Pauline point of comparison, that it is heaven and not the world which is man's proper home. But in the *Wanderer* and the *Seafarer* the image is so filled with emotional associations of the powerfully evocative ideas of transcience and loneliness, that the reader's response to it is not limited by sharp lines drawn by the poet, but only by his individual capacity to respond to the evocative and nostalgic. The emphasis upon precise correspondence in medieval allegory may also be illustrated in another way. There are very few medieval allegories which could not aptly be given a visual illustration. Indeed for Biblical allegory, art with its isolated moment of time was usually a far better medium than poetic narrative, in which moral or aesthetic discrepancies were more likely to obtrude. It is, however, self evident that *Piers Plowman* is insusceptible of illustration, a point borne out by the fact that none of the very numerous manuscript texts of the poem are illustrated. There is here a very striking contrast with the Ellesmere Manuscript of the *Canterbury Tales*, with the manuscript of the *Pearl* and *Sir Gawain*, with the many French manuscripts of the *Roman de la Rose* and of Guillaume de Guilleville's *Pèlerinage de la Vie Humaine*.

The absence of illumination surely drives home the point that *Piers Plowman* entirely lacks the visual quality which is so characteristic of medieval literature. The lack of visualisation is a point which will later be amplified: its relevance here is that Piers himself is an important allegorical figure, whom it would be unhelpful and indeed impossible to illustrate, for, after his first appearance, it would be ludicrously irrelevant to imagine him as a ploughman. When, for instance, it is said that Piers 'lered hym [Christ] lechecraft his lyf for to save' (B Text, Passus xvi, 104), to imagine this scene visually would be almost blasphemously comic, and would quite clearly be at odds with the thought of Langland. This is a very obvious example of

Langland's disregard for the literal level of his allegory: Samson or the hydrus became more intensely themselves through the reflected dignity of their relationship to Christ, but Piers, as he grows in allegorical significance, ceases to be a ploughman: all that remains of the literal level is a name. But, though Langland maintains no visual image of Piers, nor any consistent rational significance, yet by a skilful accumulation of references to him, he concentrates in the figure much of the emotional force of the poem. Piers Plowman does not appear in the poem between Passus 8–15 (B text), but in Passus 13–15 he is referred to a number of times, and is said to be a teacher of authority and the only guide to charity, and by this kind of reference Langland contrives an intense sense of expectancy, so that when in Passus 16 the dreamer is said to swoon with pure joy at hearing the name of Piers Plowman (ll. 18–19), the reader shares a sense of joy and relief, so skilfully has Langland led up to this point. The role of Piers Plowman in this passus, where he presides over the tree of charity and in the subsequent passus where he becomes closely associated with Christ, is not at all clear, and it is evident from the excision of many of these passages from the C text, that this lack of clarity was equally apparent in the fourteenth century. But with the diminishment of Piers in the C text there is lost a great deal of poetic force. As we have said before, it is possible to recognise in Piers at various points, Christ in His humanity, the Church, mankind, the virtuous life, etc., but the fact that all these can be signified by one symbol, and that there are other potent and enigmatic usages, gives to the figure a tremendous power as an intimation of security and perfection and as a promise of the Redemption. The power of the figure of Piers and the uncertainty of his significance is perhaps nowhere so clear as in the concluding lines of the poem which describes the beginning of a fresh search for Piers Plowman.

The other important character in the poem is the dreamer himself, and he too is presented in a manner which is not characteristic of medieval literature. Langland had behind him a long tradition of poetry set in the form of a dream, and the aim of this much-used convention was obviously to give a rational framework to some phantasy, and to make it seem real and personal. Langland's use of the dream-vision, however, is far less straightforward than this. Normally the content of the dream, as in Chaucer's allegories or the *Pearl*, is quite clear: the scene is self-contained and the story as orderly as that of any other narrative. The relationship of the dream-world to the real world is not that of shadow to reality, but rather that of architype to copy. The dream-world of the *Pearl*, for instance, is the natural world heightened: colours are more intense, form and sound more perfect, everything more clear and ordered than it can be in the unselectiveness of every-day life. The extraordinary point about Langland's dreams, however, is that they show the bewildering indifference to time and place which is characteristic of real dreams. The effect of this unique modification of the convention may be seen in two ways. Firstly it may be seen in the absence of the visualisation of a scene, to which we have already referred. Often the background against which characters meet is quite unknown, and this gives an impression of vagueness and greyness to the poem, in contrast, for instance, with the precision and brilliance of the *Pearl*. This lack, however, is compensated for by the effect of movement. Whilst the dominant tone of the *Pearl* and *Sir Gawain* is set by their recurrent adjectives, that of *Piers Plowman* is set by the verbs, which constantly suggest abrupt and vigorous action—action such as leaping, jumping or rushing—in a way that could not be sensibly visualised, and which bear no relation to the static scenes of art. The well-known description of the triumph of death illustrates this point:

> Deth cam dryvende after   and al to doust passhed
> Kynges and knyghtes   kayseres and popes;
> Lered ne lewed   he let no man stonde,
> That he hitte evene   that evere stired after.
> Many a lovely lady   and lemmanes of knyghtes
> Swouned and swelted   for sorwe of Dethes dyntes.
>
> (B text, Passus xx, 99–104)[3]

Though this theme was very familiar and traditional in art as well as literature, it is most unlikely that Langland could have seen an illustration of it before the end of the fourteenth century and in England, in which death swept upon man with such power and violence. Indeed the only approximate parallel to it at any date and anywhere in western Europe is the well known fresco of the Campo Santo in Pisa. Certainly if Langland had seen the theme of the inevitability of death visually treated, he would have seen something like a nobleman and a skeleton confronting each other, a scene grotesque and motionless.

The second characteristic which derives from Langland's peculiar use of the dream-convention is the abrupt shifting of time and place, which is so familiar from actual dreams, and so extremely unlike any

[3] All quotations are from *Piers Plowman*, ed. W. W. Skeat, Oxford, 1886.

other medieval use of the dream convention. There are in fact many parts of the poem, in which one cannot tell where the action is taking place or at what point in time. There is, for instance, the episode in which the dreamer and Scripture argue learnedly about salvation, when suddenly Trajan (the great example of the righteous heathen) interrupts with his contemptuous exclamation 'Yee! baw for bokes!', and proceeds to discourse on his own situation (B Text, xi, 135 ff.). Here there is obviously the relevance to idea and the inconsequentiality of event, which is typical of dreams. This disregard for limits of time and place often quickens the pace of the narrative to a disconcerting speed, or perhaps it would be more accurate to say that the narrative progresses with an alternate dawdling and darting movement. Langland's avoidance of the common need to lay a foundation in reasonable plot for the appearance or conduct of any character is clearly related to his indifference to the literal level of his allegory, and his suggestion of the disorganised nature of real dreams gives at least a technical plausibility to the inconsistencies of the literal story of the poem.

It is necessary to give the first person narrator of *Piers Plowman* some title to distinguish him from Langland the poet. It is most obviously appropriate to call him the dreamer, but he could almost equally well be called the pilgrim or wanderer, for another peculiarity of the poem is that Langland has made an unusual conflation of two forms, that of the dream and that of the pilgrimage. By far the more obvious is that of the dream vision, or rather a series of them, and in these the dreamer meets allegorical characters, some of whom personify various of his intellectual qualities; dreams which also enable him to be present at various episodes of the Redemption, as they do later authors of the religious lyric. Between his dreams, however, the dreamer is also a pilgrim, wandering on his journey through life in search of Do-Wel. This allegory of life as a journey or pilgrimage was of course a common medieval sermon theme, though now better known from its later use in the *Pilgrim's Progress*. In the first half of the fourteenth century this image had been used as the form for an extensive moral poem by the French Cistercian Guillaume de Guilleville in his *Pèlerinage de la Vie Humaine*, a poem later translated into English by Lydgate.[4] In this poem the various points of man's life from birth to death are represented as stages on a journey: the dreamer at birth sets out for the heavenly Jerusalem,

[4] Ed. F. J. Furnivall, *Roxburghe Club*, 1905.

being provided with spiritual armour by Grace of God, but is thereafter impeded at every turning by Satan or one of the seven deadly sins, and is confused by the wheel of fortune. At last, however, Grace of God intervenes to bring him to a Cistercian monastery, where he is later approached by old age and infirmity, the two messengers of death, and finally by death himself, whereupon he wakes up. In the clarity of its outline the *Pèlerinage de la Vie Humaine* is as different from *Piers Plowman* as all other medieval allegories, but it can cast some light upon the kind of poem which Langland thought he was writing, and on the extension of time within the poem. Langland's conception of his poem was that of a journey, a journey in which the dreamer or wanderer was primarily engaged, not with virtue as in the *Pèlerinage*, but with knowledge, and in which, as he inquired farther, he grew older. In the A Text the dreamer at last meets with Fever, who says 'I am messager of Deth' (xii, 83), and who advises his victim in the traditional moral way to 'do after Do-Wel'. The poem then abruptly becomes a third person narrative, and we are told how the dreamer wrote the poem and then died. Whilst the fact that the A Text ends with the dreamer's death shows very pointedly that his journeyings are an allegory of life, the progress of growing old is more emphasised in the B Text. In the latter, before his dispute with Scripture, the dreamer finds himself pursued and enticed by fortune, with her attendants, lust and avarice, and though warned by old age not to trust in them, the dreamer finds their words too sweet for him to be able to dismiss them. Similarly in Passus 20 the dreamer meets with old age, whose effects are described in the traditional manner of medieval moral satire: at age's blows the dreamer becomes deaf, toothless, stiffened by gout and impotent (xx, 188 ff.). One thread of Langland's allegory therefore is that of the dreamer as Everyman or the pilgrim through life, who is diverted from his search for virtue and heaven by the sins of the world, and, who, as the journey proceeds, in one version grows old and in the other dies.

This distinguishing of Everyman's journey as an important connecting thread in the poem brings us to the difficult but important point of the relationship of the dreamer to Langland himself. Up to the end of the fourteenth century one would not expect a poem set in the first person to contain any personal truth: the poet is not concerned with the individual, whether it be himself or another, but with what is common to everybody. In the religious lyric, for instance, the 'I' speaker expresses feelings which anybody could make their own, whilst in narrative poetry the 'I' character, as in Chaucer's

Prologue, may be quite unlike the poet, indeed ironically his opposite. Modern critics seem sometimes to think that the use of a dramatic 'I' is sophisticated, and that the simple and natural thing for a poet to do is to express truthfully his own feelings. The course of English literature, however, suggests the exact opposite, for the development is from the impersonal or dramatic 'I' of Anglo-Saxon and medieval poetry, through the semi-personal 'I' of Renaissance literature, to the completely personal 'I' of the Romantics. If Langland therefore was typical of his period, one would expect the dreamer to be as remote from the individual personality of the poet, as he is in the *Pèlerinage* or in the *Pearl*. The latter has admittedly been searched for autobiographical information, but the self-absorbed grief of the dreamer should properly be interpreted as that of anybody bereaved and unresigned. At first sight by analogy it might be supposed that the questionings of the dreamer in *Piers Plowman* are the questionings of any intelligent man of the fourteenth century: there is, however, a very striking difference between the 'I' character of the *Pearl* and that of *Piers Plowman*. In the *Pearl* the arguments of the maiden are very skilfully developed and timed, so that at each stage in his answers the dreamer becomes milder and more moderate, with the result that by the end he has emerged from his self-pitying possessiveness to a more tranquil understanding of loss and death. In *Piers Plowman*, however, the dreamer in this sense never learns, for there is no poetic resolution to the opposing arguments: they are merely accumulated and put on one side. It is hard therefore to avoid the inference that Langland, unlike the author of the *Pearl*, did not know which way his arguments were leading him, and therefore, whilst his intention may have been to show Everyman seeking a solution to the moral corruption and philosophical problems of his own age, in fact he was exploring the perplexities of his own mind.

The setting out antithetically of opposing points of view was so common a method of medieval theology and poetry, that it comes as quite a shock to find somebody, who either could not control the form or did not wish to do so. It has been pointed out that the second half of the fourteenth century was probably the first period in the Middle Ages in which laymen discussed philosophical problems, perhaps just as non-experts today take an interest in psychology. Langland seems to be an extreme example of a general tendency, for his inquiry into truth has the earnestness typical of the amateur and he does not write with the assurance of professional ease: at an earlier period he would surely not have concerned himself with problems such as those of grace or free-will. Langland's intellectual difficulties communicate themselves to the reader because there is no logical solution to them which is poetically emphasised. Until one has read the poem many times, and even then, it is difficult to remember which side in the various theological arguments prevailed: poetically the solution does not lie in a crowning argument, but in the figure of Piers and in the long and fine narrative of the Harrowing of Hell. It was not of course that Langland was intellectually feeble or that a man of sharper mind would not have shared his perplexity. In part his difficulties arose from a desire to reconcile current philosophical disputes with the issues of every day living, as, for instance, the relationship of Bradwardine's doctrine of predestination, which was the concern of philosophers, with the idea of personal moral choice, so vital an issue with preacher. Other people were not more successful than Langland in relating these two ideas, but rather with professional prudence they did not normally attempt it. It should, however, be added that the role of the plain man perplexed was not peculiar to Langland. Chaucer assumed it both for himself and for Troilus, and it is possible to think that this was not an attitude inconsistent with the depiction of Everyman in the second half of the fourteenth century. In Chaucer's work, however, such passages are minor asides, whilst in *Piers Plowman* they contribute to the dominant tone of the poem.

The extent to which we read the perplexity of the dreamer as being that of Langland himself depends finally upon the interpretation of a long passage of personal reference which was added in the C Text (Passus 6, 1–108). In this the dreamer describes himself as some kind of clerk in minor orders,[5] who earns his living by saying the office for the dead, and who is reproached by reason for living the kind of life only proper to one in a religious order. This description obviously does not sum up Langland's career, for his poem shows him to have been a learned and well-read man, and of this the C Text says nothing. Yet the passage does not have the general relevance nor the unmistakable borrowing of previous commonplaces, which occurred in the passage describing the ageing of the dreamer, so that if it does not contain genuine personal description, it is difficult to account for it. But if it is personal description, then we can see clearly in it Langland's self-conscious concern and uncertainty over himself, of

[5] Langland seems to have led somewhat the same kind of unregularised life of piety as Richard Rolle. For the latter see D. Knowles, *The English Mystical Tradition*, London, 1961, p. 50.

which the whole poem could in a sense be called a magnificent extension. It may well be that it was Langland's passionate concern with his own difficulties and their relationship to wider issues which was the driving force of the poem, contributing to both its merits and defects. The chief fault which it encouraged was confusion, for, since the subject-matter was the range of Langland's own mind, it had no inherent shapeliness which might have helped a poet whose power of imagination far exceeded his ability to organise his material. It is strikingly clear that there is a correlation between the dreamer's perplexity and the poet's confusion: that where the dreamer is most oppressed by the conflict between different philosophical arguments or by the antithesis between the contemporary world and the world as it should be, that there the poet is most likely to be diverted from his point, or to allow some allegorical figure to develop an argument inappropriate or irrelevant to his significance. This might be illustrated over and over again from the section on Do-Wel. There is here a strong contrast with the section on Do-Bet. In the section on Do-Wel Langland imitated the form of allegorical dream in which the dreamer is also one of the chief characters, but with the approach of the section on Do-Bet Langland gradually reverts to the kind which he had used for satiric purposes to begin with, that is the kind in which the dreamer is chiefly said to be present in order to give to the content an air of immediacy and reality. The very beautiful speech on poverty delivered by Patience in Passus 14 or the analysis of charity in Passus 15 are only listened to by the dreamer, whilst in the finest passus of the whole poem, that on the Harrowing of Hell (Passus 18), the dreamer is only present as an onlooker. The dream from here is no longer being used to explore the poet's mind, but as an external vision, and to this difference of method is related the confident tone of the poetry. As a poet Langland is at his greatest when not attempting an argumentative synthesis, but either when he is seeing the world through the eyes of a satirist as a place corrupted throughout by the seven deadly sins, or, by a reverse process, when he is seeing in it only Christ or His reflection.

In the development of this latter point there is a paradox, for, whilst as we said earlier, Langland disregarded the literal level of his allegory in a quite un-medieval way, yet in isolated visionary passages he sees with extraordinary poetic insight some aspect of the real world combined with its farther supernatural significance. Whilst this was the basic theory of medieval allegory, Langland seems to have been the only writer who was stirred by it in his imagination rather than in his reason. This power of Langland is particularly evident in his descriptions of the poor, in whom he sees Christ most clearly reflected, and yet at the same time shows an acute and compassionate observation of their appearance and manners. The description, for instance, of the beggar, who, with his pack on his back (symbolising his good works),[6] strides into heaven in front of the rich 'batauntliche [eagerly] as beggeres done' (Passus 14, 213), shows a striking fusion of literal observation with allegorical significance.

Langland's allegorical method and in particular his treatment of the figures of Piers Plowman and the dreamer are the most obvious non-medieval characteristics of the design and content of the poem. There remains, however, a concluding point about Langland's style, a point so important and deserving of analysis that it should properly be made the subject of an independent study. In so far, however, as it is related to the previous arguments it must be mentioned here. The relationship is this: it is not only Langland's manipulation of his allegory nor the absence of a visual imagination, which shows the lack of the typical medieval virtue of clarity, but also his style, which has none of the lucid elegance of medieval style at its best, but has on the contrary a subtle and complex texture. Associated ideas, for instance, are not set out one by one or side by side in the typical Medieval manner, but are interwoven and compressed together. A very fine illustration of this is the treatment of the image of drinking in Christ's speech to the devil in the account of the Harrowing of Hell:

The bitternesse that thowe hast browe   brouke it thi-seluen,
That art doctour of deth   drynke that thow madest!
For I, that am lorde of lyf   loue is my drynke,
And for that drynke to-day   I deyde vpon erthe.
I faughte so, me threstes yet   for mannes soule sake;
May no drynke me moiste   ne my thruste slake,
Tyl the vendage falle   in the vale of Iosephath,
That I drynke righte ripe must   *resureccio mortuorum*,
And thanne shal I come as a kynge   crouned with angeles,
And han out of helle   alle mennes soules.

(Passus 18, 361–70)

The opening lines suggest the amplification of a common proverb of the kind, 'you have made your bed and now you must lie on it', and

[6] The ultimate source of the common Medieval idea of the companionship or accompaniment of good works is, of course, Apoc. (Revelations) xiv, 13, *Opera enim illorum sequuntur illos*.

this brusque, colloquial retort is expressed in a tone of plain and righteous contempt, which nowadays recalls most strikingly that of *Paradise Regained.* With the devil's drink of death is then contrasted Christ's drink of love. In the amplification of this there are echoes of Mark xiv, 25, John xix, 28, and Matthew xx, 22, with the traditional commentaries upon them, in particular that Christ's thirst on the Cross was for man's salvation, and the whole is given a farther allegorical dimension by its incorporation within the image of the Christ-knight, which had been developed earlier in the passus. Such disentangling, however, could at best cast light on Langland's method: the magnificence of the lines is scarcely illuminated by it. It is unfortunate that in some parts of *Piers Plowman* the style seems matted, turgid or flat, but in passages such as this, Langland writes with a profundity of imagination and a strength of style beyond the range of all other poets of the Middle Ages.

VII

THE THEME OF CHRIST THE LOVER-KNIGHT IN MEDIEVAL ENGLISH LITERATURE

ONE OF the commonest allegories in medieval preaching books and manuals of instruction is that of Christ as a lover-knight. The story of the knight who dies for the sake of his lady and in order to win her love occurs repeatedly in the form of an exemplum, and within the latter the knight's plea for love is often expressed in the form of a short verse complaint. The theme, however, contained such abundant potentialities of theological allegory and so many literary associations that, whilst this simple outline may be taken as the norm, at every point in its history it was given shape in a variety of stories—sometimes, for instance, one recognizes an analogue to the Franklin's Tale[1] or the Clerk's Tale[2]—and it was expressed in a variety of styles, romantic, didactic, or witty. Moreover, the verses themselves were not limited in kind to brief mnemonic jingles summing up the main point of the exemplum, but often developed into independent and moving complaints of Christ, similar in form to the translations of the *Improperia* or to the lyrics amplifying the text 'O vos omnes ...'.

The popularity of the theme undoubtedly arose from its exceptional fitness to express the dominant idea of medieval piety, that Christ endured the torments of the Passion in order to win man's love. This stress upon a personal and emotional relationship between God and man in the work of Redemption was new in the twelfth century. Previously the nature of the Redemption had been defined as a conquest of the devil, and the practical consequence of this was

[1] The story related in the Northern Homily Collection, where the husband goes overseas and the wife is wooed by another lover, obviously has a family resemblance to that of the Franklin's Tale. The exemplum, without the allegorical exposition, has been printed by C. Horstmann, 'Die Evangelien-Geschichten der Homiliensammlung des Ms Vernon', *Archiv für das Studium der neueren Sprachen und Literaturen*, lvii (1877), 274–5.

[2] The point of resemblance here is limited to that of a man of noble birth who falls in love with and marries a maiden of poor and lowly family, as in the *Fasciculus Morum* and *Dives and Pauper*. This form of the story has been commented upon by G. Shepherd, *Ancrene Wisse* (London, 1959), p. 55, who refers to an early version of the theme in a homily of Macarius the Egyptian.

shown to the laity to consist of obedience to God's commands by the observing of moral laws and the theological instruction of the Church. But when the old doctrine of 'the devil's rights' was superseded by that of the 'satisfaction' theory (that Christ as man in some sense made reparation to God), there developed a new emphasis on personal relationship. The new feeling of the twelfth century was expressed in its most exaggerated and heretical form by Peter Abelard,[3] who maintained that the sole efficacy of the Redemption lay in Christ's demonstration of His love to man, thereby winning man's love in return. Slightly later this idea was given correct theological proportions by St. Thomas Aquinas, who defines the Redemption in terms of 'satisfaction', but in answer to the *quæstio* 'Utrum alius modus convenientior fuisset liberationis humanæ quam per passionem Christi' replies that by this method more things were achieved than the freeing from sin: 'Primo enim, per hoc homo cognoscit quantum Deus hominem diligat, et per hoc provocatur ad eum diligendum: in quo perfectio humanæ salutis consistit.'[4] The same point is made by St. Bonaventura in his Commentary on the *Sentences* (Lib. III, dist. xx, qu. 5), where he quotes in support the key text, John xii. 32, and a passage from the *De Arrha Animæ* of Hugh of St. Victor: '... Ut ostenderet tibi, quantum te diligeret, non nisi moriendo a morte te liberavit ut non tantum pietatis impenderet beneficium, verum etiam caritatis monstraret affectum.'[5] As a meditative observation, rather than as part of rigorous theology, it had already been a favourite comment of St. Bernard,[6] and used in this way it became a commonplace of medieval preaching, and is sometimes, as in the following quotation from the *Fasciculus Morum*, actually found as an introduction to the exemplum of the lover-knight: 'Christus passus est et sanguinem eius

[3] *Commentariorum super S. Pauli Epistolam ad Romanos Libri Quinque*, in Migne, *P.L.* clxxviii, 836.

[4] *Summa Theologica*, pt. III, art. xlvi, qu. 3. *Opera Omnia*, ed. Fratres ordinis praedicatorum, xi (1903), 438. The question: 'whether another method would have been more appropriate for the liberation of mankind than the passion of Christ.' Answer: 'for first, by this, man recognizes how much God loves man, and thereby he is prompted to love him; and in this consists the perfection of human salvation.'

[5] Ed. PP Collegii S. Bonaventurae, iii (1887), 428. The quotation from the *De Arrha Animae* will be found with minor verbal differences in *P.L.* clxxvi, 962. 'In order to show how much he loved you, he even died to liberate you from death, so that he could confer on you not only the benefit of pious regard, but also show his feelings of love.'

[6] See E. Gilson, *The Mystical Theology of St. Bernard* (tr. A. H. C. Downes, London, 1940), p. 78 and footnote references.

fudit pro nobis ut nos ad eius amorem et caritatem celerius alliceret.'[7]

From the end of the twelfth century onwards there developed a perfect parallelism between the theological stress upon Christ's display of love on the Cross and the conception of chivalric conduct in the Arthurian romances, wherein a knight by brave endurance and heroic encounters would save the lady whom he loved from treacherous capture, thereby hoping to gain her favour, or might joust brilliantly in front of her, hoping by his prowess to win her love. This common theme of the romances had arisen from two causes: religious morality imposed upon feudal custom emphasized the duty of a knight to protect the helpless, such as women and the fatherless, whilst romantic love fusing with chivalric courtesy exalted battle on behalf of a lady as a means of gaining her love. It is likely that the ancient and well-known image of the Crucifixion as a battle, which was relevant only to the theory of 'the devil's rights', would have disappeared in the Middle Ages had not the literary conventions of medieval chivalry enabled the idea of the warrior Christ to fuse with the idea of Christ the lover or bridegroom of the individual soul, thus making a single theme. It is, however, only partially correct to describe this fusion as new, for it is rather a medievalization of an interlocking of ideas which had taken place at a much earlier time.

The expression of God's relationship to Israel in nuptial imagery was quite common in the Old Testament: Hos. ii. 14–20 and Ezek. xvi, for instance, develop at length the allegory of Israel as an ungrateful bride, who despite her husband's generosity has become a harlot, and yet, it is said, God will forgive her and take her back. A similar current of nuptial imagery runs through the New Testament, where in the Epistles of St. Paul and in the Apocalypse the Church is redeemed and called to be the spotless bride at the marriage of the Lamb. It was possible to relate the Old and New Testament nuptial themes in two ways. The lesser tradition conformed to the common exegetic pattern of substitution, and the Church in this context was seen to take the place of the Synagogue, which chronologically had precedence, just as Jacob, for instance, received the birthright of Esau. This tradition, fairly common in the patristic period, occasionally appears in the Middle Ages, as in the allegory of Hugh of St. Victor in the *De Arrha Animæ*, where Vashti, replaced by Esther as

[7] MS. Rawl. C. 670, f. 42^{v}. Such introductions are no doubt rare only because usually the stories are not embedded in homiletic material. 'Christ suffered and poured forth his blood for us, so that he might draw us the more quickly to love and charity towards him.'

queen to Ahasuerus, signifies the Jews superseded by the Christians.[8] But the more important tradition is that expounded by St. Augustine which describes not substitution, but continuity, a continuity made possible and given extended force by recourse to the idea of Christ as the warrior-bridegroom: adulterous Israel in the power of her lover the devil is won back by Christ who sheds His blood for her. In his commentary on the Wedding at Cana in his eighth homily on St. John's Gospel St. Augustine makes this point clear:

> Habet ergo hic sponsam quam redemit sanguine suo ... eruit eam de mancipatu diaboli: mortuus est propter delicta ejus. ... Offerant homines quælibet ornamenta terrarum, aurum, argentum, lapides pretiosos, equos, mancipia, fundos, prædia; numquid aliquis offeret sanguinem suum. ... Verbum enim sponsus, et sponsa caro humana...ille uterus virginis Mariæ thalamus ejus, inde processit tanquam sponsus de thalamo suo. ...[9]

The same point is made again by St. Augustine in the *Enarrationes in Psalmos*, when he is expounding Psalm xliv,[10] which is itself one of the chief sources of the concept of the warrior-bridegroom. When in the Middle Ages the exemplum became a popular preaching form, it was obviously only a short step to disentangle the symbolic language of St. Augustine into a brief narrative and allegorical exposition. At the same time the theme was medievalized, so that on the one hand the warrior became a chivalric knight, and on the other hand, in accordance with the devotional exposition of the Songs of Songs, the bride ceased to be a corporate body, mankind or the Church, and became instead the individual soul.

The most important point in the story as it arose from the exegetic reconciliation of the Old and New Testament nuptial themes was the faithlessness of the lady which brought about the need for her husband to do battle and rescue her. Echoes of this occasionally survive in the versions of the exemplum: in the thirteenth century, for instance, in the *conte* of Nicolas Bozon, 'Du roy ki avait un amye'[11]

[8] *P.L.* clxxvi, 964–5.

[9] *P.L.* xxxv, 1452: 'So he has his spouse whom he redeedmed with his blood ... he rescued her from the bondage of the devil, he died on account of her transgressions ... Men may offer every kind of earthly treasure; gold, silver, precious stones, horses, slaves, land and estates: would anyone offer his own blood? For the Word is the bridegroom and the bride is human flesh ... that womb of the Virgin Mary was his wedding chamber, out of which he stepped forth as the bridegroom from his wedding chamber.'

[10] *Enarratio in Psalmum* xliv, *P.L.* xxxvi, 494–514.

[11] A. Jubinal, *Nouveau recueil de contes, dits, fabliaux*, ii (Paris, 1842), 308–15. It has also been printed by T. Wright at the end of Peter Langtoft's Chronicle, ii (Rolls Series, 1868), 426–36.

the lady has allowed herself to be carried off by a traitor from the king who loves her, but he is forgiving and fights to win her back. This narration of the story, however, as that of an unfaithful wife was normally unsatisfactory in theological terms in that it cast emphasis on to the battle which had lost its doctrinal significance, and unsatisfactory in literary terms, for in the conventional patterns of characterization of medieval literature there was no room for the wronged but forgiving husband. The Cistercian Isaac of Stella quotes in a sermon one of the key texts for this theme from Jeremiah iii, 'Fornicata es cum amatoribus multis, et tamen revertere ad me, dicit dominus' [you have fornicated with many lovers, yet return again to me, says the Lord], adding that whilst the Gospel allows separation for adultery, yet after a thousand adulteries God still calls back the soul;[12] and the author of the *Ancrene Riwle* likewise quotes the text from Jeremiah in his section on love, and translates it with added touches of affection: 'Ȝet, he ȝeiȝeð al dei, þu þet hauest se unwreaste idon, biturn þe and cum aȝein, welcume schalt tu beo me'.[13] But for this extravagant charity there was most certainly no literary analogue: on the contrary the subject of the husband with an unfaithful wife belonged only to satire and fabliau burlesque. One eccentric fourteenth-century sermon in fact, with an explicitness of analogy which nowadays at least seems unbecoming, compares Christ to a cuckold. The passage in which this occurs is also interesting in that it seems to contain a trivial English verse of secular origin, which has been transformed into a complaint of Christ by its context:

Cokewold relictus ab uxore sua propria iam uti poterit post pascha illa amorosa cantilena:

Ich ave a love untrewe
þat myn herte wo,
þat makes me of reufol hewe,
late to bedde go.
Sore me may rewe
þat evere hi lovede hire so.

Nam infidelis amica est inconstans anima que relabitur ad peccatum post pascha pro qua dominus totus pallidus ivit ad lectum quando corpus eius laceratum positum fuit in sepulcro.[14]

12 Sermo xl, *In Die Paschæ, P.L.* cxciv, 1824.

13 *Ancrene Wisse*, ed. Shepherd, p. 23.

14 MS. CUL. Ii.3.8, ff. 83^{v}–84^{r}. 'The cuckold deserted by his own wife might well sing that well known amorous tune after Easter ... For the faithless lover is the inconstant soul who relapses into sin after the paschal feast (?); she for whom her lord

continued

And, the sermon adds, the foregoing verse is spoken by Christ at His entombment. It is obvious, however, that this is no more than a startling byway in the history of the theme of the lover-knight. Normally Christ's redemption of faithless Israel was transformed in a manner which accorded better with the new theology and new literary tastes, and although relics of its former history sometimes remained—usually as though fossilized[15]—fundamentally it changed from the story of a husband reclaiming in his charity a lapsed and fickle wife to that of a king or knight fighting to save a lady and to win her love.

Since the point of the exemplum was the lady's response to the knight, stress naturally fell either upon the prelude to the battle or upon the subsequent events. Narratives of the first kind are by far the rarer, and the best known is of course that in the *Ancrene Riwle*. There is, however, an analogous version in the fourteenth-century preaching manuscript, Harley 7322:

> Fertur in quibusdam gestis quod quedam erat nobilis domina nomine Faustina, exulata a propria patria et omnibus hominibus spoliata et in castro quodam luteo obsessa undique ab inimicis suis, quam tamen quidem rex nobilis adamavit. Misit ergo ad eam nuntios solempnes cum literis amorem suum ad eam exprimentibus cum muneribus variis. Ipsa tamen munera recepit recusans amorem. Misit autem rex alios nuntios solempniores cum literis et muneribus, que fecit sicut prius et eius amorem omnino contempsit. Tandem iste rex fidelis et gratus in propria persona ad eam accessit, suam potentiam ei ostendens et promittens ei fore ipsam reginam in regno suo et ipsum ex corde diligere velle. Set ipsa misera omnino contempsit. Cui lacrimose ait rex: mulier, compatior tue miserie cum sis undique obsessa ab inimicis, nec ullo modo evadere potes. Ego tamen pro te pugnabo et plagas sustinebo si tamen post mortem volueris me diligere. Spiritualiter per istam reginam intelligo naturam humanam a paradiso eiectam et a diabolo, carne, mundo, et ceteris inimicis in hac valle lutosa obsessam. Rex igitur iste bonus et gratus Christus est qui nostram naturam tantum dilexit quod pro illa mori voluit, nec illum reamare curamus in vita neque in morte.[16]

went to his bed when, all pale, his torn body was placed into the sepulchre.' In l. 4 of the verse, *late* is an emendation of the MS. *lato*.

[15] E.g. two points in versions of the *Gesta Romanorum*, one that the lady is guilty of fornication (faithless Israel), the other that the knight marries the lady before entering battle (an allegory of the Incarnation). (E.E.T.S., E.S. xxxiii (1879), 23–26.)

[16] MS. Harley 7322, f. 26^{r-v}. In l. 2 the MS. has *exultata* with the first *t* subpuncted; in l. 5 for *tamen* it has the abbreviation for *enim*; in l. 9 for *velle* it reads *vellet*. 'It is told in some histories that there was a noble lady called Faustina who, exiled from her own country and deprived of all her followers, was besieged by her enemies within an earthen fortification. Yet she was loved by a noble king. So he sent to her solemn

It is interesting to compare this version with that of the *Ancrene Riwle* for, if the author is directly indebted to the latter, then it is a curious example of a basic story being reproduced, but entirely stripped of its romantic and evocative presentation. But if, as seems more likely, both versions are derivatives of a common source,[17] then the fourteenth-century text may well give some indication of the kind of material used by the author of the *Ancrene Riwle*. The revelation that the much-praised description of the backbiter in the *Ancrene Riwle* is an almost exact translation of a passage in one of St. Bernard's Sermons on the Song of Songs[18] has made it clear that modern literary sensibility alone cannot be trusted to detect passages which unmistakeably reflect the author's literary powers, and therefore any hint of a mediocre source for a particularly fine description is not quite valueless.

The *Ancrene Riwle* and Harley 7322 are unique amongst known texts in putting the stress upon the knight's wooing before the battle: usually the emphasis is upon the situation after the battle when the lady gratefully and lovingly treasures the shirt or arms of the dead knight as a memorial of him. The best-known version of this is the exemplum of the *Gesta Romanorum*, but it was widely current throughout the Middle Ages, and appears fairly frequently in lyric form. The most complete example of this is two stanzas which accompany another complaint of Christ in Cambridge University MS. Dd. 5. 64, III:

> Lo! lemman swete, now may þou see
> Þat I haue lost my lyf for þe.
> What myght I do þe mare?

embassies with letters declaring his love for her, and various gifts. She, however, while accepting his gifts, refused his love. But the king sent other, even more magnificent messengers with letters and gifts. She did as before and utterly despised his love. At last this faithful and gracious king came to her in his own person, showing her his power and promising her that she would be queen in his kingdom and that he was willing to love her from the heart. But this wretched creature entirely despised it. The king said tearfully to her, "Woman, I pity your misery, that you are besieged on all sides by your enemies and you cannot escape them by any means. Yet I will fight for you and sustain wounds if yet after my death you will be willing to love me." In the spiritual sense, I understand by this, queen, human nature expelled from Paradise and besieged by the Devil, the flesh, the world and other enemies in this vale of clay. So this good and gracious king is Christ, who loved our human nature so much that for it he was willing to die, and whom we do not trouble to love in return, in life or in death.'

[17] It is certain that the writer was not using the Latin text of the *Ancrene Riwle*, for they are verbally quite distinct.

[18] C. H. Talbot, 'Some notes on the Dating of the Ancrene Riwle', *Neophilologus*, xl (1956), 39.

For-þi I pray þe speciali
Þat þou forsake ill company
  Þat woundes me so sare;

And take myne armes pryuely
And do þam in þi tresory,
  In what stede sa þou dwelles,
And swete lemman, forget þow noght
Þat I þi lufe sa dere haue boght,
  And I aske þe noght elles.[19]

Whilst it is usually Christ's appeal which is expressed in verse, occasionally the lady's resolve of constancy and her loving recollection of what the knight has done for her is rhymed in the exemplum. In the early fifteenth-century didactic treatise *Dives and Pauper* the lady, having received the bloodstained shirt of her dead husband, thereafter replies to would-be suitors:

Whil I have his blod in myn mende
Þat was to me so goode and kende,
Schal I nevir husbonde take
But hym þat died for my sake.[20]

And almost the same verse occurs in one of the manuscripts of the *Gesta Romanorum.*[21] *In Dives and Pauper* the lady's resolve is prompted by a verse letter written to her by her husband as he is dying:

Beholde myn woundis and have hem in þine þouȝte
For al the good þat ben þine with myn blod I have hem bouȝte.[22]

An attempt is made to show the verse as appropriate to the contents of a letter by a reference to the shirt as being *ful of woundis and of holis*, but such a use of the word *woundis* is undoubtedly forced. The verse in fact properly belongs to a different form of the exemplum, in which it is imagined that the knight, though severely wounded, does not die but returns to his beloved's door. The most striking and interesting

[19] C. Brown, *Religious Lyrics of the Fourteenth Century*, p. 94. The two complaints are followed by a group of lyrics usually accepted as the work of Richard Rolle. The complaints, however, are clearly governed by the initial rubric, 'hic incipiunt cantus compassionis Christi ...', and not by the *explicit* which attributes an uncertain number of the preceding poems to Rolle. There is no reason to connect the origin of the complaints either with Rolle or with his 'school'.

[20] MS. Douce 295, f. 142^{v}. *Dives and Pauper* survives in five manuscripts and was printed by both Pynson and Wynknyn de Worde. For a description of it see H. G. Pfander, 'Dives and Pauper', *The Library*, 4th ser. xiv (1934), 299–312.

[21] E.E.T.S., E.S. xxxiii (1879), 26.

[22] MS. Douce 295, f. 142^{v}.

version of this occurs in the much-used Franciscan preaching book, the *Fasciculus Morum*,[23] a work composed in the fourteenth century, but widely current in the fifteenth, from which period all extant manuscripts save one survive:

> Unde narrat Virgilius eneydos (et similiter commentator super Alexandrum magnum) libro 4 et 6 de Enea quomodo amore cuiusdam puelle exarsit in tantum ut se ipsum pro ipsa depauperando humiliaret atque eam ditando exaltaret, quod et factum est. Accidit ergo quodam die cum de quodam bello pro ea rediret vulneribus sauciatus vix semivivus evasit. Accessit ergo ad eam tanquam ad tutiora refugia confidenter eo quod illam tantum pre ceteris dilexisset et se ipsum depauperando eam exaltasset. Sed ipsa tanquam ingrata portas seravit et aditum constanter sibi negavit. Quo facto secundum Ovidium Metamorfoseos ei sic scripsit infortunium suum allegans:
>
> Cerne cicatrices veteris vestigia pugne,
> Quesivi proprio sanguine quicquid habes.
>
> Beholde myne woundes how sore I am dyȝth
> For all þe wele þat þu hast I wan hit in fyȝt.
> I am sore woundet, behold on my skyn,
> Leve lyf, for my love, let me comen in.
>
> Spiritualiter loquendo iste miles Eneas Christus est qui istam puellam scilicet animam humanam in tantum dilexit quod ipsam ditaret et exaltaret, nostram naturam assumens pauper devenit, atque pro ea contra hostem humani generis bellum fortissimum agressus est, ubi tam horribiliter sauciatus est quod ut dicitur Isaias, A planta pedis usque ad verticem capitis non est in eo sanitas. A quo conflictu vix vivus evadens ad portam anime pro qua tanta passus est securus accessit, ut ipsa pre ceteris amore et compassione mota ipsum in tali necessitate consolaretur et refocillaret. Pulsat ergo ut ingressum habeat prout dicitur Apocalypsis, Ecce sto ad hostium et pulso. Quid plura? Revera fortissime ibi clamat ibidem, Aperi mihi soror mea, amica mea, columba mea, sed certe, ut timeo, tanquam ingrata et tanti beneficii immemor, portas anime, que sunt amor, compassio et huiusmodi affectiones bone fortiter obserando claudit dum scilicet peccando sic ingrate illum excludit, sed certe hoc non obstante ipse tanquam gratissimus et fidelissimus pulsare non desistit et clamare: Beholde myn woundes et cetera.[24]

[23] For an account of the *Fasciculus Morum* see A. G. Little, *Studies in English Franciscan History* (Manchester, 1917), pp. 139–57.

[24] MS. Rawl. C. 670, ff. 42^{v}–43^{r}. This is one of the three manuscripts which Frances Foster decided should be the basis of her proposed edition: see 'A Note on the *Fasciculus Morum*', *Franciscan Studies*, viii (1948), 202–4. In the last sentence this manuscript reads *observando*; the other three manuscripts which I have examined, Laud Misc. 213, Laud Misc. 568, and Bodley 410, all agree on the reading *obserando*. I am indebted to Dr R. W. Hunt and Mr E. P. M. Dronke for comments on this passage and on my transcription of it. 'Thus Vergil tells in books 4 and 6 of the Aeneid (and similarly the commentator on Alexander the Great) about Aeneas, how he burned with

continued

The most immediately obtrusive characteristic of this passage is its medieval classicism: first the invention that the story is that of Æneas with the reference to the probably fictitious *Commentator super Alexandrum magnum* (another version attributes the story to Ovid),[25] and secondly the quotation of the two lines from the *Amores*,[26] with a slight change in the second, so that what was in its original context a harsh reproach to Corinna that she should prefer an uncivilized soldier to the poet becomes an epitome of the lover-knight's complaint. Another point of interest which marks this story off from many other versions of the exemplum is that the lady is not of equal rank but poor. The allegorical aptness of this is plain, but such a relationship is so contrary to the patterns of courtly romance that more often, as in the *Ancrene Riwle*, the lady is shown to be of noble birth, though now dispossessed of her inheritance.[27] The same motif, however, occurs in *Dives and Pauper*, and this, together with the

love for a maiden to such a degree that he would humble himself by making himself poor for her and raise her up by making her rich, which also was achieved. Thus it came to pass one day when he returned from some war fought on her behalf, that he barely escaped half dead, covered with wounds. So he approached her confidently as a safe refuge, because he had loved her so much above all others and had made her great by making himself poor. But she, ungrateful as she was, locked the gates and persistently denied him entrance. Thereupon he wrote to her thus, in the words of Ovid's Metamorphoses, describing his misfortune: "Behold the scars, marks of the long fight. Whatever you possess I won with my own blood." ... Spiritually speaking, this knight Aeneas is Christ who so much loved this maid (that is the human soul), that he made her rich and noble and, taking on our nature, became poor and embarked for her on the most strenuous war against the enemy of the human race, in which he was so horribly wounded that, as Isaiah says: "From the sole of the foot to the crown of the head there was nothing whole in him." From this conflict barely escaping with his life he approached confidently the door of the soul for whom he had suffered so much, so that she, more than others moved by love and compassion, should comfort and revive him in his need. So he knocks to have entrance, as it says in the Apocalypse: "Lo, I stand at the door and knock". What more can be said? Truly, he calls very loudly the same words standing there: "Open to me, my sister, my friend, my dove!" But in fact, being ungrateful and unmindful of such a great favour, she closed the doors of the soul which are love, compassion and good feelings of this kind; with strong locks she closes the doors while she locks him out viz. by sinning so ungratefully. But he notwithstanding this, being most gracious and faithful does not cease to knock and to call: "Behold my wounds" etc.'

[25] This is in the *Convertimini* (MS. Royal 7 C 1, f. 116^{v}) where the story is told with the quotation from Ovid, but without the English verse and the elaboration of the allegory by reference to the 'ecce sto' text. The whole exemplum occurs independently in a fifteenth-century manuscript, B.M. Add. 6716, f. 8^{v}.

[26] *Amores*, 111. viii. 19–20, where the second line reads, 'quæsitum est illi corpore quicquid habet'.

[27] The lady in the *Ancrene Riwle* had been rich ('hire lond al destruet'), and, in that she needs the help of a knight, she is in a typically romantic situation.

quotation *Cerne cicatrices* & c., suggests a common ancestry. In the *Fasciculus Morum* there is obviously an inconsistent conflation of two versions: the one where the dying knight writes a letter (*sic scripsit* in the *Fasciculus Morum*) and the lady cherishes his memory; the other in which the knight returns to his lady's door, and she, hard-hearted and unkind, bars her gates against him. The accusation that the lady is *ingrata et tanti beneficii immemor* [ungrateful and unmindful of such great favour] has point on both the literal and allegorical levels. On the allegorical plane the individual, intent on his own pleasure, is indifferent to Christ, and on the literal level within the conventions of romantic love the lady is unkind. Whilst in the extreme forms of the courtly love convention a lady, such as for instance Guinevere in the *Chevalier de la Charrette* of Chrétien de Troyes, might lack completely in gratitude and generosity to her lover and still be above reproach, commonly—and certainly in England—it was thought that the unbounded loyalty of a lover deserved a reciprocal courtesy and consideration in his mistress, and that a lady lacking in these would show a churlishness particularly unfitting in one of gentle birth: the author of the *Ancrene Riwle*, for instance, after relating the death of the knight, asks with the confidence of a rhetorical question, 'Nere þeos ilke leafdi of uueles cunnes cunde, ȝef ha ouer alle þing ne luuede him her efter?'[28]

The source of the episode in which the knight comes to his beloved's door is made plain by the scriptural texts quoted, the one from the Apocalypse, the other from the Song of Songs. Whilst this image was used fairly frequently in lyrics and exempla during the fourteenth century, its only occurrence before the *Fasciculus Morum* is in an exceptionally moving poem from the late-thirteenth-century manuscript Lambeth 557, where it is copied with Latin sermon notes on the Passion. It was later included in John of Grimestone's preaching book with an inferior addition in different metre.[29] The Lambeth text is as follows:

Allas, allas, vel yvel ye sped,
For synne Jesu from me ys fled,
  Þat lyvely fere.

[28] *Ancrene Wisse*, ed. Shepherd, p. 22. 'Would not this lady be of an evil sort of nature, if she did not love him above all things thereafter?'

[29] Brown, *Fourteenth Century*, p. 86. The text of the Lambeth MS. is preferable in its readings and stanza-order, except for the reading *at one* for *alone* in l. 4.

At my dore he standeth alone
And kallys, undo, yit reuful mone
  On þis manere:

Undo my lef, my dowve dere,
Undo, wy stond [y] stekyn out here,
  Iyk am þi make.
Lo my heved and myne lockys
Ar al bywevyd wyt blody dropys
  For þine sake.[30]

The manner in which this poem anticipates the exemplum in the *Fasciculus Morum* can be clearly seen if it is compared with the eleventh-century Latin poem, *Quis est iste qui pulsat ad ostium*, based on the same episode from the Song of Songs. In the Latin poem, as in its source, the lady eagerly arises to answer her lover's knocking, only to find that he has fled. But in the English the flight—by implication the exclusion of Christ from the heart—has already taken place, and now like the knight of the *Fasciculus Morum* Christ 'tanquam gratissimus et fidelissimus pulsare non desistat et clamare ...' [being so gracious and most faithful, does not cease knocking and calling out]. Moreover the tone of Christ's address is quite different from that of the Latin, which is as follows:

Ego sum summi regis filius,
primus et novissimus;
qui de caelis in has veni tenebras,
liberare captivorum animas:
passus mortem et multas iniurias.[31]

The Latin is much more dogmatic and impersonal, the English more tender and lovingly reproachful. But the most relevant difference between them is that in the Latin, although there is a reference to Christ's sufferings in the last line quoted, there is no suggestion that they are visible on Him, whereas the author of the English poem, by an ingenious interpretation of Cant. v. 2 ('... quia caput meum plenum est rore, et cincinni mei guttis noctium') [because my head is covered with dew, and my locks with the drops of the nights] and by the addition of the emotive phrase 'for þine sake', shows with delicacy and clearness that it is a lover-knight who speaks.

[30] Lambeth 557, f. 185ᵛ. The text printed in the *Catalogue* is not quite accurate.

[31] *The Oxford Book of Medieval Latin Verse*, ed. F. J. E. Raby (Oxford, 1959), p. 158. 'I am the son of the high king, the eldest and youngest; I come from the sky into these shadows, to set free the souls of those enslaved. I suffered death and many injuries.'

In all the versions of the exemplum so far quoted and in the complaints of the lover-knight the main point has self-evidently been Christ's appeal for love in return for His own, and, despite minor details deriving from some earlier theological intention, there has been no important modification of the story and no device of style which was not intended to heighten the effect of this. But there remain a number of poems and narrative allegories in which there is a distinctive element more likely to please the intellect than the emotions. The battle image, as we have seen, was strikingly appropriate to the old doctrine of the Redemption in that the result of the Crucifixion was the result normally peculiar to battle, an enemy defeated, and so long as art represented Christ on the Cross as a hero triumphant, the self-evident differences between the Crucifixion and a battle remained satisfactorily unobtrusive. But once the moment of the Crucifixion chosen for representation was the time when Christ hung dead and blood-stained from the Cross, the latent but violent discrepancy became manifest. In some traditions this discrepancy was not ignored but exploited, and was developed into a series of paradoxes and conceits. This treatment is remarkable in that it passed from Latin into English verse at an earlier date than the period at which intellectual ingenuity was commonly put at the service of Passion poetry. But it shares with the later, fifteenth-century, style a common characteristic: that is that its elements of shock and surprise do not, as in seventeenth-century metaphysical poetry, derive from the invention of a startling and hitherto unthought-of term of comparison, but from the choosing of some ancient and well-established similitude, and then pressing every possible detail of it into the comparison. The conceits in the Christ-knight literature depend upon an implicit question: if Christ on the Cross is likened to a knight in battle or tournament, in what manner then was He armed? A temperate paradoxical answer to this is that of the opening lines of a verse in John of Grimestone's preaching book:

I am iesu, þat cum to fith
With-outen seld and spere—[32]

but more often in the sermon narratives it is answered with length and ingenuity. It may well be that St. Paul's allegory of the 'armour of God' had some influence upon the minutely detailed description of Christ's arming, and it may be noted that an allegorization of

[32] Brown, *Fourteenth Century*, p. 82.

knightly armour in terms of the virtues was very popular in the later Middle Ages, being copied amongst the short prose works of Richard Rolle or as part of the treatise compilation *The Pore Caitiff*:[33] in this, for instance, the horse is the body, the saddle mansuetude, the spurs fear and love. The literary precedent, however, is quite clearly the favourite set passages in the romances, in which the arming of a knight is described. The earliest extensive allegory of this kind is the Anglo-Norman poem of Nicolas Bozon already referred to: of this two texts survive in the famous collection of Anglo-Norman literature, Phillipps 8336 (now B. L. Add. 46919), one of them in a group which includes a prose passage entitled *Modus ad armandi milites ad torneamentum*, and the *Ordre de Chevalerie* by Hue de Tabarie.[34] This grouping reflects the obvious point that only those who knew the technical terms normally made familiar by the romance convention would appreciate a witty extension of these. The main point of Bozon's poem consists of a fairly uncommon allegory, wherein God's assumption of a human body in the womb of the Blessed Virgin is imagined as a knight's arming with the assistance of a maiden:

Si entra en la chaumbre cele damoisele
Qe de totes altres estoit la plus belle,

. . . . . .

La damoisele l'arma de mult estraunge armure:
Pur aketoun li bailla blaunche chare et pure.

. . . . . .

Pour chauces de fere de nerfs mist la jointure,
Ses plates furent de os qe sisterènt à mesure.[35]

Usually, however, it is not Christ's human flesh which is His armour, but the outward signs of His sufferings and the instruments

[33] *The Pore Caitiff* was an exceptionally popular compilation of the late fourteenth century. See M. Deanesly, *The Lollard Bible* (Cambridge, 1920), pp. 346–7, and Sister Mary Teresa Brady, 'The Pore Caitif', *Traditio*, x (1954), 529–48.

[34] For a description of the manuscript see P. Meyer, 'Notice et extraits du ms. 8336 de la bibliotheque de sir Thomas Phillipps à Cheltenham', *Romania*, xiii (1884), 497–541.

[35] Jubinal, *Nouveau Recueil*, ii, 310.

So this young lady enters the room,
The one who was of all others the most beautiful,
The young lady armed him with very strange armour:
For a jacket she gave him pure white flesh.
For hose of metal she made the seam with nerves,
His breastplates were of bone, and fitted perfectly.

of the Passion. A typical allegory is one which occurs in a number of fourteenth-century manuscripts in a sermon on the text *amore langueo*, where the Passion is described under the seven secular signs of love-longing. The allegory occurs near the beginning, where the familiar story of Christ-knight is thus interpreted:

> ... pro istum militem nobilem intelligo Cristum qui est ex nobili genere procreatus quia dei filius strenuissimus, et fuit sicut patuit hodierna die in bello contra diabolum. Et ecce qualiter mirabiliter iste miles fuit armatus ut procedet ad bellum. Primo habuit suum actoun corpus mundum, et pro sua hawberk quod est ful of holes habuit corpus suum plenum vulneribus; pro galea habuit coronam spineam capiti inpensam, et pro arotheas de plate habuit duos clavos fixos in manibus; pro calcaribus habuit clavum fixum in pedibus. Pro equo habuit crucem super quam pependit; pro scuto apposuit latus suum, et processit sic contra inimicum cum lancea, non in manu sed stykand in his side.[36]

The English phrases so oddly scattered through this, like the French sentence in a Latin exemplum related by the friar Albert de Metz,[37] suggest a vernacular version known to the author.

The main details of this allegory may be seen entirely in English in the rhymed version of the exemplum in the Northern Homily Collection. In this a lady, like Dorigen in the Franklin's Tale, is wooed though not seduced by a suitor, whilst her husband is overseas; the husband on his return decides, unlike Arviragus, to defend his wife's honour by fighting the suitor, and he is killed in battle. The allegorical interpretation exceeds in length the literal story, and contains a detailed allegory of the armour:

> Bote how þis kniht and Jhesu
> was armed good is þat we kneuh.
> Schon he hedde of iren and steel,
> harde nayles, wyte we hit wel,
> weore þorwh boþe his feet idryven

[36] MS. Balliol 149, f. 32ᵛ. The same sermon occurs in MSS. Magdalen 93 and Trinity Dublin 277. '... by this noble knight I understand Christ who is descended from a noble race because he is the most vigorous son of God and as such he was revealed in this present day in the war against the Devil. And look how wonderfully this knight was armed as he goes to war. First he had as his "actoun" [a padded jacket under armour] a human body, and as his "hawberk" which is "ful of holes" he had his body full of wounds; as a helmet he had two nails fixed into his hands; as spurs he had a nail fixed in his feet. For a horse he had the cross on which he hung; for a shield he presented his side, and he advanced thus against the enemy with his lance, not in his hand, but "stykand in his side".'

[37] For this exemplum see W. Gaffney, 'The Allegory or the Christ-Knight in *Piers Plowman*', *P.M.L.A.* xlvi (1931), 155–68.

þat bones and senewes al to-ryven.
Leg harneys and haburgon also
and brases of o sute dude he go.
Al was kevered wiþ red blood
and mony a wounde þerin stod.
A gurdel he hedde aboute hym fast,
a rop þat harde to him was wrast,
when he was drawe fer and neer
and bounden to an heih pileer.
A peire gloves he wered of plate,
two nayles þorwh his hondes sate.
His basenet was, is nouht to sayn,
a croune of þorn sat to þe brayn.
His wepenes bar he mildelye
wiþ mekenesse wiþouten envye.
Þer oþur men beer heore schelde
bifore heore breste hemself to welde,
his scheld at his bac bar he
þat was þe harde rode tre.
Þer oþur man bere heore spere
þe poynt forþward hem to were,
he bar þe poynt in his syde
and to his herte he let hit glyde.
And þus he overcom þe fende
wiþ mekenes as kniht ful hende.[38]

In descriptions of this kind (though it does not occur above) the most important and recurrent allegory is that of Christ's Cross as the horse or saddle upon which He rode. Apart from the text of MS. Balliol 149, it occurs also, for instance, in the subsidiary allegory of Nicolas Bozon's poem ('Sa sele fu trop dure, et mout l'ad anguise'), and in an interesting biblical allegory in a Latin sermon of MS. Bodley 649, which has as its text Luke xi. 21, 'Cum fortis armatus custodit atrium suum, in pace sunt ea quæ possidet' [when a strong armed man guards his home, his possessions are in peace].[39] The *fortis armatus* is identified with the angel of 2 Macc. iii. 25, and both, of course, signify Christ. In the allegorical exposition of the Maccabees story, Israel is mankind and Antiochus the devil, and the *miles equitans in equo* [knight riding on a horse], sent by God to help the Jews, is Christ riding upon the Cross. The image of the Cross as a horse is the main point of a complaint of Christ in MS. Harley 2316—a Dominican preaching manuscript of the second half of the fourteenth century; at

[38] Vernon MS., f. 185^{v}.
[39] MS. Bodley 649, f. 34^{r}.

first sight it may seem an unpromising poetical theme, since it has neither the startlingly grim appropriateness of Christ's body, covered with a multitude of wounds, as a shirt of mail, nor the ironic poignancy of the lance, not carried point outwards, but driven inwards to Christ's heart. Nevertheless the use of the image in 'Men rent me on rode' is extremely moving:

Biheld mi side,
Mi wndes sprede so wide,
Rest-les i ride.
Lok up on me! Put fro ȝe pride.

Mi palefrey is of tre,
Wiht nayles naylede ȝwrh me.
Ne is more sorwe to se—
Certes noon more no may be.[40]

One reason for the success of the image here is its isolation: since it is not the member of a series, it does give the effect of springing from unrestrained inventiveness, but conveys a sober pathos and a mournful reproach of the kind of those in the *Improperia*, and it therefore does not seem unfittingly spoken by Christ. The tone of the image has been changed from triumph to melancholy, and nowadays at least it seems more decorous as part of a lament than as part of a chivalric panoply. The ironic incongruity between the pride of a horse and the humiliation of the Cross is exploited most strikingly in the Towneley Crucifixion play.[41] In this, before the actual nailing to the Cross, the executioners with harsh jesting liken their task to the horsing of a king. To the modern reader this seems the best and most proper use of the image, but clearly to the audiences of the mystery plays it remained only one of various possible usages, for whilst the audience of the Towneley cycle heard it as a brutal joke, in York the people heard Christ, when He appeared to Mary Magdalene in the garden, speak a typical complaint in the conventions of this allegory.[42] It is not from modern prejudice alone, however, that we may judge that the author of the Towneley play had a keener

[40] Brown, *Fourteenth Century*, p. 67.

[41] E.E.T.S., E.S. lxxii (1897), 261. It has been argued by Sister Jean Marie, 'The Cross in the Towneley Plays', *Traditio*, v (1947), 331–4, that this image implies a projection on which Christ was seated. But the evidence, including that of the Towneley Play itself, is so abundantly against this that it is quite unacceptable. The point of the analogy was the raising, not the seating, as is clear in the passage quoted from MS. Balliol 149, 'Pro equo habuit crucem super quam pependit'.

[42] *York Mystery Plays*, ed. Lucy Toulmin Smith (Oxford, 1885), p. 424.

dramatic sense in his use of the image than had the York writer.

The allegory of the lover-knight occurs in so many places that it would be tedious to enumerate and examine each one; and no doubt a thorough search of Latin sermon manuscripts would produce further illustrations. There is in fact only one well-known preaching book which does not include the exemplum: The *Summa Prædicantium* of John Bromyard. In this massive work, however, under the heading of *Passio*, there occurs a closely related story,[43] which may be commented upon as an epilogue to a consideration of the theme of the lover-knight. The tale is of a man who is deprived of his inheritance by a tyrant, and who regains it with the help of a friend himself slain in battle. Whereupon the restored heir places the *vestes et arma sanguine aspersa* [clothes and armour sprinkled with blood] in his room, and thereafter, when he is tempted by the wiles of the tyrant to sell or make over his inheritance to him, he gratefully looks on the armour of his friend and is strengthened to resist. This is self-evidently the plot of the bloody-shirt exemplum, but transferred from a knight and his lady to a pair of friends. The history of the concept of friendship in the Middle Ages and of its application to Christ could profitably be traced at length.[44] But briefly it may be said that the Middle Ages inherited the classical idea of friendship and that this illuminated the traditional exegetic application of John xv. 13 to Christ. Not surprisingly, it was in the twelfth century that the idea of friendship was substantially developed in Christian literature: its chief source was, of course, the *De Amicitia* of Cicero, though references to the ultimate source, Book VIII of the *Ethics* of Aristotle, throughout the Middle Ages adorn discussions of the subject. The *De Amicitia* was the basis of the *De Spirituali Amicitia* of Ailred of Rievaulx, and the influence of its theme can be seen in the section on love in the *Ancrene Riwle*, where the author recognizes friendship as a clear and binding relationship, and illustrates it with a story anticipating that of *The Merchant of Venice*. From this period also dates the western Christian use of three exempla which illustrate the theme, and which are all included in the *Summa Prædicantium* under *amicitia*. The first derives from the *Dictorum Factorumque*

[43] *Summa Prædicantium* (Venice, 1586), ii. 176^{r}, col. 2.

[44] L. J. Mills, *One Soul in Bodies Twain* (Bloomington, 1937), is moderately helpful. More useful is R. R. Purdy, 'The Friendship Motif in Middle English Literature', *Vanderbilt Studies in the Humanities*, i (1951), 113–41. Some valuable comments on the application of the idea to Christ are made in R. Egenter, *Gottesfreundschaft* (Augsburg, 1927), pp. 258–62.

Memorabilium Libri Novem of Valerius Maximus[45]—a work much quoted from the twelfth century onwards—and it is the story of Damon and Pythias; another, with a fairly similar story, concerns two merchants of Lombardy and Bagdad, and comes from another much-used source of exempla, the *Disciplina Clericalis* of Petrus Alphonsus;[46] whilst the third, referred by Bromyard to the *Speculum Historiale* of Vincent de Beauvais, is that of a man who kills his own children in order to provide a blood-bath which will cure his friend of leprosy—an episode which is more familiar from the romance of Amis and Amiloun, but which goes back to Franco-Latin saints' lives earlier in date than the *Speculum Historiale*.[47] In their sources these three exempla have only a moral application, but in Bromyard the faithful friend symbolizes Christ.

The point of the lover-knight theme is so obviously Christ's demonstration of love in the Redemption that further evidence for it may seem superfluous. But, if it were needed, the exchange of one relationship of love for another in the exemplum of the *Summa Prædicantium* would provide an admirable illustration.

[45] Cap. vii, 'de amicitiæ vinculo'; edn. of Venice, 1691, pp. 190–1.

[46] Ed. A. Hilka and W. Söderhjelm (Heidelberg, 1911), pp. 4–6. The story was popular in the fourteenth and fifteenth centuries and occurs in the *Gesta Romanorum* (pp. 196–205), in the *Fabula Duorum Mercatorum* of Lydgate (ed. G. Schleich, *Quellen und Forschungen*, lxxxiii (1897)), and in the story of Tito and Gisippo in the *Decameron*, x. 8.

[47] The story of Amicus and Amelius occurs in the *Speculum Historiale*, xxiii. 162–6, edn. of Venice, 1591, ff. 329^{v}–330^{r}. For reference to twelfth-century Latin saints' lives see L. Gautier, *Épopées françaises*, i (Paris, 1865), 308–18.

VIII

THE LOST OPENING TO THE *JUDITH*

THE probable length of the lost opening to the *Judith* is a problem which has never been fully discussed. Most scholars, including the most recent editor of the poem, Dr Timmer, have assumed without question that the 350 lines which remain represent only a small part of the original;[1] whilst the only serious opponent of this view, A. S. Cook, was content to state his theory, that little had been lost, as a personal opinion, only substantiating it by pointing out a verbal similarity between the opening lines of the fragment and the conclusion:[2] a fact which could be too easily explained as a coincidence to bear the slightest weight. The point, however, deserves a detailed treatment, rather than a brief dismissal in a categorical aside or a curt footnote, which is all that it has hitherto been given, for it is not merely a matter of academic interest: any critical opinion of the poem depends on it.

The extant Anglo-Saxon poems on Biblical subjects fall into two classes. The first type may be called the chronicle poem, in which the poet followed with historical fidelity all the incidents in his original (rarely supplementing or deducting), and preserved its proportions almost exactly: *Genesis A* and *Daniel* are of this type. In the second type the poet chose some incident from the Bible, extracted it with a selective eye from its context, and transmuted it into a dramatic shape: the *Exodus*, which corresponds only to some parts of chapters 13 - 15 of the Book of Exodus, is an example of this method. The essential difference between these two is, of course, a concept of form and unity, the presence or absence of which is very relevant to any assessment of the total literary value of a work. It is therefore interesting to try to discover to which category *Judith* belongs. But before it is useful to analyse the poet's treatment of his source and the aesthetic impression produced by the poem, it is necessary to consider the sectional numbering, for according to the manuscript the poem

[1] *Judith*, ed. B. J. Timmer, footnote to line 1.
[2] *Judith*, ed. A. S. Cook, note to line 1.

begins towards the end of section 9, and, if it can be proved that the sectional numbers in the manuscript represent the numbering in the poet's autograph, then no amount of general argument can outweigh the hard fact that approximately 1000 lines of the work must have disappeared.[3]

Now there are two schools of thought, both of which attribute the numerals in Anglo-Saxon manuscripts to the poet's handiwork, but for different reasons. The earlier of these was formed by Henry Bradley,[4] followed by Sir William Craigie,[5] who contended that the numbers originally served the purpose of marking the order of the poets' loose parchment leaves. After Gollancz's sound refutation of this view,[6] there is little need to reopen the case against Bradley at any length. It need only here by noticed that his brilliantly ingenious calculations are quite discredited by the fact that they involve the incredible assumption that the Anglo-Saxon poet laboured to end each sheet at a major pause in the narrative. Bradley himself asks the question why, and cannot even suggest an answer. Moreover, if the numbers had served a mainly mechanical purpose, there is the further question why the scribes so often preserved them. If the answer is that they were aware of the poet's self-imposed discipline of always ending a sheet at the close of a paragraph, in fact that they considered this to be the main function of the numerals, then doubt is immediately cast on whether they ever served any other purpose.

The second school of thought is represented by Klaeber, who believes that the numbers correspond to the author's own structural divisions,[7] and by Dr Timmer, who calls them 'psychological units' and likens them to the chapters of a novel.[8] The latter is an unfortunate comparison, for it blurs the distinction between his theory and Klaeber's. Moreover, whilst Dr Timmer's major point that the poems were not conceived in the terms of the structural divisions indicated by the numbers is most important and illuminating, his deduction from this that they coincide with the temporary flagging of the poets' inspiration is without proof and

[3] This calculation is made by Bradley in 'The Numbered Sections in Old English Poetic Manuscripts', *Proceedings of the British Academy*, VII, 179.

[4] *Ibid.* pp. 165–83.

[5] 'Interpolations and Omissions in Anglo-Saxon Poetic Texts', *Philologica*, II, 5–19.

[6] *The Cædmon Manuscript*, London 1927, Introduction, section iv.

[7] *Beowulf*, ed. Klaeber, London 1922, Introduction, pp. c–ci.

[8] B. J. Timmer, 'Sectional Divisons of Poems in Old English Manuscripts', *M.L.R.* XLVII, 319–22.

intrinsically improbable: it means in fact that a poet whenever he recommenced writing inserted a number—for the sake of order, Dr Timmer suggests—but why the poets preferred this to the clearer paginal numeration, and why scribes should have troubled to copy the numerals (the objection made above to Bradley's theory also applies here) is not explained. It also involves the postulation that most poets were quite extraordinarily regular in the amount of inspiration they enjoyed at every sitting,[9] and whilst there is no need to suppose them composing erratically in bursts of poetic fervour of uncertain duration, it yet remains improbable that a number of different poets succeeded in maintaining such astounding uniformity in the amount they composed at one time.

Since the sectional numbers indicate suitable pauses in the narrative, but often not structurally important points, I would support Gollancz's view that the numerals were used to indicate suitable breaks in the story, where the hearers might momentarily rest their attention. This theory is corroborated by the sentence from the *Præfatio in librum antiquum lingua Saxonica conscriptum*, quoted by both Gollancz and Dr Timmer, in which the writer equates the sectional divisions of Anglo-Saxon poetry with *lectiones*, a monastic term referring to reading portions of the Bible or other religious works, which suggests that he recognized some similarity of purpose in both. Where I disagree with Gollancz is in his assumption that these numerals must have been the work of the poet,[10] for, granted this use of the numbers, it is at least as likely that a copyist or reviser inserted them, as that the poet did, and granted the fact that they are not fundamentally appropriate, it is more likely that they were inserted by someone reading through the poem than by the person who conceived the whole.

Moreover, even if the poet had normally divided his work into sections, it could not be certain that the scribes would preserve the numbers accurately. They undoubtedly showed respect neither for his spelling, nor his punctuation, as may be deduced from Dr Sisam's collation of those Anglo-Saxon poems which survive in more than

[9] Although there is some variation in the length of sectional divisions, particularly in *Beowulf*, the frequency with which, in most poems, they conform to an internal average is remarkable. For tables see Bradley, op. cit. pp. 175 (*Genesis*), 178 (*Exodus*), 179 (*Elene*). In *Judith* the numbers of lines in the sections are respectively 107, 114, 113.

[10] Although Gollancz (op. cit.) concludes that the sectional divisions 'were originally structural divisions due to the poet', he admits that there is no positive evidence that the numbers were inserted in fact by the poet himself.

one manuscript.[11] That the scribes did not reproduce exactly the figures of their original (if these figures existed) is clear from the Junius Manuscript, where the first three poems, *Genesis, Exodus* and *Daniel*, are numbered consecutively from 1 to 55, with no fresh set of numbering for each poem. So unless one assumes that these works were all written by the same author in that precise order, which no scholar would dream of accepting, it must be admitted that a scribe, when copying a group of poems, would continue numbering, irrespective of the fact that his exemplar or exemplars, if they numbered at all, must have begun afresh, or that he inserted numerals as he went through, and did not bother to indicate by a new sequence of numbers the beginning of a different poem. Whilst either explanation is possible, the second suggestion is the more probable, since a scribe inserting sectional marks, as he copied or on revision, might well number several poems continuously, if there were only punctuation marks or no sectional divisions at all in his original, but would be less likely to make the actual effort—for no valid reason—of adjusting the numbering in his exemplar to his own system.

Under these circumstances it becomes clear that the numbers in *Judith* by no means necessarily represent the poet's autograph. Since the scribe of the Cotton Manuscript was presumably copying an incomplete text, they might either represent his guess at the amount lost, in which case by a comparison with the Apocryphal Book he made a reasonable estimation of the total length of the poem, if it had preserved the proportions of its source exactly; or they might mean that in an earlier manuscript *Judith* had succeeded a poem that was numbered up to eight, and that this sequence had been continued in it. A scribe copying the poem, once its beginning was lost, would, of course, automatically repeat the numbers before him, without realizing that an adjustment was necessary.

It is now possible to return to the poem itself, and to consider whether a writer would be likely to base his work on only a part of the Apocryphal Book. As has already been pointed out, the *Exodus* provides an admirable example of a poet's selection of an episode with its relevant historical background, without paraphrasing the whole of his Biblical source; whilst that it might occur to an Anglo-Saxon poet to treat the subject of Judith in this way is shown by the fact that the story was known with all the preliminary historical

[11] 'Notes on Old English Poetry', *R.E.S.* XXII, 285 ff.; reprinted in *Studies in Old English Literature*, pp. 31 ff.

material subtracted: in his *de laudibus Virginitatis* Aldhelm uses the life of Judith as one of his exempla, and begins his brief account with a description of Judith's conduct after the death of her husband.[12] Since the Apocryphal version glorifies the Jewish race, and Judith only as their representative and saviour, it begins the history, at the logical and chronologically correct place, with Nebuchadnezzar's anger against those nations who would not support him in his war against the King of the Medes, and his decision to take vengeance on them. But since Aldhelm's theme is the virtue of Judith, he naturally begins with her and inserts the relevant historical material afterwards. That the Anglo-Saxon poet's approach was very similar to Aldhelm's is indisputable (see below), and it is therefore not improbable that he would choose the same point at which to begin his narrative.

Since a general case can be made out for the possibility that the poet only followed the last part of the Apocryphal Book, it is now worth while to discover whether any more precise deductions can be made from a comparison of the Old English poem with its source. Any references in the later chapters of the Apocryphal Book to personages who had previously been introduced in the early parts are omitted by the poet. When Judith returns to Bethulia with the head of Holofernes, she is saluted and blessed by Ozias, one of the two rulers of the city, who is first mentioned in chapter 6 of the Apocryphal version. But in the Old English version she is greeted only by the crowd. In the Apocrypha Judith then summons Achior, a renegade supporter of Holofernes, who had seceded to the Jewish side, in order to demonstrate to him that his faith in the Jewish God had been justified (Achior's history is given in chapters 6 and 7 of the Apocryphal *Judith*), but this incident again is not found in the Old English peom. The events preceding Judith's expedition are thus linked with those succeeding it in the Apocrypha, and it is difficult to avoid the inference that the Anglo-Saxon poet did not round off his story in this way because he had never introduced these characters (otherwise one must assume that, despite the guidance of his source, he casually abandoned them). But that he should have omitted Ozias in a lengthy poem is odd; that he should have omitted Achior in a poem which preserved, even roughly, the proportions of his original is impossible, for his story fills two chapters of the Apocryphal *Judith*; and if the Anglo-Saxon poet did give this story, then it is most

[12] Section lvii.

unlikely that he would have excluded this scene, which so properly concludes Achior's history with a triumphant vindication of his faith.

The poet's attitude to his theme supports the deduction drawn from the treatment of his source. The Apocryphal Book is pervaded by the nationalistic spirit of the Jews, their sense of being the chosen race. The author presents his story as a struggle between the Jewish nation and the enemies of Jehovah. But the Anglo-Saxon poet, almost certainly influenced by patristic tradition and by saint's lives in both English and Latin, has radically altered this attitude in his work. The issue is no longer between countries, or even armies, between Judith the representative of her people, and Holofernes, who deserves death because of his office as leader of the force seeking to destroy the Jews, but between two individuals, the chaste and virtuous Judith and the evil and dissolute Holofernes, who deserves to die because there is nothing but the brutish in him. The fate of a nation is at stake on the night of the banquet, but the Anglo-Saxon poet so limits the implications in his narrative that he creates the impression that it is Judith's chastity alone which lies in jeopardy.

The effect of this severe limitation of implication in the narrative method, this exclusion of characters and sense of nationalistic importance, is the achieving of increased intensity. The poet gains a sense of immediacy in the action and of dramatic compactness in the whole. The effect of the poem may be compared to that of the short epic lay, such as the *Finn Fragment* and the *Battle of Maldon*, in contrast to *Beowulf* and the so-called religious epics, which are characterized by their leisurely quality and sense of remoteness. It is this intensity and compactness which suggest very strongly that, apart from some lines relating a few details concerning Judith's identity and her motive for visiting the camp of Holofernes, none of the poem is missing. Short of the discovery of a manuscript containing the whole work, no speculation concerning the lost portion of the *Judith* can be quite final. But I hope to have proved that the prima facie case of those who suppose that over eight sectional divisions have been lost does not rest on secure foundation, and that the opposite view is, at least, equally tenable.

IX

THE CONSTRUCTION OF *IN A FRYHT AS Y CON FARE FREMEDE*

THIS poem, found amongst the Harley Lyrics,[1] is the earliest extant and also the best of the English pastourelles. Unfortunately its merits have been obscured by textual and verbal difficulties in the last twelve lines—the very point at which the punch in a good pastourelle normally comes—and it has therefore not received the praise that it deserves: many readers would probably agree with Arthur Moore's judgment that '*In a fryht* is clumsy beside the really good *pastourelles*, in both conception and execution' and that 'The end is obscure and inconclusive'.[2] But it requires only a small emendation in l. 40 and the elucidation of the reference in ll. 45–6 for the coherent and subtle construction of the poem to become plain. Indeed, though its slightly cumbersome stanza form, made heavy by alliteration, deprives it of the metrical gaiety and grace normally found in French pastourelles, in the spiritedness of its dialogue and witty manipulation of argument, it is the equal of its French counterparts. Furthermore the greater leisureliness of the stanza form allows for a thoughtful and imaginative expansion of argument in a way that the French metre does not.

Up to l. 32 the development of the poem is clear: the poet-narrator woos, bribes, and wheedles, whilst the maiden first dismisses him with the colloquial directness characteristic of the initial stage of a pastourelle ('Heo me bed go my gates lest hire gremede'), and then progresses to an admirably moral resolve:

Betere is were þunnė boute laste
    þen syde robes ant synke into synne.

Stemmler has compared the tone of these lines with an unusually moralistic macaronic (Latin/Anglo-Norman) pastourelle,[3] which concludes with the maiden's resounding affirmation of virginity:

[1] *The Harley Lyrics* ed. G. L. Brook (Manchester 1948) pp. 39–40.
[2] *The Secular Lyric in Middle English* (Lexington 1951) p. 60.
[3] Theo Stemmler, *Die englishchen Liebersgedichte des MS. Harley 2253* (Bonn 1962) pp. 152–4.

Tute ma vie sans lecherie vixi puella tenera;
Saynt Marie, ke ne sey hunie, me puram pura tollera!
Si cest ribaud par mal me asaut mallem adesse funera,
kar byen say ke dunc averay eterna Christi munera.[4]

As in all good pastourelles, however, placing is all-important, and a better comparison would therefore be with a Latin dialogue, in which the maiden near the beginning replies:

Virginitas placuit, volo parcere virginitati;
Res inmunda Venus, virginitas placuit.[5]

but who, by the end of the poem, has thrown this thought to the winds. In both poems the placing is sly, and the idea of virtue is introduced as a moral attitude to be slipped away from: the tone is ironic rather than moralistic.

Up to this point, and indeed up to l. 28, 'In a fryht' conforms to the familiar pattern of a pastourelle, but thereafter a new method of argument develops, one apparently peculiar to this poem. This method consists in each character drawing upon typical dramatic situations from allied lyric genres to give alarming prophecies of the future. The maiden sees herself in the role of the betrayed maiden who so often speaks a lyric complaint:

Þenne mihti hongren on heowe,
  in vch an hyrd ben hated ant forhaht,
ant ben ycayred from alle þat y kneowe,
  ant bede cleuyen þer y hade claht.

As a parallel to these lines Stemmler has quoted a Provençal pastourelle, in which the maiden says that she does not wish to exchange her virginity *per nom de putayna* [for the name of a whore];[6] and similar parallels can be found in allied Latin dialogues. In the one already quoted *Amica* protests:

Fama ream faceret si non rea criminis essem,
Et licet inmerita fama ream faceret.[7]

[4] Stemmler op. cit. 154; and, for the whole poem, F. J. E. Raby, *A History of Secular Latin Poetry in the Middle Ages* (Oxford 1957) II 336–7. 'All my life without lechery I have lived a delicate girl; Holy Mary, so that I may not be blamed, pure herself, will keep me pure! If this fellow with evil intent attack me, I would rather be at [my] funeral, For well I know that thereby I shall enjoy the eternal gifts of Christ.'

[5] M. Delbouille, 'Trois poésies latines inédites tirées du manuscrit Bibl. Aedilium Florentinae eccl. 197 de la Laurentienne', *Mélanges Paul Thomas*, (Bruges 1930) 182. 'I have chosen virginity, I want to save my virginity; An unclean thing is Venus, I have chosen virginity.'

[6] Stemmler op. cit. 151 and, for the whole poem, Carl Appel, *Provenzalische Chrestomathie* (Leipzig 1920) pp. 101–2.

[7] Op. cit. p. 182. 'Reputation would make me guilty, even if I were not guilty of the crime; And reputation would make me guilty deservedly.'

Whilst in another *Amica* explains her resistance as follows, 'Cum prohibet tactum vult ne meretrix videatur'.[8] The lines in 'In a fryht', however, are not quite the same as these straightforwardly expressed fears of the maiden that she will gain the reputation of a harlot, as the fears are far more precisely and dramatically conceived. For, with the reference to future heartbreak in the first line of the quotation and the emphasis upon social ostracization in the next two, they are strikingly reminiscent of the lyric genre of the complaint of the betrayed maiden, and the predicament which the maiden here foresees is most probably that of bearing a fatherless child: it is for this that she will become an outcast from all whom she knows, in every family hated and scornfully rejected.[9] A poem in the *Carmina Burana*, 'Huc usque, me miseram', describes with extraordinary vividness a situation of this kind:[10] the girl has to sit alone at home, though bitterly reproached by her parents; when she goes out, people look at her as though she were a monster, nudging each other, and pointing their fingers at her. Lyrics that allude to this fate in a more melancholy and less realistic way span mediæval English literature from what is probably an early fragment, 'Byrd on brere, y telle yt to none othur, y ne dar'[11] to the lyrics set to music in Ritson's Manuscript:

A wanton chyld
Spake wordes myld
To me alone,
And me begylyd,
Goten with child
And now ys gone.
. . .
Now may I wynd
Withoute a frynd
With hert onfayn;
In ferre cuntre
Men wene I be
A mayde agayn.[12]

The would-be lover caps this argument with an equally horrifying

[8] Raby, op. cit. p. 244. 'By forbidding to be touched, she wishes not to appear a harlot.'

[9] For the translation of *forhaht* see *Early Middle English Verse and Prose* ed. J. A. W. Bennett and G. V. Smithers (Oxford 1968) pp. 324–5.

[10] *Carmina Burana* ed. Alfons Hilka and Otto Schumann I 2 (Heidelberg 1941) p. 209.

[11] *The Early English Carols* ed. R. L. Greene (Oxford 1935) p. 448.

[12] John Stevens, *Music and Poetry in the Early Tudor Court* (London 1961) pp. 346–7; cf. also 348–9.

picture of the future, one drawn from another lyric genre, that of the *chansons de mal mariées*, in which a married woman complains of her life with an aged and jealous husband and longs for her young lover from whom she is now cut off or whom it is dangerous to see. In England there is a scrap of such a verse in Anglo-Norman preserved in MS. Rawl. D. 913: 'Amy tenetz vous ioyous / si moura lui gelous',[13] and in the *Red Book of Ossory* there is a more appropriate parallel:

Alas hou shold Y singe? Yloren is my playnge.
Hou shold Y with that olde man
To leuen, and let my leman,
  Swettist of all thinge[14]

The ingenuity of this reply has been obscured by a textual corruption in l. 40, as a result of which scholars and critics have either supposed these lines to be spoken by the maiden or else have produced tortured explanations of ll. 39–40 that necessarily diminish the force of the whole.[15] It would, however, be a small and reasonably conservative emendation if 'þah he me slowe ne myhti him asluppe' were changed to: 'þah he *þ*e slowe ne myht*u* him asluppe'. Whenever lyrics survive in more than one manuscript, there are substantial textual variations between them, and one of the most recurrent mistakes is the misapportioning of speeches in dialogue poems. This of course is not the kind of mistake that arises from manuscript copying but from copying from memory, but again the texts of lyrics indicate that this was very common indeed in the Middle Ages.

At this point in 'In a fryht as y con fare fremede', the narrator is shown to become emboldened by his own argument so that he gives an open and colloquially expressed invitation:

þe beste red þat y con to vs boþe
  þat þou me take ant y þe toward huppe.

[13] Peter Dronke, 'The Rawlinson Lyrics', N & Q NS viii (1961), 245; cf. *Altfranzösische Romanzen und Pastourellen* ed. Karl Bartsch (Leipzig 1870) p. 37.

[14] Greene op. cit. xci.

[15] Brook and Smithers (by implication) assume ll. 37–44 to be spoken by the woman; K. Böddeker, *Altenglische Dichtungen des MS. Harley 2253* (Berlin 1878), pp. 158–60, gives the stanza to the man, putting a colon after *wroþe*, and explaining of l. 40, 'Der Mann versetzt sich in Gedanken an die Stelle des Mädchens'; so also does Stemmler op. cit. 150, translating ll. 37–40 by 'Es ist besser, einen geziemend gekleideten Mann (wie ich es bin) zu umarmen als einen Kerl, mit dem man so schlecht verheiratet ist. (Ich rate dir dieses), obwohl er mich erschlüge, wenn ich ihm nicht entwischte'. Peter Dronke (*MÆ* xxxii 150) has tried to reconcile symmetry with sense by dividing the stanza, allotting the first half to the woman, the second to the man.

And at this, as in so many pastourelles, the maiden suddenly yields. Her capitulation, however, is at first allusively expressed, and the point of the allusion has nowadays not been understood. She says:

Mid shupping ne mey hit me ashunche;
  nes y never wycche ne wyle.

This may be translated: 'I cannot escape by shape-shifting:[16] I am not a witch or sorceress'. This conceit is derived from the so-called *chanson des transformations* which Jeanroy regarded as a popular forerunner of the pastourelle:[17] in some versions this consists of a verbal game, in which the maiden posits various shapes that she will assume in order to elude her suitor, and the suitor outwits her by inventing shapes for himself that will capture hers (for instance, if she becomes a star, he will become a cloud). In other versions, such as the unique surviving example in English, the ballad of 'The Twa Magicians', the metamorphosis actually takes place:

Then she became a turtle dow,
  To fly up in the air,
And he became another dow,
  And they flew pair by pair.

She turnd hersell into an eel,
  To swim into yon burn,
And he became a speckled trout,
  To gie the eel a turn.[18]

Child describes this as 'a base-born cousin of a pretty ballad known all over southern Europe'. The versions containing a magical transformation seem to be close to folklore, those, which are verbal games, are sophisticated variants. The author of 'In a fryht' may have known either or both kinds. The allusion to the *chanson des transformations* is also interesting in that it casts light upon the imaginative development of the preceding argument, in which evasion and capture are expressed, not by postulating metamorphoses, but by the citing of typical social situations portrayed in other lyric genres.

In 'In a fryht' this capitulation, so ingeniously expressed, leads straight into the strikingly frank admission: 'ych am a maide, þat me of þunche'. The *Virginitas placuit* argument is usually retracted by

[16] For the translation see Bennett and Smithers op. cit. p. 325.

[17] Alfred Jeanroy, *Les origines de la poésie lyrique en France* (Paris 1965) pp. 14–15; cf. also W. P. Jones, *The Pastourelle* (Cambridge Mass. 1931) pp. 114–15.

[18] F. J. Child, *English and Scottish Ballads* (London 1904) p. 78.

actions rather then words, but the unexpected verbal explicitness is a dramatically effective departure from convention. The final line, 'luef me were gome bute gyle', which misled Stemmler into thinking that the maiden finally refused the narrator,[19] is also unusual in carrying a hint of wistfulness, since the maiden is so obviously about to make do with something less desirable. It may, however, be that 'gome boute gyle' was an alliterative collocation that did not then bear the weight of meaning that we now find in it.

This interpretation shows that the poem is carefully constructed throughout and does not trail away after l. 37. It is also interesting in that it reveals a poet who was at home in the traditional French genres, which are so sparsely represented in mediæval English literature. It may also suggest a knowledge of Latin dialogues between *Amicus* and *Amica*, for in its wit it is reminiscent of the French and in its thoughtfulness and solidity it recalls the Latin. It is anyway clear that the poet thoroughly understood the form and was thus able to invent freely and ingeniously within it.

[19] Op. cit. p. 150.

X

THE TEARING OF THE PARDON

Piers Plowman is one of the most difficult poems ever written: it is a work that constantly challenges but evades interpretation; and in it there is no scene that is more important or more elusive than that in which Piers tears the Pardon. Modern critics have been unanimous on one point only, that the scene has a dramatic resonance that extends far beyond the limits of passus vii and therefore that it is central to the whole meaning of the poem; on all other points their disagreement with one another ranges from the partial to the complete.

The course of the action, which begins in passus v, is on the surface deceptively simple. After the repentance of society expressed in the confessions of the Seven Deadly Sins, Piers Plowman sets himself to organize a just, ordered and ideal society, in which each member will conscientiously carry out the duties appropriate to his rank or profession. Thereupon God sends a 'pardon' to Piers; but, when the contents of the 'pardon' are revealed, it turns out to be Verse 41 of the Athanasian Creed, 'Et qui bona egerunt ibunt in vitam eternam; Qui vero mala, in ignem eternam'. A priest then tells Piers that this is not a pardon and Piers in 'pure tene' tears up the document. This summary, however, deceives, for it conceals both the problems and the dramatic intensity of the sequence. The difficulties are roughly as follows: how the words in the document are to be reconciled with the description of it as a pardon; whether the priest speaks as a representative of Christianity or as a corrupt priest only too ready to sneer at good works; what Piers himself at this stage of the poem symbolizes; and whether his tearing of the document is a trivial action belonging chiefly to the literal level of the story or whether it is an action of serious allegorical meaning.

The diversity of modern opinion on all these issues may be illustrated by a brief summary of three substantial analyses of the scene. Professor Coghill, who, in his British Academy lecture of 1945,[1] was the first scholar to attach adequate weight to the scene,

[1] 'The Pardon of Piers Plowman', *Proceedings of the British Academy* xxx (1944) 303–357.

supposed the pardon to be the pardon bought on Calvary, the text from the Creed to be 'a catch-phrase about Salvation', the priest to be 'the villain of the piece' and, by implication, the tearing of the pardon to be insignificant. The apparently disconcerting emphasis upon 'qui bona egerunt' he explains in terms of the allegorical reference of Piers: Piers in this part of the poem signifies 'Do-Well, or in Latin *qui bona egerunt*; it is his very name, and the pardon is truly his', and his followers, who have made confession and are seeking to carry out his commands, justly share in it.

Professor Lawlor's more recent interpretation of the scene is almost the exact reverse of this.[2] The pardon he takes to be a sign of admonition rather than forgiveness; the priest is a figure of the same order as Clergy or Scripture in the later passus, 'what they say is true, but fails to meet their interlocutor's real need'; whilst Piers himself is the best man that the corrupt society of this world can produce, and yet even he fails to meet the conditions of the pardon. Piers therefore throws himself on the mercy of God, finding only despair in the justice of the pardon: his recognition of the need for mercy is dramatically symbolized by his tearing of the pardon. What Professor Coghill understands as a scene of Redemption, Professor Lawlor takes to be a scene of judgement and condemnation.

Midway between these poles is Professor Frank's interpretation.[3] Like Professor Coghill he believes the pardon to be a true pardon, and reconciles this with its character of judgment by maintaining that the society depicted by Langland has by and large done good works and therefore can be aptly rewarded with this text: there is no question in this instance of God's justice being at odds with His mercy. Like Professor Lawlor, however, he has laid stress upon the tearing of the pardon. According to his view, in the scene between Piers and the priest, Langland's intention is to attack the system of indulgences, and the tearing of the pardon therefore symbolizes the rejection of papal pardons: 'the pardon contains a message which is by implication an attack on pardons', and Piers trusts to the message whilst rejecting the form.

It is in accord with the peculiar power of the poem that the two theories that in content are most irreconcilable seem truer to the text than the moderate one, which does not do justice to the stature of the scene. The dubiousness of indulgences was undoubtedly in Langland's mind as he wrote, and the Dreamer explicitly draws this

[2] '*Piers Plowman*: The Pardon Reconsidered', *MLR* xlv (1950) 449–458.

[3] 'The Pardon Scene in *Piers Plowman*', *Speculum* xxvi (1951) 317–331.

moral. But excessive trust in pardons was a sermon commonplace of the time, and it is a meaning too banal to warrant the dramatic tension that Langland has contrived. It is surely a reflection on the limited understanding of the Dreamer that he can only extract so slight a significance from the majestic enigma of his vision. Professor Frank's interpretation has the further disadvantage that it finds two solutions to one mystery. The paradoxical relationship between the pardon and its contents leads to the aesthetically satisfying action of the tearing, and a disjunctive explanation is therefore insufficient.

The solutions proposed by Professor Coghill and Professor Lawlor do not divide the mystery into two but do not fully account for all its elements. Professor Coghill's explanation of why, contrary to immediate appearances, the pardon is a pardon (because it is sent to Piers, the personification of *qui bona egerunt*) is subtle and moving, but it leaves the tearing of the pardon unexplained. By contrast, Professor Lawlor's explanation of the tearing of the pardon satisfyingly accounts for the dramatic power of this episode, but leaves the earlier element in the puzzle unresolved, namely why a judgement—and one that is shown to be entirely damnatory—should have been called a pardon. This cannot be ignored as though it were a random piece of mystification.

At the heart of many interpretations of the Pardon scene there lies a misstatement of the problem. The question asked is, 'Was it a valid pardon?' and to so tendentious a question there can only be one answer, yes, for the pardon that the priest demands to read is said to have been sent by Truth, who is God, and it contains a text drawn from one of the authoritative creeds of the Church. That the text itself is the word of God is incontestable: not only does it come from the Athanasian creed, but the creed itself at this point is closely echoing the words of Christ in *Matthew* xxv. What Christ spoke can indeed be presented as a message from God. The correct form of the question, however, is, 'Can this text be described as a pardon?' for, if it cannot, the true conclusion is, not that Truth has lied, but that the poet for his own purposes has misled us: it is the poet in his own voice, not God as a character in the poem, who describes the document as a pardon: it is the Dreamer and Piers and his followers who believe the document to be a pardon and, if it is not, we can say that Langland in writing the first lines of passus vii ('Treuthe herde telle herof ... And purchaced hym a pardoun') gave himself the licence to deceive, deliberately allowing us to hear in them the omniscient narrative voice of the poet, when in fact he is only reporting a misconception of his created characters. But it would be an elaborate deception and one that would require a substantial justification.

That Langland intended a shock and a mystery, of which an elaborate deception would form an essential part, is suggested by the very careful construction of the passus. There is first of all the very marked delay between the mention of the pardon in the third line of the passus and the revelation of its content more than one hundred lines later. The intervening space is taken up by the narrator's homiletic exposition of the glosses upon the text of the pardon, which (in accordance with medieval scribal custom) are imagined to be written in the margins of the document.[4] These glosses (like, for instance, the glosses on decretals) show how a general statement relates to precise circumstances, in this instance how the pardon applies to various types of society. The narrative order here is markedly odd, for the exposition of the pardon is given before the text of the pardon itself. The material itself, however, is reassuringly familiar, for by implication it is at least semi-satirical, and Langland uses the fiction of the glosses to revert to his favourite themes of the avarice of lawyers and merchants or the fraudulence of the lazy poor.

As so often in the poem Langland in this passage only fitfully remembers the literal level of his allegory,[5] and indeed the idea of the glosses provides only a narrow base for the discursive warning to the followers of Lady Meed on how they must amend their lives before they may profit from the pardon. It is therefore easy to read the passage as a typical and rather repetitious disquisition on the kind of subject that so often diverted Langland from the steady development of his theme. It is, however, more likely that Langland was here manipulating his own digressive tendencies, for the effect of the digression is to build up suspense, a suspense that is fulfilled in the dramatic emphasis upon the words of the pardon. Piers for the first time opens the document, so that the priest may read it, and the

[4] 'Marchauntz in the margyne hadden many ȝeres' (line 18), i.e. it was written in the margin that merchants were given many years of remission of purgatory.

[5] It has recently been stressed by Professor Przemyslaw Mroczkowski ('Piers and his Pardon. A Dynamic Analysis', *Studies in Language and Literature in honour of Margaret Schlauch* (Warsaw, 1966) pp. 273–291) that this disquisition on the contents of the pardon does not appear in the pardon itself when it is unfolded ('Al in two lynes it lay and nouȝt a leef more'), and from this he infers that it is Piers's own improvisation. That Piers, rather than the narrator, has been the speaker is an interesting but (despite line 16, 'this pardoun Piers sheweth') unlikely suggestion. It could of course be insisted that although the text of the pardon consisted of two lines only and not a word more, the margins of the document were crammed with commentary: this, however, would diminish the visual effect of the sudden sight of the pardon, and Langland is constantly willing to shift the literal level of the narrative in order to attain effects more important than that of simple consistency.

Dreamer as it were peers over his shoulder ('And I bihynde hem bothe bihelde al the bulle'). This is a most extraordinary treatment of the Dreamer: normally he is either a detached observer of the vision or he is present in the dream in lifelike contact with the other characters. Here, however, the reader sees him in physical relationship with the other characters but they are unaware of this, as though he were a ghost in his own dream. The effect is to bring the words of the pardon into startling focus: the poet manifestly intends us to be surprised.

We are not only surprised but also bewildered, and so too is the Dreamer at the end of the scene. He lies awake at night pondering what kind of a pardon it was and debating within himself the value of dreams. This passage on dream theory may seem unremarkable, for Chaucer, who makes it an almost invariable element of his dream-visions, has accustomed us to the acceptance of this as a traditional element. But this is the only point in the poem in which Langland wonders about the nature of dreams, and the placing of the passage is therefore very important. Moreover, it is significant that out of a fund of traditional dream material he draws out the two great enigmatic dreams of the Old Testament, the dreams of Joseph and Nebuchadnezzar,[6] dreams that have to be expounded with divine inspiration before they are understood. Langland never overtly expounds the dream of the pardon, but the many critics who assume that the exposition lies hidden in the tenor of the rest of the poem have surely rightly unfolded Langland's method of working.

The kind of dream that Langland uses in passus vii is that which Macrobius described as follows: 'By an enigmatic dream we mean one that conceals with strange shapes and veils with ambiguity the true meaning of the information being offered, and requires an interpretation for its understanding.'[7] There are two parts to our attempt to unravel this enigmatic dream, the first to define exactly the nature of the problem, the second then to penetrate beneath the strange shapes to the inner meaning. The surest way of approaching the first part is to try to reconstruct how a medieval audience would have understood it. It is certain that they would have been puzzled by the scene in a way not intended: omission of the tearing of the pardon in the C-text strongly suggests that this action caused bewilderment,

[6] As Skeat points out, Langland seems to have confused Nebuchadnezzar's dream with Belshazzar's vision of the writing on the wall, also expounded by Daniel. Which of these two was uppermost in Langland's mind as he wrote makes no difference to our argument.

[7] Macrobius, *Commentary on the Dream of Scipio*, trans. W. H. Stahl (New York, 1952) p. 90.

for over and over again one finds that the rugged mysteries of the B-text have been smoothed out in the C-text. But, though they were puzzled, this does not mean that their confusion was identical with ours, and a consideration of the literary and semi-theological background to the scene suggests that whilst they were probably no abler (indeed, probably less able) than us in discovering a solution, they were probably able to formulate the problem more clearly.

The best point at which to begin this reconstruction of a medieval audience's reactions to the scene is at the long pause, already noticed, between the announcement of the pardon and the revelation of its content. For this pause, which is filled with material of only moderate interest, offers an opportunity to the reader to pursue his own thoughts and to anticipate, at least semi-consciously from the progress of the poem and his knowledge of traditional allegorical procedures, what the pardon will be in both form and significance.

The term 'pardon' nowadays is largely familiar as an abstract noun synonymous with forgiveness or, if used to mean an act of forgiveness, the nature of the act remains unclear. In the Middle Ages, however, it had a precise and generally known sense of a document conferring a royal pardon.[8] The latter would be for some offence committed, and the recipient would keep it in his possession to guarantee his future immunity from officers of the law in regard to his crime. Walter Hilton in the *Scale of Perfection* begins an allegorical example as follows:

> For if a man had forfeited his life against a king of this earth, it were not enough to him as for a full security for to have only forgiveness of the king, but if he have a charter the which may be his token and his warrant against all other men.[9]

In the *Scale* this is used to show the need for confession and absolution as opposed to private contrition, an application that is unusual and lacking in the pointed aptness normally characteristic of medieval allegorization. But the narrative manner suggests that this is one of the many instances in which Hilton draws upon what is familiar in everyday life in order to illustrate a devotional point, and it therefore confirms, what one would anyway expect, that a pardon was the kind of legal document that people knew of and understood in the Middle Ages.

[8] It could of course also mean a papal pardon, but, as we shall see, the allegory of God sending a pardon would have suggested the analogy of a royal pardon.

[9] *The Scale of Perfection*, ed. E. Underhill (London, 1948) p. 246.

Whilst on the one hand a pardon might be known from common experience, on the other hand it might be known as a literary image, one of the many signifying the redemption. To prove this it is necessary to make a brief excursus on the development of the theme. The invariable element is that of a legal document written in Christ's blood, a document sometimes called a charter, sometimes a pardon. As we shall see, there was confusion between the two, for though to a lawyer they would seem completely distinct, from the literary point of view their field of reference was identical, and their significance the same: a charter would confer heaven on man, a pardon would give him release from hell.

The earliest extant allusion to this image is in the allegory of the lover-knight in the *Ancrene Wisse*, in which the Christ-knight is said to bring his beloved letters patent (charters were written in this form) 'and wrat wið his ahne blod saluz to his leofmon'.[10] In this allegory the letters patent are the gospels (in contrast to the Old Testament in the form of letters close): this probably represents a primitive stage in the literary development of the image, as later the charter itself was invented as a literary form. Of this, however, there is no evidence until the beginning of the fourteenth century, when in his punning lyric 'Þou wommon boute uere',[11] William Herebert describes how Love has written the charter of the Redemption, using as an inkhorn the wound in Christ's side. A similar reference occurs in Chaucer's 'ABC':

> And with his precious blood he wrote the bille
> Upon the crois, as general acquitaunce,
> To every penitent in ful creaunce.[12]

Chaucer's use of this conceit is noteworthy as it does not occur in his French source.

The Charter to which William Herebert and Chaucer refer is probably that described in the poem known as 'The Charter of Christ'.[13] There is no extant text of this before 1350, but since manuscripts only provide a *terminus post quem*, the work itself may well date from the first quarter of the fourteenth century. According

[10] *Ancrene Wisse*, ed. G. Shepherd (London, 1959) p. 21.

[11] *Religious Lyrics of the Fourteenth Century*, ed. Carleton Brown (Oxford, 1957) pp. 18–20.

[12] *Works*, ed. F. N. Robinson (London, 1957) p. 618, lines 59–61.

[13] For the text and an account of the development of the charter image see M. C. Spalding, *The Middle English Charters of Christ* (Bryn Mawr College Monographs, 1914).

to the allegory in this poem the charter was made by Christ on the Cross and it endowed man with the kingdom of heaven. Every detail of the appearance of the document and materials used was interpreted allegorically: the parchment was Christ's skin, the pen the lance or nails, the letters His many wounds, and the seal His wounded heart. The actual conferment of heaven begins with a familiar charter opening and proceeds in legal language, including a translation of the crucial phrase, *habendum et tenendum*:

> *Sciant presentes et futuri & cetera.*
> wytt yhe þat bene & sall be-tyde,
> I Ihesu crist with blody syde,
> Þat was born in bethleem
> And offerd in-to Ierusalem,
> Þe kyng[es] son of heven oboufe,
> With my fader will and lufe,
> Made a sesyng when I was born
> To þe mankynd þat was forlorn.
> With my chartre here present,
> I mak now confirmament
> Þat I have graunted & given
> To þe mankynd with me to lyfen
> In my rewme of heven blys
> To have & hald withouten mys,
> In a condicioune if þou kynde
> And my luf-dedes haue in mynde,
> ffre to haue & fre to hald
> With all þe purtenaunce to wald
> Myne erytage þat es so fre.[14]

This poem soon became popular, and it survives in a large number of manuscripts, though many belong to the fifteenth century. Amongst the fourteenth-century manuscripts to include it is the Vernon Manuscript.

Another current version of the allegory was that embodied in *The Pore Caitiff*, a didactic and devotional treatise written in the last quarter of the fourteenth century, and very popular, as the number of surviving manuscripts indicates. In this version the idea of the charter becomes blended with that of a pardon, for the document is said to be 'þe chartre of his [man's] eritage & þe bulle of his euerlastinge pardoun':[15] some manuscripts, taking their rubric from this sentence, describe what follows as 'a notable chartour of pardon'. This chapter often circulated separately in manuscripts and when it was printed as

[14] Spalding, pp. 28–30. 'Let both present and future men know ...'
[15] Spalding, pp. 100–102.

an independent work in the sixteenth century it was given the title *A General Free Pardon or Charter of Hevyn Blys*. The substance of this passage is the allegorical conceits and it does not contain the formal conferment of heaven. The author seems to have been confused and to have had in mind three kinds of documents, charters, pardons and wills, for there are allusions to all three. It is, however, unlikely that the author would have introduced the notion of a pardon if he had not had a source in which the conceits were associated with this form of document instead of a charter that was a grant of land. The blending or confusion may have been facilitated by a verbal connection in that a pardon was frequently referred to as a charter of pardon, *carta perdonationis*.

Both 'The Charter of Christ' and *The Pore Caitiff* may be called popular literature, popular in the sense that they were intended for a less than learned audience, and popular in the sense that the ideas that they contain may well have been floating commonplaces. There is, however, one very important fourteenth-century description of a pardon that would be known only to the educated. It occurs in the *Pèlerinage de l'âme*, a long French allegorical poem, written by Guillaume de Guilleville between 1340–50. This poem is the middle one of a trio, the others being the *Pèlerinage de la vie humaine* and the *Pèlerinage de Jesus-Crist*. These poems circulated in English manuscripts from the last quarter of the fourteenth century: Chaucer knew the first (and therefore probably the others), for his 'ABC' is a translation from it. More important is the fact that Langland probably knew Guillaume's trilogy, for it contains so many possible sources for individual allegories in *Piers Plowman*, and even for the outline structure of the wandering pilgrim, that it would be a strong coincidence if Langland had gathered the allegories that he has in common with Guillaume from other scattered sources. This work therefore will not only have guided the response of some of the most educated of Langland's audience, but also gives a precise significance to the word 'pardon', which was in all probability known to the poet himself.

In the *Pèlerinage de l'âme* the soul of the pilgrim after death is transported to heaven where it is led to the particular or individual (as opposed to the general) judgment (that an individual judgment awaited every soul was an accepted belief). A debate ensues between the Four Daughters of God, Justice, Righteousness, Mercy and Peace, concerning its fate. Satan and Conscience accuse it whilst the wretched soul asks for mercy. Pity urges that no pilgrim has ever kept to the right road and therefore none can be saved except through

Christ and the Blessed Virgin, but Justice insists that Christ did not die for those who persist in their sins but only for those who have amended their lives. At this point St. Benedict proposes the weighing of the soul, the good deeds to be put in one scale, the evil in the other. Though apparently proposed impartially, this is a solution that favours the cause of Justice, for the scale with the good deeds flies up, whilst the other sinks down heavily laden. Thereupon Mercy turns to Christ and the Blessed Virgin for help, and returns with a letter. In the later prose translation of the *Pèlrinage* and in the translation of this particular part ascribed to Hoccleve, this letter is called a 'chartre of pardon'. But, though Guillaume does not himself describe the letter in this way, he manifestly intends a legal document, for he gives it the formal opening characteristic of letters patent:

> Je Jhesus, haut seigneur du ciel,
> A nostre lieutenant Michiel
> Et a tous les coassistens
> Qui la sont pour nos jugemens
> Salut.[16]

Furthermore, from its contents the document is plainly a conditional pardon: all those who make confession and ask for mercy shall escape the due penalty of hell:

> D'especial grace accorde
> Que d'enfer soient relaschies
> Ceux qui en la fin leur pechies
> Aront dit en confession.[17]

With this letter goes a casket filled to overflowing from the Treasury of Merit,[18] and thus a suitable symbolic object to be placed in the scales, and by this means the scale of the pilgrim's good deeds weighs heavy, whilst that of evil deeds flies up as though it contained scarcely any weight. Though the decision to combine the two allegories of the charter of pardon and the Psychostasis has here necessitated the

[16] Ed. J. J. Stürzinger (Roxburghe Club, 1895) p. 83. 'I, Jesus, supreme lord of the heavens, to our lieutenant Michael and to all the assessors present for our judgment: greetings.'

[17] Stürzinger, p. 84. 'By special grace I grant that those, who at the end have made confession of their sins, shall be freed from hell.'

[18] The casket contains 'a bountiful sufficiency from the treasury of my Passion of which there remains so great abundance, from the merits of my Mother, to whom none may be compared, from the merits of all my saints of which great are the stores in heaven'. (Stürzinger, p. 85). This allusion to the Treasury of Merit suggests that Guillaume in composing his literary imitation of a royal charter of pardon was reminded also of papal pardons.

intermediary symbol of the Casket of Merit, the poetic attention given to the charter far exceeds that given to the casket, the latter becoming, a little awkwardly, a subordinate symbol of the Redemption.

The evidence assembled in this digression on the charter-pardon image shows that by the end of the fourteenth century the intended audience of *Piers Plowman* would certainly be familiar with the idea of a legal document symbolizing and conferring the benefits of the Redemption, and probably knew that this document could be either a pardon or a charter. Their expectation that the contents of Piers's pardon, when revealed, would be a remittal from the pains of hell expressed in legal formulae and written in the blood of Christ, would be sharpened by the fact that this kind of allegorical episode would be consonant with the allegorical methods already used in the poem. In the early passus of *Piers Plowman* Langland made use of precisely and minutely worked allegories, such as the road of the Ten Commandments at the end of passus v. More particularly he had shown himself interested in the literary potentialities of legal formulae. Of this kind is the last will and testament made by Piers at the beginning of passus vi, a legal form more often used for moral, satirical and devotional purposes,[19] but here serving rather as a model disposition for a virtuous Christian; and, more strikingly, the allegorical charter of Favel in passus ii: indeed a medieval reader with a literary turn of mind might well have thought that the poet's intention was to set against the charter of the seven deadly sins the charter of the Redemption.

Before we consider the audience's probable understanding of the unexpected contents of the 'pardon', it is necessary to assess the spiritual state of the pilgrims up to this point. The pardon episode in the *Pêlerinage de l'âme* is again helpful here, because it too is set in a narrative context, and it is specifically said to be for pilgrims (*les pelerins*), pilgrims who have come to judgment and do not merit heaven through their own good deeds. In the later translation of their charter of pardon ascribed to Hoccleve, the situation of the sinful pilgrims is described even more emphatically than in Guillaume's French original:

> Ther be pilgrymes (as thei certifie)
>   That to meward hire weies had [i]take,

[19] On this see E. C. Perrow, 'The Last Will and Testament as a Form of Literature', *Transactions of the Wisconsin Academy of Sciences, Arts and Letters* xvii (1913).

Wich have mysgon, and erred folily
Be steryng of the foule bestis blake,
That some of hem hire iourney had forsake,
And efte hire iourney have a-geyn begunne,
But sudei[n]gly hath failed him the sonne.

Some have be lettid be foule temptacioun
And steryng of hire fleschly wrechidnesse;
So, be disease and tribulacioun
Thei have [i]falle in-to huge hevynesse;
And some also to this worldes besynesse
So greuously hire hertes ouersette,
So þat thei have of hire iourney be lette.[20]

This description of the pilgrims who so desperately need the bestowal of mercy leads one to ask the question of whether Langland's pilgrims are in any better spiritual state: in other words, do they need a charter of pardon if they are to be saved or would their scale of good deeds weigh heavily enough without the merits of Christ?

The story of Langland's pilgrims begins in passus v with the strangely self-contradictory allegory of the seven deadly sins who go to confession and express contrition, a contrition that is belied by the tone of their confessions and in particular by the revelatory continuous present tense in which most of the confession is couched. There would seem to be two ideas in this passus that clash with one another. One is that of a society in which all ranks and orders are riddled with the seven deadly sins, and the form of confessions is little more than a convenient mode for the satirist: one should no more ask how the personification of a sin can repent than one should ask why Chaucer's Pardoner so revealed his wickedness to his travelling companions. The other idea is that of the field full of folk who, though guilty of all the seven deadly sins, are moved by the sermon of Reason to go to confession and then moved by Repentance's preaching of the Redemption to amend their lives, that is, according to the first allegory to set out on the pilgrimage to Truth, and, according to the allegory that supplants it, to serve Piers well in his half-acre.[21] The problem is the relation of the two ideas, and whether the impression of continousness that is given by the confessions of the sins casts an ominous shadow over the pilgrims' resolve of amendment. The solution to the problem is revealed in passus vi.

[20] EETS ES 72, p. xxix.

[21] On Langland's continuous substitution of one allegory for another, see the illuminating article of John Burrow, 'The Action of Langland's Second Vision', *EC* xv (1965) 247–268.

A commentary upon the Athanasian Creed provides guidance in the interpretation of this passus: it defines *qui bona egerunt* as those who have persevered in virtue.[22] The function of perseverance is clearly described by St. Thomas, 'Sustinere autem difficultatem quae provenit ex diuturnitate boni operis, dat laudem perseverantiae'.[23] In this virtue is crystalized what is known from common experience, that the difficulty lies, not in the performance of isolated acts of virtue, but in the continuous practice of virtue day in day out without backsliding. In passus vi of *Piers Plowman* Langland shows dramatically and with psychological probability that it is this virtue of perseverance that the pilgrims lack. The first defection occurs at the end of passus v, where some pilgrims turn back instantly after the arduous journey to Truth has been described and its goal in the house guarded by the seven virtues:

'Now, bi Cryst,' quod a cutpurs, 'I have no kynne there!'
'Ne I', quod an apewarde, 'be auȝte that I knowe!'
'Wite god,' quod a wafrestre, 'wist I this for soth,
Shulde I neuere ferthere a fote for no freres prechynge.'

. . . .

'By seynt Poule,' quod a pardonere, 'perauenture I be nouȝte knowe there,
I wil go fecche my box with my breuettes and a bulle with bisshopes lettres!'
'By Cryst,' quod a comune womman, 'thi companye wil I folwe,
Thow shalt sey I am thi sustre.' I ne wot where thei bicome.

This is the rabble, lay and religious, satirically dismissed: thieves, low entertainers, prostitutes and pardoners are allowed to show their contempt for the journey in the colloquialism of their speech. But even though this is the rabble, the company of a thousand pilgrims seems the less secure for their departure.

The main body of the pilgrims, however, do not relapse so instantly but submit themselves to Piers's advice and agree to work in his half-acre, and Piers is shown to be attempting to build a just and well-ordered society, one which in the reader's eye will counter-balance the corrupt society depicted in the previous passus:

Now is Perkyn and his pilgrymes to the plowe faren;
To erie this halue-acre holpyn hym manye.
Dikeres and delueres digged vp the balkes;
Therewith was Perkyn apayed and preysed hem faste.

[22] A. E. Burn, *The Athanasian Creed and its Early Commentaries*, Texts and Studies iv (1896) p. 10.

[23] *Summa Theologica*, II, ii, qu. 137, art. 2: 'The difficulty of persisting in a good work for a long time gives merit to perseverance.'

Other werkeman there were that wrouȝten ful ȝerne,
Eche man in his manere made hymself to done,
And some to plese Perkyn piked vp the wedes.

(B vi 107–113)

However this ideal order lasts for only three lines of the poem, for, when Piers goes amongst his labourers to see how each is working, he finds those who helped 'erie his half-acre with "how! trollilolli!"' and *wastours* who are feigning illness. From here on the order of the just society, symbolized by conscientious labouring on Piers's farm, disintegrates. The wasters are once more made to work through the compulsion of hunger, but with the harvest they take again to idling, and with the harvest too the people do as 'Glotoun tauȝte'. Gluttony's contrition and Reason's advice to Waster (v, 24–25) have come to nothing.

In the first part of passus vi Langland temporarily broke the bounds of his allegory to show ladies sewing altar-cloths and knights protecting the poor; but in the later part of the passus he returns to sustained alleogry so that all sins and all society are represented by the greedy and idle workmen. In the field of reference of the allegory there is perhaps a hint of the parable of the labourers in the vineyard,[24] but here there is no one who 'stod þe long day stable'. Furthermore, in accordance with medieval thought, and in particular with Langland's thought as revealed in passus xiv, to indicate the sinfulness of the whole of society through the sinfulness of the poor is especially pointed, for if the poor are not virtuous there is no hope for the rich. In passus xiv it is the poor man with the pack of good deeds on his back who strides into heaven ahead of the rich who are too heavily cumbered by their possessions to move at his speed. And in this passus too Langland movingly expresses the traditional medieval view that the poor through their endurance of hardship have purgatory here on earth and could therefore deserve their heaven immediately. In medieval descriptions of the Last Judgement the poor are often given a special place: sometimes they are amongst the accusers of the rich, sometimes they sit by Christ Himself as assessors, thus escaping the Judgment altogether. Langland has therefore chosen a most telling allegory, for he has symbolized the failure of the whole of society by the failure of the one part whom we might have expected to endure in virtue.

The seriousness of the labourers' relapse into sin is driven home by

[24] The parable is alluded to in Piers's first speech, v 559, 'He ne withhalt non hewe his hyre that he ne hath it at euen'.

the ominous note on which passus vi ends:

Ac I warne ȝow, werkemen, wynneth while ȝe mowe,
For Hunger hiderward hasteth hym faste,
He shal awake with water wastoures to chaste.
Ar fyue ȝere be fulfilled suche famyn shal aryse,
Thorwgh flodes and thourgh foule wederes frutes shul faille,
And so sayde Saturne and sent ȝow to warne:
Whan ȝe se the sonne amys and two monkes hedes,
And a mayde haue the maistrie and multiplie bi eight,
Thanne shal Deth withdrawe and Derthe be iustice,
And Dawe the dyker deye for hunger,
But if god of his goodnesse graunt vs a trewe.

Langland here is not the bewildered dreamer, but the prophet-poet exhorting his characters to repent whilst there is yet time. The last five lines—added in the B-text—though inferior poetically are most important to the sense, for they draw on the strange contemporary prophecies of the coming of the Anti-Christ, whose arrival would herald the end of the world and the Day of Judgment.[25] It is therefore a sinister warning to the people in Piers's half-acre, whose intention of amendment had lasted so short a time. Despite the weirdness of the esoteric imagery, the warning is the same as that of the famous and more awe-inspiring opening of the *De contemptu mundi* of Bernard of Cluny:

Hora novissima, tempora pessima sunt, vigilemus.
Ecce minaciter imminet arbiter, ille supremus.[26]

In sharp contrast, passus vii opens in an apparently sunnier way, 'Treuthe herde telle herof ... And purchased hym a pardoun'; though coming straight after the dark, apocalyptic conclusion of passus vi, it may sound a little bland, and certainly the word 'herof' is slyly ambiguous, for it could refer either to the attempt at amendment or the relapse. Nevertheless, the pardon undoubtedly sounds reassuring, for the thousand pilgrims, who made confession and who at least momentarily sought amendment of life, might at their death hope to have Guillaume's charter of pardon added to their pitifully light scale of good deeds. The shock to the medieval audience must therefore have been intense when they found that the time for mercy was apparently past, and that the pilgrims are to be confronted with

[25] Cf. M. W. Bloomfield, *Piers Plowman as a Fourteenth-century Apocalypse* (New Brunswick, 1961) pp. 91–94, 212.

[26] Ed. H. C. Hoskier (London, 1929) p. 1: 'The hour is very late and the times very wicked, let us keep watch. Behold threateningly near is the most high judge.'

the sentence of the Last Judgment, the day of wrath that had been foreseen at the end of passus vi.

It is beyond all shadow of doubt that Verse 41 of the Athanasian Creed refers solely and emphatically to the Last Judgment: it has to be read with the preceding verse:

> At whose [Christ's] coming all men shall rise again with their bodies, and shall give account for their own works.
> And they that have done good shall go into life everlasting: and they that have done evil into everlasting fire.

The second verse is of course based on the Last Judgment parable of the sheep and the goats in *Matthew* xxv, and on the rare occasions when it is quoted in medieval literature, as in *The Castell of Perseverance* and an anonymous sermon on Psalm cxxix, 3 ('Si iniquitates obseruaueris, Domine, Domine, quis sustinebit'),[27] it is in the context of the Judgment. Moreover, though the text itself seems to be quoted rarely, its content in the form of direct address is the common substance of Advent sermons and plays of the Last Judgment in the mystery cycles.

The Athanasian Creed is the only one of the three creeds to be so explicit about the Last Judgment, and its emphasis upon good and evil deeds may perhaps support the recent view that it was composed in a semi-Pelagian milieu. Admittedly even this distribution of reward to the good was held to have been made possible by the Crucifixion alone (so that even this verdict could be said to have been 'purchased' [vii, 2] by Christ), for before the Redemption the patriarchs and prophets of the Old Testament awaited their release in the Limbo of the Fathers, which was the outermost part of hell. But stated so baldly, and in such a position, this judgment has a discomforting, if not a heretical, ring.

In their treatment of the Redemption and the Judgment medieval theologians and preachers had to reconcile two apparent paradoxes. The first is that, according to St. Thomas (whose view may be taken as the orthodox teaching of the Middle Ages), every good deed was initiated by grace, sustained by grace, and in the end, despite its deficiencies, held to be good through grace. Nevertheless co-operation with grace was necessary, and this co-operation between man and the movement of grace is especially elusive to the understanding, being indeed potentially misleading to the un-theologically-minded Christian. For, whatever the truth, the average man feels that, when he has acted rightly, the initiative and effort were

[27] EETS 209, p. 29; this reference is given by Frank, *Speculum* xxvi, 322.

his own, and to learn that they were not might well prove an encouragement to acquiescence in one's own worst impulses. The solution to this in popular didactic literature was to divide the paradox into its parts, sometimes, as we shall see, showing that man is saved through Christ's mercy, sometimes, as in the Last Judgment plays, showing that his salvation depended upon good works.[28]

The second paradox is a related one, namely the relationship of God's justice to His mercy. It was a traditional view that God's mercy would be supreme until the moment of the Last Judgment, but then no longer, for at the end of time all would be ordered in accordance with His justice. This had been the view of St. Augustine, who expressed it in a much-quoted comment on Psalm CI ('Misericordiam et iudicium cantabo'), saying '... modo tempus esse misericordiae, futurum autem tempus judicii'.[29] Such a distinction was of course repugnant to the scholastic theologians, such as Peter Lombard in the *Sentences* and the authors of subsequent commentaries upon this work, but they made it philosophically acceptable along the lines of the comment on the same psalm in the *Glossa Ordinaria*: 'Semper haec simul in eo sunt: sed per tempora secundum effectus distinguuntur, misericordia nunc, judicium in futuro.'[30] There was here a distinction easy to embody in popular literature: Christ's mercy was displayed at the personal judgment, His justice at the Day of Doom.

In order to appreciate the medieval understanding of the Last Judgment it is worth pursuing these theological paradoxes a little further, not in theology, but in the works of didactic and devotional edification. It was of course always the method of this kind of literature to simplify in order to present the unimaginable vividly to the imagination. In drama, art, and narrative the apparently contradictory cannot be presented simultaneously. Therefore, for instance, the simultaneous triumph and suffering of the Redemption are portrayed successively: the suffering in the Crucifixion, the

[28] This kind of distinction had been made by St Augustine in his comment in Psalm xxiv, 10: 'Et ideo universae viae Domini, duo adventus Filii Dei unus miserantis, alter judicantis.' *PL* 36, 185. ('"All the ways of the Lord" refers to the two comings of the Son of God, the one when He shows mercy, the other when He judges.')

[29] Ibid. 1282. '... now is still the time for mercy: the future will be the time for judgement.'

[30] *PL* 113, 1010. 'These two are always united in Him, but at different times different effects manifest themselves, mercy now, judgement in the future.' For the discussion of God's justice in relation to His mercy (as an introduction to the subject of the Last Judgment) in the *Sentences* and in Bonaventura's Commentary on this work, see Bonaventura, *Opera omnia* iv (Quaracchi, 1889) 955 and 964–965.

triumph in the Harrowing of Hell. So also mercy and justice could be displayed successively: the good deeds that would be all-determining at the Last Judgment are, when inadequate, shown to be superabundantly augmented at the particular judgment. This was done at the cost of narrative discrepancy, as for instance, in *The Castell of Perseverance*. In this play the hero, *Humanum Genus*, after various moral vicissitudes, is in his old age tempted out of the Castle of Perseverance by Avarice:

> How, Mankynde! I am a-tenyde
> for þou art þere so in þat holde.
> Cum & speke with þi best frende,
> Syr Coueytyse! þou knowyst me of olde.
> What, deuyl schalt þou þer lenger lende
> with grete penaunce in þat castel colde?[31]

Humanum Genus then abandons perseverance in virtue until struck down by Death. His soul is transported to the weighing, which is to be done by Righteousness ('þanne wey I his goode dedys and his synne'). In the debate between the Four Daughters of God, Justice maintains that he must be damned for he has not performed the seven works of mercy and the gospel says that such cannot enter heaven. But Mercy pleads the pains of the Passion, and at her prayer God receives the soul into heaven. At this point God, in a speech that is preceded by the text from the Athanasian Creed, foretells how at the Last Judgment He will divide the sheep from the goats. In terms of narrative this is pure contradiction: *Humanum Genus*, deficient in good deeds, is received at God's right hand, for sin is quenched by mercy as is a single spark by the sea, and yet God foretells how in the future He will reject all those lacking good deeds.

A similar discrepancy, though not within a single work, is found in the versions of the exemplum of the man with four friends.[32] In most allegories of this the condemned man is abandoned by all his friends save the fourth (the last and least valued), and the faithful friend is Christ; but in the play of *Everyman*, which has this exemplum for its plot, the last and only faithful friend is Good Deeds. Contradictions of this kind reflect both the apparent antithesis in God between His justice and His mercy and also the dual needs of man, who must exert all his efforts towards virtue, whilst recognizing that it is through the mercy of Christ alone that he can hope to be saved.

[31] *The Macro Plays*, EETS ES 91, p. 149.

[32] For an example see *Middle English Sermons*, EETS 209, pp. 86–89.

The Castell of Perseverance was written later than *Piers Plowman*, but its themes are ancient and traditional, and it provides a compact illustration of the two issues that concern us: the one, the failure in perseverance being met by God's mercy, the other, the adamantine justice of the Day of Judgment. This play is also interestingly linked to the scene of the Pardon in the *Pèlerinage de l'âme*, for it is in these two works alone that the popular allegory of the Four Daughters of God[33] is applied exclusively to the judgment of the soul. This debate is much more commonly applied to the doctrine of the Redemption formulated by St. Anselm: Justice demands that man should die, Mercy that God should show compassion; the Sisters are reconciled by God the Son proposing the Incarnation. According to St. Anselm's theory God found in the Incarnation a unique way of harmonizing justice with mercy: the significance of the allegory is therefore the nature of the Redemption. In the *Pèlerinage* and *The Castell*, however, its aim is to demonstrate how sinners may be saved, how the Redemption will work for each man, however sinful he may have been. But, though the use of the debate in the *Pèlerinage* is uncommon, the complementary theme of the weighing of the soul occurs frequently in both exempla and in art. Invariably in the Psychostasis (as this theme is technically called) the weight of the scale of good deeds is increased by some symbolic object: sometimes it is a rosary (this has been shown to be characteristic of English iconography) or sometimes the Virgin puts in the hem of her dress or actually depresses the scale with her hand. The significance of the Psychostasis is always, not merit rewarded, but mercy prevailing.

Moreover, not only was the Day of Judgment a day of strict justice, according to the theologians, but also in the devotional tradition of liturgy, sermon and hymn it was a day of terror, the day on which even the just will tremble. Two verses from Zephaniah provided the starting point for meditative expansions of this subject: 'Iuxta est dies Domini magnus, iuxta est et velox nimis; vox diei Domini amara, tribulabitur ibi fortis. Dies irae dies illa, dies tribulationis et angustiae, dies calamitatis et miseriae ...'.[34] These words are echoed in the moving responsory, *Libera me, Domine*, which was part of the Mass for the Dead, and in the opening of the famous hymn, *Dies irae*,

[33] For the history of this theme see Hope Traver, *The Four Daughters of God* (Bryn Mawr College Monographs, 1907).

[34] *Zephaniah* i, 14–15. 'The great day of the Lord is near, it is near and all too swift; the voice of the day of the Lord is bitter, there will the strong man be troubled. That day is a day of wrath, a day of trouble and distress, a day of disaster and wretchedness.'

which was probably sung on the first Sunday in Advent.[35] In both of these and elsewhere is found the idea that on that day of wrath the just man will tremble, for even he will scarcely be saved:[36] 'vix justus salvabitur' [Even the just shall barely be saved];[37] 'quid sum miser tunc dicturus ... dum vix iustus sit securus' [How wretched I am is then to be said ... when scarcely is the just person safe];[38] 'et si iustus vix evadit, / impius ubi parebit?' [And if the just man will escape with difficulty, where will the evil be?].[39]

It is certain, therefore, that the appropriate response to the thought of the Day of Judgment was that of fear, and it was not a theme that could be used to demonstrate the rewards of the virtuous. The rich and complex body of Christian thought was matched in the Middle Ages by an equally rich and abundant store of themes and images, and they could not be mixed. Langland was an eccentric writer, but he never confused traditions in this way. The company of pilgrims, therefore, even if they had been more perseverant in virtue, could not have come to the sentence of the Last Judgment with equanimity or trust in their own good deeds. It is inconceivable that Langland would have used a Last Judgment text in a way that would seem reassuring to his characters and complacent to his audience.

An investigation of the literary theological background of the pilgrims and their pardon shows very clearly how the scene should be read up to the moment of the tearing. Society corrupted by the seven deadly sins makes a fleeting attempt at amendment. Nevertheless (or therefore), a 'pardon' is sent by God, a pardon that should be a promise of forgiveness and a symbol of the Redemption; but the content of the 'pardon' turns out to be a threat and a symbol of the Day of Judgment. Langland can thus be seen to have created two pairs of intolerables; a society pessimistically conceived and darkened with the devices and exaggerations of the homiletic satirist is juxtaposed to a text that in its isolation presents an equally partial truth, and this juxtaposition means damnation; yet this sentence of damnation for more than a hundred lines is deceptively alluded to as a pardon.

From here on the viewpoint of the medieval audience, in so far as it can be reconstructed, is no longer helpful. The priest's exclamation 'I can no pardoun fynde' would have expressed their own feelings, but

[35] For the texts of the responsory and the *Dies irae* see F. J. E. Raby, *A History of Christian-Latin Poetry* (Oxford, 1953) pp. 445–448.

[36] Cf. 1 *Peter* iv, 18.

[37] Raby, p. 446.

[38] Raby, p. 448.

[39] Raby, p. 448.

beyond this we know only that some people were so bewildered by the next action, the tearing of the pardon, that Langland omitted it in the C-text. Nevertheless a paraphrase of the scene in terms of the probable medieval understanding of it serves to define the issues so sharply that only one solution remains. For if it is accepted that the document which Piers held and the priest looked at was not a pardon but a condemnation, then there is only one way of justifying Langland's description of it as a pardon and the lengthy deception in which he describes the glosses upon it: the document was not a pardon when it was received, but it was a pardon after Piers had torn it. The suggestion that the tearing of the document symbolizes the mercy and forgiveness shown in the Redemption may seem startling, but even at first sight has a certain propriety. A sentence of death, when torn up, might appropriately be called a reprieve. To call it a reprieve in advance would be normally impermissible but could be justified in terms of poetic anticipation and illuminating paradox.

This proposed interpretation prompts two closely related questions: What does Piers signify? and, Can a parallel be found in other parts of the poem for so strange an allegorical method? Up to now there has been one point on which all critics have been agreed, namely, that whatever divine affinities Piers may reveal later in the poem, at this stage he represents no more than the simple, virtuous Christian, in other words that he is scarcely an allegorical figure, the literal level of the story containing almost the entire meaning (Professor Coghill's theory that Piers here represents Do-Wel gives depth to this view but does not radically change it). But, though in passus vi there is a very strong literal level to the allegory—Piers has a wife and children and land to plough—and, in contrast to this, when Piers much later re-enters the narrative, the literal level is almost entirely stripped away so that he becomes a mysterious figure unlocalized in time or place, there is nevertheless some suggestion in passus vi that Piers has dignity and powers that are not those of the virtuous active layman, for he speaks and acts with an authority whose source is not revealed.

Piers orders and preaches to the company of pilgrims, which contains all ranks of society from knights to beggars, and this they accept reasonably and courteously. When, for instance, he has instructed the knight to act justly towards his tenants and to protect the poor, he goes on to remind him of the levelling power of death:

For in charnel atte chirche cherles ben yuel to knowe,
Or a kniȝte fram a knaue there; knowe this in thin herte.

And the knight replies:

> 'I assente, bi seynt Iame', seyde the kniȝte thanne,
> 'Forto worche bi thi wordes the while my lyf dureth.'
>
> (B vi 50 ff.)

To understand this episode as one in which the little man of simple virtue admonishes the mighty is possible, but is probably anachronistic and certainly diminishes the power of the scene. Piers's treatment of the lower ranks of society could be explained in terms of social realism for he might be thought of as a just though severe overseer, but yet more strikingly exceeds this simple interpretation, since he has powers that are not those of an ordinary farm-bailiff. For the seasons of the year with their consequent famine and fullness are at his command: in anger he summons Hunger to force the lazy to work, and then in compassion for the people's misery dismisses Hunger again. The simple meaning of this passage could have been presented naturalistically through the normal passing of the seasons, and unless there was some further significance, there was no need to give Piers command over natural forces. It would be unwise to ask at this point what Piers signifies: like the Green Knight he seems to be a dispenser of justice without any explanation being given for this authority, and if an explanation were given, the powerful but indefinable effect of awe in both poems would be dispelled.

In the figure of Piers in passus vi, however, there are no more than almost imperceptible intimations of divine power, and it is only when we look back at this passus in the light of the later parts of the poem that they become more readily discernible. But, if Piers seems Christ-like in his tearing of the Pardon, then it can certainly be held that there are adumbrations of this in the preceding passus. It is, however, in the much later scene of the Tree of Charity in passus xvi that Piers's divine prerogatives shine out unmistakably, and this episode is particularly relevant to the Pardon scene, for it has the same mysterious and dramatic intensity, and for the same reason in that in both Piers acts violently and strangely. In the passage beginning at line 75 of the B-text, Piers at the request of the dreamer shakes the tree so that the fruit may drop off, and the apples, which symbolize all mankind, and in particular the patriarchs and prophets who lived under the Old Dispensation—Adam, Abraham, Isaiah and others—all drop from the tree and the devil gathers them up: at this, Piers seizes one of the props of the tree, which symbolizes the Second Person of the Trinity, and hurls it after the devil, and the Annunciation begins. Just as Piers's tearing of the Pardon is cut out from the C-text, so also in the C-text here his rôle disappears, and it is Old Age who shakes the tree and Libera-Voluntas-Dei who throws the prop. In the C-text therefore the meaning of the action is plain but commonplace: men die of old age, God in His utter free-will chose to redeem man. Not only is the meaning of the two individual actions made commonplace but also the fact that they are performed by different figures much diminishes the force of the whole. The meaning of the B-text cannot be so readily translated into non-allegorical terms, but it is clear that what God has done Piers does. God has decreed that all men shall die, for He said 'in the day that thou eatest thereof thou shalt surely die', and it is God who appoints to each man the hour of his death. In *Everyman*, for instance, God summons Death and sends him to Everyman[40] and in the Play of Herod in the *Ludus Coventriae* Death announces himself as God's messenger.[41] So Piers shakes the tree. But the God who ordained death also ordained the Redemption, and therefore Piers hurls the prop.

In this episode, as in the Pardon scene, the literal and allegorical levels are interwoven in a bewildering and unpredictable way. Rosamund Tuve has pointed out that most medieval allegorical narratives are only allegorical intermittently and that they therefore cannot be read as continuous and consistent allegories.[42] But in the best passages of *Piers Plowman* the transitions from literal to allegorical are so swift and startling that, even with Rosamund Tuve's warning, it is not easy to identify them. In the two scenes that we are discussing Piers does something of most august singificance in response to some trivial action which belongs solely to the literal level: the priest asks to see the pardon and then dismisses its worth in the condescending manner and contemptuous tone of a trained theologian dealing with an ignorant layman, so Piers tears the Pardon; correspondingly the Dreamer, standing by the fruit tree, asks casually for an apple, so Piers shakes the tree. Moreover, just as the action is stimulated by a simple comment or request, so also in both instances Piers seems to be motivated by fairly trivial emotions: on the occasion he is dismayed and humiliated by the priest's words, on the second occasion he is cross that a sneak-thief should steal his fruit; in feelings he is no more than a disappointed, simple man, or an angry farmer. It is, however, noticeable that both times Piers acts out of *pure tene*. This could be a verbal coincidence (Langland has a device

[40] Ed. A. C. Cawley (Manchester, 1961) p. 3.
[41] EETS ES 120, p. 174.
[42] *Allegorical Imagery* (Princeton, 1966).

of animating his allegorical figures by attributing extremes of emotion to them, particularly anger: only a moment before Piers had stared at the Dreamer *egrelich*), and he was not a meticulous writer. It is, however, likely that this verbal echo that resounds between two such carefully worked scenes was not merely the fortunate chance of careless writing.

The triviality of the stimulus for the action and of Piers's emotional response are matched by the triviality of the symbolic actions on a literal level: nothing could be more ordinary than to tear a letter or throw a stick. Again it is characteristic of Langland to choose the most everyday of human actions to bear the most sublime significances. However, although these actions are commonplace, it would be reasonable to expect to find in them some propriety between their nature and the thing signified. But since what is signified has no corporal pattern, the parallelism has to be sought between these actions and more traditional imagery. For the hurling of the staff this is easy, for in its violence and movement it suggests the great leap that Christ made when He descended from heaven to earth. For the tearing of the pardon the analogies are more involved. In the act of tearing there may well be, as one critic has already suggested, an allusion to the rending of the veil of the temple. But the crucial point here is probably not the precise action of tearing but the more general idea of a document destroyed. In some ways very close is the image in *Colossians* ii, 13–14 of the 'chirographum peccatorum nostrorum, quod erat contrarium nobis' [the manuscript of ordinances that was against us], which Christ annulled by nailing it to the Cross. The *Legenda aurea* explains the *chirographum* as a debt incurred by Eve,[43] increasing with interest throughout the ages until cancelled by Christ; Ludolf the Carthusian more illuminatingly describes it as 'chirographum peccatorum nostrorum et mortis' [the manuscript of our sins and death].[44] The contents of the *chirographum*, however, is different from that of the pardon, but it resembles it in being a document containing a sentence of damnation that was destroyed by the Redemption.

Theologically, however, a closer parallel is to be found in the traditional allegory of Church and Synagogue. In this, when represented iconographically, Church on the right side of the Cross holds a chalice into which flows the blood from Christ's side, whilst

[43] *The Golden Legend*, translated William Caxton, ed. F. S. Ellis (Temple Classics, 1900) I, p. 79.

[44] *Vita Jesu Christi*, ed. L. M. Rigollot (Paris, 1878) iv, 97.

on the left side stands Synagogue from whose hands fall the tables of the law.[45] This analogy is helpful because it shows that there was nothing doctrinally repugnant in demonstrating in artistic form the dispossession of the Old Law under the New Dispensation. That the Ten Commandments fall from the hands of Synagogue does not mean that they are not binding on the Christian: the Ten Commandments were, for instance, an important element in medieval penitential treatises, such as *Handlynge Synne* and the *Parson's Tale*. Similarly the text from the Athanasian Creed can be torn up without its validity in other contexts being questioned. Their destruction in individual scenes is but a striking way of demonstrating that with the Redemption it is mercy and not the Law that is at the heart of the matter.

If this is a true interpretation of the tearing of the pardon, Langland did not deceive his audience with his implied promise that the back-sliding pilgrims would through God's mercy be saved. But he executed the promise, not in the conventional and traditional way that the term 'pardon' had suggested, but in a unique allegory, which can more illuminatingly be called myth. For it is often a characteristic of myth that trivial actions have cosmic consequences: to tear a letter, to throw a stick, to open a box, to eat an apple, are all equally commonplace. It is also of the nature of myth that there are no clear allegorical equivalences: allegory is not necessary when one is dealing with the absolute sources of power. Furthermore, myth has a far closer and more mysterious relationship to what is signified than does allegory. If Piers's document had contained, not two lines of condemnation, but a long charter of pardon, this would have been an allegorical equivalent to a statement that men though sinful are saved through Christ. But by the brilliant invention of a myth, Langland makes the Redemption happen precisely in the social world that he has created, not far away on Calvary, not in the mysterious garden of the Tree of Charity, but in the field full of folk. But the myth though located in time is also timeless in that the nexus of the seven deadly sins and the tearing of the pardon is always present in the world.

The further profit of rejecting the conventional allegory of the charter of pardon is that this allegory by its roundness and definiteness would have brought the poem to a close: there would have been nothing more to say. Structurally, however, Langland has only come to the end of his prelude, and therefore his method is to

[45] E. Mâle, *L'Art religieux du xiiie siècle en France* (Paris, 1948) pp. 191–192 and fig. 100.

state a main element of his theme at first enigmatically, and then repeating it with a gradually increasing explicitness, until it is boldly and majestically revealed in its full grandeur in passus xviii on the Harrowing of Hell. Langland's concern in the whole poem is with the relationship between the world and its Redemption in every facet. In passus vii he brings the two into a momentary, striking conjunction. But, because this conjunction is startling and mysterious, it poses the problem rather than solves it, and therefore the poet and his audience, the Dreamer and Piers, are not contented, and the search continues with greater intensity of enquiry and determination.

XI

THE WANDERER, *THE SEAFARER*, AND THE GENRE OF *PLANCTUS*

The Wanderer and *The Seafarer*, though now commonly referred to as elegies, may more helpfully be seen to belong to the distinctively mediaeval genre of *planctus* or complaint. The characteristics of this genre that divide it from elegy are firstly that the speaker is invariably fictional and secondly that, whilst the subject of the lament may be a death, it can equally well be any kind of loss that is experienced intensely. The fictional speaker may be either an individual or a representative type. In various western European literatures there survive on the one hand laments of Dido, Orpheus, Guðrun, Eve, Mary Magdalene and, in abundance, the Blessed Virgin, on the other hand, for instance, complaints of an old man or a young woman betrayed by her lover or separated from him.[1]

Our knowledge of the Old English *planctus* is of two kinds: that which derives from extant poems and that which is inferred obliquely from other sources of which the most important is *Beowulf*. Both types of *planctus* existed: complaints of individual speakers are represented by *The Wife's Lament*, *The Husband's Message*, and *Wulf and Eadwacer*.[2] No one would dispute that the latter two are spoken within the context of specific situations. This is made especially plain by the fact that the recipient of the complaint is also a fictional person within the story. In the case of *Wulf and Eadwacer* it would be inappropriately realistic to ask how the lament was conveyed to the person addressed; but it is interesting to note that in the *Husband's Message*, the message is either carved upon a rune staff or is delivered verbally by a messenger.[3] This variation in the form of the *planctus*

[1] *The Wanderer* and *The Seafarer* are included in the valuable list of western European *planctus* provided by Peter Dronke, *Poetic Individuality in the Middle Ages* (Oxford, 1970), pp. 27–28.

[2] I exclude here poems that are commonly or sometimes described as elegaic, such as *The Ruin*, which, despite its theme, is not a *planctus*, and poems such as *Deor* and *Resignation (The Penitent's Prayer)*, which, though they are narrated by an I-speaker, for different reasons present a problem concerning genre. At this stage it seems safest to assume that Old English literature contained a body of poems that were offshoots of the genre of *planctus*, not members of it.

[3] Cf. *Three Old English Elegies*, ed. R. F. Leslie (Manchester, 1961), pp. 12–15.

reminds one of Ovid's adoption of the epistolary form for his series of complaints of unhappy women, a sophisticated device which nevertheless does not always work realistically. *The Wife's Lament*, however, does not quite so unmistakably have a narrative context. Nevertheless, there seem to be too many personal references which are tantalisingly unclear for us to be able to classify it simply as the lament of a women deprived of her husband. It is not, however, addressed to a particular person—in this, of course, resembling the complaints of representative types. Nowadays, when we read these poems on the printed page, we may be inclined to think of ourselves as overhearing an interior soliloquy; but in a period when poetry was read aloud it is much more likely that poets who wrote complaints thought of the audience as being the recipients. For the *Wife's Lament* they would as it were be a confidant: their relationship to the complaints of the Wanderer and Seafarer is less simply labelled, but is important in that it has a bearing upon the tone of voice heard in these poems at the beginning and the end.

The evidence of these surviving poems is usefully amplified by the allusions to *planctus* in *Beowulf*, which incidentally makes plain that the *planctus* was a varied and flourishing form by the eighth century: a valuable piece of information since most Old English poems are so difficult to date. As has often been suggested, the opening of the Finn Episode may well reflect the existence of a *planctus* spoken by Hildeburg: if it does, it provides a useful illustration of the way in which complaints could be related to heroic stories and could therefore be integrated into narratives if a poet so wished; Chaucer's treatment of the *Heroides* in the *Legend of Good Women* comes to mind as an analogy. A literary tradition of a lament for the death of a hero may also lie behind the last three moving lines of *Beowulf*: an earlier analogue to this is the lament for Christ in the *Dream of the Rood*. Such laments had already become part of the eastern devotional tradition, but it is easier to suppose that this represents a parallel development from folkdirge to Christian literary lament than to postulate any direct influence.[4] The end of *Beowulf*, however, is distinguished from the common type of complaint through being eulogistic, and it is therefore possible that, rather than being literary in origin, it reflects historical custom, some funeral address, for instance, at the death of a king.

[4] For the eastern tradition see Margaret Alexiou, *The Ritual Lament in Greek Tradition* (Cambridge, 1974).

An equally interesting hint at another type of *planctus* occurs in the account of Hroþgar's composition or narration of various kinds of poetry (lines 2105–14). *Eldo gebunden* [shackled by old age] he lamented the loss of his youth (*ongan ... gioguðe cwiðan*). The complaint of a typical figure, that of an old man, seems here to have been recited with self-reference by the aged Hroþgar. No doubt Old English *planctus* of this type were far more generalised and decorous than the Middle English analogues which insist upon the disgusting detail of physical senility. The loss of strength (cf. *Beowulf*, line 2113) or the outliving of friends (cf. *Seafarer* 92–93) may have been typical themes rather than those of deafness and a shuffling walk. By the end of the Old English period the disabilities of old age had become a recurrent homiletic theme, deriving directly or indirectly from patristic sources. It would be interesting to know whether there was an entirely native Old English tradition of complaints of an old man and, if so, for how long it remained uninfluenced by Christian didactic literature.

Besides these three brief references to *planctus* in *Beowulf* there are two famous elegiac passages, one of which is in form a short *planctus*, the other a summary of a *planctus*. The first is the so-called elegy of the last survivor (lines 2247–66). Though there are many differences between these lines and *The Wanderer*, the modern differences of title suggest a distinction that is not there: for the 'last survivor' appears to be an exile (*unbliðe hwearf / dæges ond nihtes* [went about sadly by day and by night, 2268b–69a]), while the narrative implications of the poem are that the Wanderer is also a last survivor. The lament of the last survivor is cast in the form of an apostrophe to the earth (this opening is required to adapt the lament to its narrative context); but much of the lament itself is reminiscent of *The Wanderer* and may well give an accurate impression of what were the simpler antecedents of *The Wanderer*.

The second passage is the so-called elegy of the bereaved father. Its opening suggests that, unlike the elegy of the last survivor, this is the *planctus* of an individual, for the father mourns for a son who has been hanged. This cannot be a typical situation and scholars have sought to identify the story.[5] The rest of the lament, however, is generalised and rather interestingly, at its close shows an insight into

[5] Like the story relating to *The Wife's Lament*, however, it remains unidentified. Klaeber's objection (cf. note to line 2444) to the theory that the father is Jǫrmunrekkr is fully convncing.

the psychological responses to bereavement of a kind that, as we shall see, is also to be found in *The Wanderer*. This insight occurs in the narrative summing up, *þuhte him eall to rum, / wongas ond wicstede* [the fields and the dwelling place now seemed to him all too large, 2461b–62a]: and experience that a room or house of a person who had died suddenly seems to become large and empty is surely a common one, though the author of *Beowulf* is perhaps the only English poet to have recorded it.

The abundant references to *planctus* in *Beowulf* show that the genre was current in the eighth century. A slightly earlier date for its currency can be inferred from Bede's famous story of the conversion to Christianity of one of the leading pagan counsellors of King Edwin of Northumbria. According to Bede this counsellor justified his abandonment of the old religion for the reason that Christianity brought a solution to the pagan view of life, which he likened to that of a sparrow which flies from outer wintry darkness through a warm and lighted hall out into wintry darkness again.[6] The source of this image, which is movingly elaborated, is surely a *planctus* concerning the transience of life. Whether a tradition had reached Bede that this image had been used or whether Bede himself turned to the tradition of *planctus* in order to make the counsellor's understanding of the doctrine of the Resurrection articulate is of little consequence, though the latter is perhaps more likely.

The story of the sparrow is also of value in indicating the nature of the first relationship between Christianity and native *planctus*. If this image of the sparrow is indeed pre-Christian in origin, it shows how extraordinarily apt was the Anglo-Saxon imagination for an immediate responsiveness to the Christian doctrine of eternal life. Pagans are not necessarily so acutely aware of the shortness of human life nor of the poignancy of the passing of all that one values. It seems safe to assert that the Church would have fostered a native tradition of *planctus* rather than have attempted to suppress it. Ingeld may have nothing to do with Christ but the Last Survivor in his lonely exile undoubtedly does. It is perhaps paradoxical that Christianity encourages, at least in poetry, a deep and melancholy response to transience. In later English literature some of the finest poems of Christian authors have been on this subject, and Anglo-Saxon poets would similarly have found that Christianity provided a natural

[6] Cf. *Bede's Ecclesiastical History of the English People*, eds. Bertram Colgrave and R. A. B. Mynors (Oxford, 1969), pp. 182–84.

home for traditional laments.

The Church, however, did more than provide fortunate conditions in which a purely native tradition could flourish. With the Old Testament and later didactic works indebted to it, it provided fresh sources upon which Anglo-Saxon poets could draw. Many books of the Bible, including the Psalms, Isaiah, Jeremiah, and Ecclesiasticus, had expressed most powerfully and movingly the idea of the brevity of human life and of all man's achievements. Many such Christian sources have now been identified for *The Wanderer* and *The Seafarer*, and it is clear from these poems that the native and the biblical could be mingled together in a most natural and seemly way.

It is sometimes thought that even if Christianity did contain within the Bible and its later homiletic literature so many imaginatively moving expressions of the theme of transience, there must nevertheless be an obligation upon the Christian poet who writes upon transience to include in his poem some equally moving expression of his trust in eternal life. Such a view would probably be confirmed by a study of the practice of later mediaeval poets. In the 'Love Ron' of Thomas of Hales, for instance, which contains in its lament a beautiful use of the *ubi sunt* formula, less than half the poem is occupied with lament;[7] similarly, in Dunbar's 'Of Luve Erdly and Divine', which also deals with the superiority of sacred to profane love, the lament for the transience of human love turns midway through the poem to a confident acknowledgement of the unendingness of divine love.[8] Reflection upon the poems of later Christian authors, however, shows this assumption to be wrong. Some seventeenth-century lyrics, for instance, contain at most fleeting or perfunctory reference to the fact that for the Christian transience must yield to eternity. Herrick's 'To Daffadills', for instance, contains only a momentary and oblique allusion to a Christian frame of reference, whilst Herbert's 'Vertue' and 'Life' both end on a Christian note, but in them, as in *The Wanderer*, the imaginative vitality does not extend beyond the lament. In Hopkins's 'Spring and Fall' there is no reference to Christianity at all.[9] All these

[7] *English Lyrics of the XIIIth Century*, ed. Carleton Brown (Oxford, 1932), pp. 68–74.

[8] *Poems*, ed. Mackay Mackenzie (London, 1932), pp. 101–04.

[9] Robert Herrick, *Poetical Works*, ed. L. C. Martin (Oxford, 1956), p. 125; *The Works of George Herbert*, ed. F. E. Hutchinson (Oxford, 1941), pp. 87–88, 94; Gerard Manley Hopkins, *Poems*, ed. Robert Bridges, 2nd ed. by Charles Williams (Oxford, 1930), p. 50.

are moving lyrics written by poets who are famous for their explicitly Christian poetry, and this fact makes clear that speculation about a poet's religious convictions—the question of how deep or how well-informed was his faith—was pointless when we have only a single poem to interpret. In this situation an assessment of the equilibrium sought in the poem between a lament for transience and its Christian solution will be an inevitable part of a critical interpretation, but it cannot provide the foundations for any inference about the poet's personal beliefs.

If a Christian poet may write about the experience of transience with little or no interest in the Christian promise of eternal life, this must be especially true of a Christian who writes in the genre of the *planctus*, in which the speaker is by definition someone other than himself. Recollection of this may help in understanding the structure and progress of thought in *The Wanderer* where the question of whether or not the poet felt his Christianity deeply is an irrelevant one that distracts from more pertinent issues. One of the apparently most difficult problems that arise (and certainly a genuine problem for the editor who is compelled by the modern system of punctuation to take a definite view) is that of the number of independent speakers in the poem and of which of them is speaking at a number of different points. In a personal response to the poem it seems that the *swa cwæþ* construction at lines 6 and 111 is so conspicuously intrusive that it must serve an important function, whilst paradoxically the question of who is speaking at the beginning of the poem (poet or Wanderer) and at the end (poet, Wanderer, or contemplator of the ruin) seems scarcely to affect one's understanding of the poem. The primary purpose of the *swa cwæþ* construction may therefore be to block off the first and last passages about the consolation of God's mercy from the main body of the poem.[10]

To suggest that these passages are deliberately blocked off is not to imply that they are irrelevant, but that despite their relevancy the poet did not wish them to undercut the power and poignancy of the main part of the *planctus* which they frame. It would furthermore follow that the poet, whilst achieving a logical and lyrical continuity, was not seeking to analyse a subtle pyschological continuity of thought. Though there are in the poem moments of sensitive perception, it is

[10] For a recent discussion of the force of *swa cwæþ* considered from a syntactical point of view see *The Wanderer*, eds. T. P. Dunning and A. J. Bliss (London, 1969), pp. 30–36.

no use searching it for an examination of the long, slow movements of the heart which may bring a man to a certain peace and resignation. The very fact that it would only take about ten minutes to read aloud whilst the passage of time within the poem (though past is time recalled) is unchartably long, reveals that the poet is not concerned to show, with any pyschological precision, how a person learns: one may contrast it with *The Pearl*, where the dreamer's slow and zigzag progress towards acceptance of bereavement and submission to God's will strike a familiar chord.

Once the reader ceases to wonder whether the Wanderer himself was capable of the various degrees of wisdom presented in the poem, it is possible to find a pattern in the poem without resolving the question of who the speaker is at various points, a question which may well be without answer. The reason that it is unanswerable is that at the beginning and end either the Wanderer speaks partially with the voice of the poet-narrator or the poet-narrator speaks partially with the voice of the Wanderer. The authorial voice may be heard clearly but unobtrusively in the use of *us* in the last halfline, *þær us eal seo fæstnung stondeð* [where all our security lies, 115b]. At this point an audience is manifestly addressed and probably this linking of speaker and hearers has a homiletic resonance. Nevertheless the last four lines (of which this half-line is the climax) cannot be interpreted solely as the author's didactic epilogue, for they contain two important indications of the Wanderer's final state of mind. Firstly, of course, they contain the second reference to *ar*, God's mercy, which by implication the Wanderer now seeks (*seceð*) and therefore, according to Christ's promise, will find. Whether this represents a development upon the statement *Oft him anhaga are gebideð* [Often the solitary one experiences, or awaits, God's mercy, 1] depends upon the meaning of *gebidan*.[11] If it means 'experience' then the first line as it were sets the seal upon the penultimate one: we know the end at the beginning. If, however, *gebidan* means 'wait,' a development has surely taken place, for actively to seek God's mercy must represent a spiritual stage beyond passively awaiting it. Moreover if the sense is 'await', there is probably some hint that the Wanderer at this stage mis-understands the nature of God's mercy, supposing that it will take the form of his finding a new lord. In that case a wiser

[11] It does not seem possible to solve the meaning of *gebidan* in *The Wanderer*: as argued above on literary grounds either interpretation is possible, whilst Bruce Mitchell, 'Some Syntactical Problems in *The Wanderer*', *NM*, 69 (1968), 172–75, has convincingly shown that the linguistic evidence shows either meaning to be acceptable.

understanding of *ar* has been reached at the close of the poem.

The last four lines of *The Wanderer* are thematically related not only to the first five lines but also to the argument of the succeeding twelve lines; indeed at first sight lines 111–12 seem to be mere repetition of the earlier and elaborate statement (probably of classical orgin)[12] that it is a noble and virtuous custom for a man not to reveal his sufferings however intense these may be. The recurrence of this idea may appear ill-placed for it seems a bathetically inadequate response to the awe-inspiring vision of a deserted world, ruined walls representing the last trace of man, and the snow falling perpetually. But the repetition is significant because of a sudden qualification that it is given, ... *nemþe he ær þa bote cunne* [unless he knows the remedy beforehand, 113b]. The *bot* is surely the affirmation in the last line and a half, *Wel bið þam þe him are seceð / frofre to Fæder on heofonum, þær us eal seo fæstnung stondeð* [Well is it for him who seeks favour, consolation from the Father in heaven, where all our security lies, 114b–15], and this relationship should be indicated by punctuation (i.e., a colon after *gefremman* in line 114). This observation resolves the problem that is sometimes raised, namely of how the speaker can so emphatically maintain that a man must keep his sorrows to himself and then reveal them.[13] As we have said before, the theory that with a *planctus* we are listening to man's inner thoughts is not quite happy in a social context in which the poem is recited to an audience. It is more satisfactory to assume that the poet intended an apparent discrepancy between the reticence demanded in lines 11–18 and the poem itself, and delayed the resolution of the discrepancy until his concluding climax.

If *The Wanderer* is interpreted as the lament of a typical figure, namely a last survivor and an exile, the question of whether there may be more than one speaker within the main body of the monologue becomes irrelevant, no matter how subtly it may be investigated.[14]

[12] For the classical-Christian origin of this theme see J. E. Cross, 'On the Genre of *The Wanderer*', *Neophil*, 45 (1961), 65, repr. *Essential Articles for the Study of Old English Poetry*, eds. J. B. Bessinger, Jr. and Stanley J. Kahrl (Hamden, Connecticut, 1968), pp. 517–18.

[13] There are of course other and plausible explanations such as that of Dunning and Bliss, ed. cit., p. 93.

[14] The most convincing argument for two speakers is that of John C. Pope, 'Dramatic Voices in *The Wanderer* and *The Seafarer*', *Franciplegius: Medieval and Linguistic Studies in Honor of Francis Peabody Magoun, Jr.* (New York, 1965), pp. 164–93; repr. *Essential Articles*, pp. 533–70. For a thoughtful and sometimes telling criticism of Professor Pope's arguments see *The Wanderer*, ed. R. F. Leslie (Manchester, 1966), pp. 9–25.

For any argument for two speakers presupposes that the poet is displaying the idiosyncracies of an individual consciousness, so that the reader may properly feel that one individual person could not make the psychological progress towards wisdom that the poem is concerned with. But this type of realistic response is mistaken if the speaker is a typical figure who will describe himself, not through a probing self-knowledge, but rather from the point of view of a thoughtful onlooker: there is no difference of attitude or understanding between the speaker of the *planctus* and the hearer who wisely considers the speaker's plight. Indeed the poet has taken considerable care to prevent an audience identifying themselves too instinctively and uncritically with the Wanderer's loss. The poet at one point, for instance, describes a common but private experience, namely how a bereaved person for many years (or longer) will dream with special intensity that the dead are alive again: lines 30–50 record this experience and in particular how the awakening from such a dream seems to be fresh bereavement. The latter is expressed well by the contrast between the warm world of the dream and the wintry scene to which the *wineleas guma* [lordless man, 45b] awakens. Nevertheless the possibility of an intimate sympathy developing between speaker and hearer is prevented through a deliberate act of distancing. This dream is only by implication the Wanderer's, for it is ascribed by the Wanderer to a hypothetical *wineleas guma* and this figure is therefore an imaginary creation who stands anyway at one remove from the audience. This is only one striking instance of a general peculiarity of the poem, which is that the Wanderer most often describes, not how he feels, but how someone in a comparable situation would feel. Over half the poem is set in this form. The intention of the poet must be to distance and generalise, and it is achieved at the deliberate expense of naturalism, for real people do not think in such a stylised way.

In the place of psychological development the poem has a definite thematic patterning and one that is paradoxical in relation to the old issue of the Christian versus pagan or secular elements in the poem: for it is the first part of the poem, which is usually described as heroic, that bears the Christian meaning, whilst it is the second part, which seems to be constructed out of an assemblage of Christian borrowings, that is secular in tone. The secularisation of the passages of Christian origin has been achieved by stripping their normal doctrinal or didactic contexts from them. The *sum*-series in lines 80–84, for instance, is a rhetorical figure and Christian theme; various ways of disposing of the earthly body are listed in a prelude to a demonstration that nevertheless the dead rise up.[15] But as used in *The Wanderer* this theme has nothing to do with the refutation of heretical objections to the doctrine of the resurrection of the body. It stands simply as a melancholy list to remind one that whilst methods of burial may be manifold, dead and buried every man will be.

Similarly the *ubi sunt* passage derives immediately from a Christian sermon tradition in which it serves to emphasise contempt for the world. The preacher asks where various splendours have gone and answers his own rhetorical question by enjoining his audience to visit the tomb where dust and bones will provide the true but frightening answer.[16] But in *The Wanderer* there is no suggestion that the *maþþumgyfa* [giver of treasure, 92b] rots in the grave or that the *beorht bune* [bright cup, 94a] may be rusted through. Standing on their own, as they do in *The Wanderer, ubi sunt* questions have the reverse effect. Far from suggesting that their subjects are worthless they confer a deep nostalgic value upon them, and the very fleetingness which the questions call to mind enhances rather than diminishes their preciousness. Such passages following upon the description of the Wanderer's former life in his lord's hall make clear that he has to learn detachment from that life, not because it was worthless and undeserving of his affections, but because it is inevitable that everything that is loved on earth, however precious it may be, must be lost. Such an understanding of life is of course capable of being translated into Christian terms, yet in itself is neither Christian nor unChristian but a straightforward recognition of the nature of things; as expressed, however, in the second half of *The Wanderer* it has resonances of melancholy and wistfulness which make it poetically moving but with more concern for natural feelings than for pure Christian teaching.

The first half of *The Wanderer* has properly been called heroic in that its background is probably the kind of literary-heroic society that is depicted in *Beowulf*. Not only is the background probably literary but also the treatment of the Wanderer himself is literary and stylised. There does not seem to be any historical reason why a man who had lost his lord should not sooner or later in his travels find another (one critic who has considered this question has found too

[15] Cf. J. E. Cross, 'On *The Wanderer* lines 80–84, a Study of a Figure and a Theme', *Vetenskaps-Societetens i Lund Årsbok*, 1958–1959, pp. 77–110.

[16] Cf. J. E. Cross, '*The Dry Bones* Speak—A Theme in Some Old English Homilies', *JEGP*, 56 (1957), 434–39.

realistic an answer to it, namely that the Wanderer had abandoned his lord in cowardly fashion);[17] certainly there is no reason why the Wanderer should live in a world where the weather is perpetual winter. From outside the poem one can say that the situation is thus depicted because the Wanderer is not an individual, who would experience the normal alternations of loss and gain to which all are accustomed, but the typical figure of an exile living in a typical exile's world. But to dismiss the matter in this way is perhaps to miss the crucial point of how the Wanderer's change of heart comes about. For near the beginning of the poem the Wanderer conceives of himself as a member of a real world where another lord and another meadhall might reasonably be found: in the course of the poem he comes to accept that his lot as wanderer is irreversible. It might therefore be not too farfetched to say that the wisdom that the Wanderer acquires is that of coming to understand the Christian truth of which he himself is accidentally a figure, namely that all men are exiles on earth and that the only true home lies, not behind one, but before.[18]

Many quotations assembled by Professor Whitelock with reference to her interpretation of *The Seafarer* show that Anglo-Saxon writers liked to play verbally upon the paradox of a man choosing to become an exile on earth in order more surely to reach his native land thereafter (e.g. *multo tempore pro aeterna patria exulauerant*).[19] Those to whom Professor Whitelock refers are men who deliberately chose the life of exile or pilgrim: the reason is plainly that they may in fact live the life which allegorically all Christians live. Manifestly, a man who lives in contentment all his life in his lord's hall or in his own home with his wife and children is not likely to feel the truth of the Christian image. The devout therefore change their lives. In *The Wanderer* the poet depicts an exile who has not initially chosen to change his life, but, having this change forced upon him, comes to understand its significance, and through the mouth of an imaginary man, *frod in ferðe* [wise in heart, 90a] expresses the recognition of the permanence of his situation. The very last line of

[17] For this view see R. W. V. Elliott, 'The Wanderer's Conscience', *ES*, 39 (1958), 193–200.

[18] For quotations illustrative of this tradition see G. V. Smithers, 'The Meaning of *The Seafarer* and *The Wanderer*', MÆ, 26 (1957), 137–53.

[19] 'For a long time they had been exiles, in order to gain the eternal homeland.' 'The Interpretation of *The Seafarer*', in *The Early Cultures of North-West Europe (H. M. Chadwick Memorial Studies)*, eds. Sir Cyril Fox and Bruce Dickens (Cambridge, 1950), pp. 268, 271–72; repr. *Essential Articles*, pp. 442–57.

the poem perhaps also captures his understanding of that which he is a figure and of that which the figure promises. It has been ingeniously suggested that *fæstnung* in the last line is a concrete noun and thus reverses the image of the ruin.[20] But the line would provide an even more effective close if the ideas of *frofor* and *fæstnung* are related and are taken to establish a relationship between what the Wanderer originally sought on earth, a lord who would comfort (*frefran*) him and the security of life within the hall, and what he now looks for in heaven.

The Wanderer is an elusive and delicate poem: any interpretation must be based on hints and oblique implications and therefore must be tentative. *The Seafarer* by contrast is a strong and boldly designed poem and therefore well able to withstand firm critical investigation. The problems of interpreting it are in the main similar to those of *The Wanderer*, though the solutions are sometimes different. To begin with there is the issue of the number of speakers. In this respect *The Seafarer* has a paradoxical relationship to *The Wanderer*. In the latter, the poet by his *swa cwæþ* construction seems to indicate a change of speaker though there is no sharp difference in tone to suggest that the speaker must have changed, whereas in *The Seafarer* the attitude to seafaring seems to change so abruptly and inexplicably at line 33a that it has seemed necessary to assume a change of speaker although the poet does not indicate one. The failure of the poet to interpose a narrative aside to mark the opening of a new speech must be taken seriously, for the presence of such authorial interjections in *The Wanderer* shows that they were not considered unsuited to the genre (as they presumably were to the more impressionistic emotional style of the *Advent Lyrics*).[21] The significance of this omission is confirmed by the style of the opening line of the poem, *Mæg ic be me sylfum soðgied wrecan* [I can recite a true lay concerning myself]. This is surely the introduction to the whole poem; if the *soðgied* ends at line 33a, what comes after that? There is thus good justification for supposing that there is no break at line 33a and indeed that, as others have pointed out, there is a strong dramatic sweep which carries the reader forward to the climax in lines 64–66.

If there is no change of speaker at line 33a, one must assume that

[20] Cf. S. I. Tucker, 'Return to *The Wanderer*', *Essays in Criticism*, 8 (1958), 229–37 and Dunning and Bliss, ed. cit. p. 50.

[21] For the dialogue between Joseph and Mary in which no change of speaker is indicated see R. Burlin, *The Old English Advent, A Typological Commentary* (New Haven and London, 1968), pp. 112–14.

the poet intended the subsequent lines to come as a surprise: the man made wretched by seafaring now chooses to go to sea. But clearly this kind of literary surprise cannot be random: close attention to the text must show it to be justified. The justification for the surprise appears to be that whilst the speaker's attitude to the sea startlingly changes in midline, his attitude to the land remains constant throughout. There are all together four passages (two before line 33a and two after) in which it becomes increasingly plain that life on land is to be despised. The first is in lines 12–13 where the Seafarer complains that the man *þe him on foldan fægrost limpeð* [to whom it befalls in the fairest manner on land] does not understand his sufferings on the sea. This statement is at most mutedly pejorative; but it would seem that happiness brings blindness or indifference to the miseries of others, and the poet's method here is markedly different from that of the author of *The Wanderer*, who constantly introduces the thought of other people who will share and understand the Wanderer's desolation.

The next occurrence of the theme is at lines 27–29 where the Seafarer again imagines the prosperous and carefree man, *wlonc ond wingal*, living *in burgum*, who again will not understand the sufferings of the man who journeys by sea. Despite the apparently neutral use of the collocation *wlonc ond wingal* in *The Ruin* (line 34), it is difficult to accept that this phrase is free of pejorative connotations in the present text.[22] Whether terms such as *wlonc* [proud] or *wingal* ['drunken' or at best 'having abundantly drunk'] are pejorative will depend upon the moral seriousness of the poem in which they occur. But nobody doubts that *The Seafarer* is serious to the point of overt homiletic didacticism, and even in a more obliquely moral work such as *Beowulf*, one could not imagine that even in the triumphal festivities at Heorot Beowulf could be described in these terms. The same idea in *The Seafarer* is repeated in lines 55–56: here it is the *sefteadig secg* who cannot understand the miseries of the exile. *Sefteadig* is an

[22] The evidence about *wlonc* is uncertain: both in Old English secular and religious poetry it may be used of either hero or villain; it is worth noting, however, that in *The Wanderer* (line 80) it seems to suggest simultaneously the value and ultimate uselessness of pride, whilst in *Beowulf* the related noun *wlenco* is invariably used in a depreciatory sense. The pejorative associations of *wingal* are much clearer. If we take together the seven occurrences of *wingal* and the analogous formation *medugal* (excluding *wingal* in *The Seafarer*), the non-pejorative use in *The Ruin* is unique. Particularly notable is the application in *Daniel* of *wingal* to Nebuchadnezzar (line 116) and *medugal* to Belshazzar at his feast (line 702), and of the phrase *modig ond medugal* (a collocation similar to *wlonc ond wingal*) to Holofernes in *Judith* (line 26).

emendation and a nonce word, but the grounds for accepting it in the text are good,[23] whilst the implications of the first element *seft-* are plain: one who is *sefteadig* enjoys a life that is soft or indolent.

The fourth of these passages is the climax: the Seafarer no longer hints that a contented life in the world is worthless but states it explicitly and powerfully:

forþon me hatran sind
Dryhtnes dreamas þonne þis deade lif
læne on londe.
(64b–66a)

It is from this dead life, transient on land, that the Seafarer wishes to escape by embarking on his sea-voyage. The force of the paradoxical collocation *deade lif* has of course often been noticed; but the phrase *laene on londe* is equally pregnant. In other contexts it could of course mean 'transitory in this world' (as opposed to the next), but in this context it surely means 'on land' (as opposed to on sea). The poet seems in fact to have given an individual twist to the traditional images of man as an exile (as used in *The Wanderer*) and of life as a sea-voyage.[24] According to his stylised figurative pattern the man who lives a life on land is always in a state of security and contentment: he is therefore mindless of the Christian image of man as an exile; indeed the poet's insistence on this point suggests that there is a resolute rejection of it. The sea, however, is always a place of isolation and hardship: the man therefore who chooses to be literally what in Christian terms he is figuratively must forsake the land and live upon the sea.

It will be clear from this argument that there are major differences in tone and situation between *The Wanderer* and *Seafarer*. The latter is a much harsher and more didactic poem. Though the life of seafaring exile is full of hardship, what alternatives there are may not fittingly be grieved for, nor have they accidentally been lost: they have been deliberately rejected and rejected with contempt. A consequence of this is that when the poet passes in the second half of the poem to his generalised instances of transience, which are borrowed like those in *The Wanderer* from Christian homiletic sources, he does not rid

[23] See *The Seafarer*, ed. I. L. Gordon (London, 1960), note to line 56. The alternative emendation to *esteadig* would yield a less obviously pejorative sense.

[24] For evidence of the currency of the latter image see Smithers, p. 150, where he cites texts noted by earlier scholars and adds further instances. To these examples should be added *Christ*, lines 850–66 (already noted by Schücking).

them of their original meaning.[25] The second half of *The Seafarer* is therefore not only of sermon origin but grimly didactic in tone. Fittingly, therefore, the conclusion of *The Seafarer* from line 117 onwards is openly homiletic. There has been a single hint of this in *The Wanderer* in the use of the word *us*, but this preacher's use of *we* is hammered home at the end of *The Seafarer*, occurring six times in eight lines, whilst its first use in conjunction with *Uton* is pure sermon style. Whilst it would be possible to assume that the author spoke in his own voice from line 117 onwards (the arguments against a change of speaker at line 33a would not apply here), it is not necessary to do so. As in *The Wanderer* there is the same possibility of the author speaking partly with the voice of the Seafarer or the Seafarer speaking partly with the voice of the author. The Seafarer's personal voice is heard for the last time in lines 66–67: *Ic gelyfe no / þæt him eorðwelan ece stondað* [I do not believe that earthly prosperity will last forever, 66b–67]. There follow the generalisations about the decay of the world and the inevitability of old age, death, and God's judgment. All these are entirely fitting to the character of the Seafarer, but they could also prepare the way for the Seafarer at the close of the poem to stand aside a little from his dramatic role and to give to the audience a Christian exhortation that takes its force from all that has preceded it.

This interpretation of *The Seafarer* leaves open the significance of the sea-voyage except insofar as it is the opposite of life on land, in which a man is spiritually dead and subject to transience. It could, for instance, be the life of the voluntary exile, as Professor Whitelock suggested, but it is unlikely to be exclusively so, for a voluntary exile travels over both land and sea and the poet's potent but artificial distinction between them would become obliterated. Since it is also virtually certain that the voyage itself is metaphorical, it could equally take place in a monastery or hermit's cell. Nevertheless the untempered emphasis upon the hardship of the seafaring life seems slightly inapposite if the voyage is a symbol for the religious life. That a religious lives 'where no storms come' may be a moving but over-sentimental idea, but that he lives in an especially storm-tossed place (*Stormas þær stanclifu beotan* [there storms beat on rocky cliffs, 23a]) is slightly disconcerting. Alternatively the voyaging could, as Professor Smithers and others have argued, represent death. This interpretation makes good sense of the fluctuations in mood that recur between lines 26–65. The Seafarer both expresses a religious

[25] Professor Smithers, p. 142, provides a convenient list of these sermon topics.

longing akin to St. Paul's declaration, 'I desire to die and be with Christ' and yet acknowledges the natural human fear of death, *Timor mortis conturbat me* [fear of death disturbs me]. Such a reading is also supported by the general impression that the poem is much concerned with death and that its meaning is summed up on the gnomic line, *Dol biþ se þe him his Dryhten ne ondrædeþ: cymeð him se deað unþinged* [foolish is he who dares not fear his Lord: death comes to him unexpected, 106]. It remains certain, however, that *The Seafarer* is not a carefully worked out allegorical poem and that whilst figurative meanings are distinct in outline, they are opaque in detail. Indeed some of the power of the poem resides in its resistance to consistent exposition. It is therefore possible that the poet intended no single meaning for the sea-voyage except insofar as it is anything that is the opposite of life on land. The understanding hearer would provide a referend in terms of his own experience.

An analysis on *The Wanderer* and *Seafarer* as poems belonging to the genre of *planctus* may serve not only as a method of examining each poem individually but also as a means of comparing the two. There is a tendency to consider the poems as companion pieces, bearing perhaps the same relationship to each other as *L'Allegro* and *Il Penseroso*. As *planctus*, however, they are markedly distinct. *The Wanderer* is a genuine *planctus*. Ignoring the modern title we may say that the speaker is a typical figure, that of an exile, and that what he laments is equally clear: in the past the loss of his lord and the miseries of homelessness, and in the present the ever-spreading desolation around him. As is not uncommon in Christian *planctus* (e.g. 'An Old Man's Prayer' from *The Harley Lyrics*),[26] the speaker experiences some reconciliation to his loss without the sense of loss becoming attenuated. By contrast *The Seafarer* is a poem that exploits the genre of *planctus*. Whilst the poem may imply, to begin with, that the speaker is again the typical figure of exile, it gradually becomes clear that he is exemplary rather than typical, a subordinate feature of *planctus* thus becoming dominating and exclusive. Furthermore, whilst there is much in the work that could find a place within a *planctus* (even those passages that have most affinity with the theme of *contemptus mundi*), such laments are given a different tone by the fact that the speaker has deliberately chosen a life of earthly deprivation. There is thus no clear way of characterising the speaker

[26] *Religious Lyrics of the XIVth Century*, ed. Carleton Brown, rev. G. V. Smithers (Oxford, 1952), pp. 3–7.

and no clear sense of loss.

Of course no value judgments are implied either in the general classification of these poems as *planctus* nor in the distinction that is drawn in these terms between *The Wanderer* and *The Seafarer*. The value of the classification lies in its hindrance to the asking of unuseful questions. For a remarkable characteristic of the poems is that, though differing critical interpretations are imposed upon them, they remain unchanged. Later poetry may be ironic, oblique, and ambiguous or it may be densely metaphorical, and so the text may seem to reflect varying and indeed sometimes self-contradictory meanings. But this is not so with *The Wanderer* and *The Seafarer*. Whoever the speaker, whatever the figurative meaning, they remain grave, sombre formal laments, powerful poems, and in contrast to their themes, immutable.

XII

THE IDEAL OF MEN DYING WITH THEIR LORD IN THE *GERMANIA* AND IN *THE BATTLE OF MALDON*

THERE is a well-known resemblance between the heroic behaviour described in the *Germania* and in *The Battle of Maldon*: in his account of the material code of honour of the Germanic tribes Tacitus says, 'Iam vero infame in omnem vitam ac probrosum superstitem principi suo ex acie recessisse',[1] whilst in *Maldon* the poet has the followers of Byrhtnoth affirm one after the other that it would be a disgrace to leave the battlefield now that their lord lies dead. For a long time it was assumed that this resemblance reflected historical fact, ties of loyalty and heroic aspirations having remained unchanged over 900 years. A more plausible modification of this view has been that, whilst the society of the tribes in first-century Germany had to be firmly distinguished from that of the Anglo-Saxons in tenth-century England, Old English poetry archaically preserved some of the ideals of conduct that characterized a much earlier form of society.[2] But more recently still the harking back to Tacitus by students of Anglo-Saxon history and literature has been shown to be fallacious, originating in the ethnic romanticism of German scholars in the late nineteenth century.[3] Nevertheless the long-standing view that there is a particular resemblance between the *Germania* and *The Battle of Maldon* cannot be lightly abandoned. Indeed the more one becomes aware that there is no evidence that the obligation of a retainer to die with his lord was a pervasive ideal in Germanic society which could well have lived on into tenth-century English life or literature, the more striking and curious the resemblance becomes. My aims in the present article are first to demonstrate the apparently total lack of historical or literary-historical continuity between the *Germania* and

[1] *De Origine et Situ Germanorum*, ed. J. G. C. Anderson (Oxford, 1938), c. XIV. 'Moreover to survive the leader and retreat from the battlefield is a lifelong disgrace and infamy.'

[2] This view is, for instance, expressed in passing by Frederick Whitehead, '*Ofermod* et *Desmesure*', *CCM* 3 (1960), 115–17.

[3] See E. G. Stanley, 'The Search for Anglo-Saxon Paganism', *N&Q* 210 (1965), 9–17; repr. in his *The Search for Anglo-Saxon Paganism* (Cambridge and Totowa, N.J., 1975).

Maldon and second, nevertheless, to seek an explanation for a resemblance which is too remarkable to be dismissed as pure chance.

Though it is customary for modern Anglo-Saxon scholars to refer to Tacitus for evidence of the heroic duty of a warrior to die with his lord, he was not the first classical historian to record this custom.[4] A hundred to a hundred and fifty years earlier than the composition of the *Germania* in A.D. 98, Caesar had noted it as a custom amongst the band of *soldurii* who were in the service of the Aquitanian leader. Of them, he says, 'neque adhuc hominum memoria repertus est quisquam, qui eo interfecto, cuius se amicitiae devovisset, mori recusaret'.[5] At about the same time Sallust in his *Historiae* had made the same observation about the Celts in Spain, though the latter reference has to be reconstructed from Plutarch's *Life of Sertorius* and Servius's commentary upon the *Georgics*.[6] In both these works the custom, though admired as brave, was primarily seen as part of the fanatical and alien conduct of the barbarians and it is given a sacrificial colouring, the followers' refusal to outlive their lord being in part or in whole an act of self-immolation.

Though both Caesar and Sallust describe this custom, they nevertheless do not provide in context an actual example of such determination to die a suicidal death but only an example of less spectacular and more practical acts of loyalty: in Caesar the *soldurii* give loyal support to their leader Adiatunnus in his attempt to break through the Roman siege, while in Sallust the followers of Sertorius rescue him from his enemies and carrying him in turn upon their shoulders take him to a place of safety. Despite this peculiarity, however, there seems no reason to doubt that Caesar and Sallust aimed to make a true historical record in their respective works. Tacitus's aim in the *Germania*, on the other hand, is ambiguous. In terms of literary genre this is a hybrid work, part ethnographical treatise, part primitive Utopia. One strain in it contrasts the civilized but degenerate Romans with the noble savages of Germany, the men brave and loyal to the point of dying with their chief, the women free

[4] Most of the references that follow (both to classical and Germanic authors) have been derived from Axel Olrik, *The Heroic Legends of Denmark*, trans. Lee M. Hollander (New York, 1919), pp. 158–60; cf. also Rudolf Much, *Die 'Germania' des Tacitus*, 3rd ed. (Heidelberg, 1967), pp. 227–30.

[5] *De Bello Gallico* (III.22), ed. St George Stock (Oxford, 1898) II, 115–16; 'nor within human memory has anybody been found who has refused to die when he to whom he was bound by a vow of friendship had been killed'.

[6] For the references to Plutarch and Servius, see below, p. 177, nn. 9 and 11. Plutarch's use of the *Historiae* for his *Life of Sertorius* is discussed by Ronald Syme, *Sallust* (Cambridge, 1964), pp. 178–9 and 203–5.

of vanity and irreproachably chaste, and all indifferent to gold and silver. Since, according to modern scholars, Tacitus did not always seek historical precision in the long stretches of non-Utopian narrative, it is the less likely that he did so in the Utopian parts. Therefore, whilst it is quite possible that Tacitus learnt of the shame attached to members of a *comitatus* who did not seek death with their lord from Roman soldiers who had returned from the frontier, it is also possible that in designing his primitive Golden Age he borrowed this heroic ideal from Caesar and Sallust and, purging it a little of fanatical connotations, transferred it from the peoples of Spain and south-west Gaul to those of Germany.[7]

In the following centuries a number of writers referred to the self-sacrificial deaths of the Spaniards, all undoubtedly deriving their information from Sallust.[8] Plutarch, as by inference Sallust, mentions the custom in order to contribute to his eulogistic account of the Roman general Sertorius, who was so esteemed by the Spaniards that they offered him the supreme act of loyalty which they normally reserved for leaders of their own race.[9] Valerius Maximus in his characterization of the Germanic peoples makes a brief aside about the Spaniards of whom he says, 'Celtiberi etiam nefas esse ducebant proelio superesse, cum is occidisset, pro cuius salute spiritum deuouerant.'[10] Finally Servius was reminded of Sallust's observation on the Spaniards when commenting upon Vergil's description of the loyal devotion of the bees, saying of the phrase *pulchram mortem* [a beautiful death] (*Georgics* iv.218), 'gloriosam, quippe quae pro rege suscipitur. Traxit autem hoc de Celtiberorum more, qui, ut in Sallustio legimus, se regibus devovent et post eos vitam refutant.'[11] None of these authors has any claim to be considered an independent witness to barbarian custom.

Two Byzantine historians must also be mentioned. One is

[7] Tacitus's sources for the *Germania* cannot be fully identified, though it is generally agreed that they were literary; cf. Ronald Syme, *Tacitus* (Oxford, 1958) I, 127–8.

[8] For a useful listing of the evidence for the currency of the *Historiae* in the first five centuries, see Ezio Bolaffi, *Sallustio e la sua Fortuna nei Secoli* (Rome, 1949).

[9] 'Life of Sertorius', *Plutarch's Lives*, ed. Bernadotte Perrin, Loeb Classical Lib., VIII (1919), 38.

[10] *Factorum et Dictorum Memorabilium Libri Novem*, ed. K. Kempf (Leipzig, 1888), p. 80. 'The Spaniards too held it to be a disgrace to survive in the battle when he, to whose welfare they had vowed themselves, had been killed.'

[11] *Servii Grammatici qui feruntur in Vergilii Carmina Commentarii*, ed. G. Thilo and H. Hagen, III.1 (Leipzig, 1887), 336; 'glorious because it is undergone for the king. He [Vergil] transferred this from the custom of the Spaniards, who, as we read in Sallust, vow themselves to their kings and refuse to survive them.'

Ammianus Marcellinus, who, though a Greek of Antioch, wrote his *Historiae* in Latin. In his narrative of the wars in Gaul in the fourth century he says of the followers of Chonodomaric that when he surrendered to the Romans they too surrendered, 'flagitium arbitrati post regem uiuere uel pro rege non mori si ita tulerit casus'.[12] The actual context, in which others who had sought to escape were all killed by the Romans, does not require the imputation of so noble a motive. Therefore, whilst Ammianus may have acquired independent historical evidence of this custom amongst the Gauls, the probability that he was borrowing from one of the authoritative Roman historians is high (he certainly knew the works of Sallust and Tacitus).

The second historian is Agathias who in the sixth century wrote a continuation of Procopius's *History of the Goths*. The relevant passage describes the death of Fulcaris and his followers and it is exceptionally interesting in that it is the only surviving instance where it is possible to infer the custom from the deed (in all other examples either the custom does not match the deed or the custom is described without illustrative action). Agathias is primarily interested here in the grave but foolish impetuosity of Fulcaris (leader of the Eruli in the Byzantine army), who preferred to dash into battle alone in front of his men rather than to draw up a prudent and strategic plan of attack: Fulcaris in fact appears to be the typical barbarian chieftain as seen through Roman and Byzantine eyes. The implications of Agathias's brief description of the followers of Fulcaris, who, after their leader has been killed, die *τύχον μὲν ἐθέλοντες, τύχον δὲ καὶ ὑπὸ τῶν πολεμίων εἰργόμενοι*, are not quite clear but are very intriguing.[13] It could mean no more than that in a situation where flight was impossible some fought so bravely that they seemed to welcome death whilst others were killed as they tried to escape; alternatively, however, it may show the application to a particular event of Caesar's account of the deaths of the *soldurii*, some of whom were, like their leader, violently killed, whilst others killed themselves. In support of the latter interpretation it may be noted that Caesar's description of the Aquitanian custom had been embodied in the *Historiae* of Nicholas of Damascus and had thus become part of the eastern historical

[12] Ammien Marcellin, *Historiae* (I.xiv–xvi), ed. and trans. E. Galletier and J. Fontaine (Paris, 1968), pp. 186–7; 'having judged it a disgrace to live after the death of their king or not to die for him if the opportunity occurred'.

[13] Agathias, *Historiarum Libri Quinque*, ed. Rudolf Keydell (Berlin, 1967), pp. 28–9; 'some willingly, some cut down by the enemy'.

tradition.[14] The sources of Agathias's knowledge of the Byzantine campaigns in Italy are unknown; but it is clear that his *History* was designed as a literary and moral work, and therefore its interpretation of event and motive is more likely to reflect deliberate patterning than an attempt to understand them realistically.[15]

It is clear from a study of these references that Roman historians understood this act of loyalty in different ways. For Caesar and Sallust it had a heathen religious colouring: both use of it the verb *devovere* ('to dedicate to a god'), whilst Plutarch refers to it by the noun *κατάσπεισις* ('libation'). In the *Germania*, however, the custom seems free of heathen connotations and indeed Tacitus has taken some care to make sense of it within the forms of society that he describes. The men who thus scorn to outlive their lord are members of a raiding band. Their wealth derives from plunder: though they own land it is cultivated unproductively and agricultural pursuits are regarded as women's work. The whole life of the *comitatus* lies in successful warfare and in the luxurious bouts of feasting that punctuate it. It would follow that, if such a band depended upon the coverage and initiative of their leader and in some battle he was killed and they were put to fight, the only way of life that they valued would be lost. In these circumstances the resolve of the men to die with their lord would make some sense in purely practical terms.

It is of course out of the question that the poet and audience of *The Battle of Maldon* saw in the heroic deaths of Byrhtnoth's retainers the relics of pagan suicide. But it is equally impossible that the retainers' determination to die could have fitted the social context as it did in the *Germania*, for at least from the eighth century onwards the organization of society in England must have been entirely different. Contrary to the impression that is given by some Old English poems it is clear that a thegn's life did not reduce itself to fighting, feasting and receiving treasure from his lord's hands. There is a famous passage in Bede's *Letter to Egbert* in which he reproves the foolishness of kings who so dispossessed themselves of their land that they had none to confer upon their young fighting men, who therefore either went overseas (and were thus lost to the service of their native land) or remained at court leading a life of idleness and sexual promiscuity.[16]

[14] F. Jacoby, *Die Fragmente der griechischen Historiker* IIA (Berlin, 1926), no. 80, p. 379.

[15] Cf. Averil Cameron, *Agathias* (Oxford, 1970), pp. 30–56.

[16] 'Epistola Bede ad Ecgbertum Episcopum', *Venerabilis Baedae Opera Historica*, ed. Charles Plummer (Oxford, 1896) I, 415.

The unmistakable implication of this is that, although the sons of noble families lived at the king's court in their youth, they expected to be given land once they were of age. On this land they would live with their families and from it they would depart to fight for the king or perhaps to attend at court. There is another famous passage dealing with the same issue in Asser's *Life of King Alfred*: according to this work Alfred had organized his court in such a way that in every three-month period a man lived two months at home and one at court.[17] This was obviously a thoughtful and systematic way of solving the problem of conflicting obligations.

It is interesting to note that in the tenth-century continental *Waltharius* these conflicting obligations are made precise and explicit. Near the beginning of this work the poet describes how Attila seeks to tie Walther to him in such a way that he will not return to his native country which he had left as a child to become a hostage at Attila's court: the method that he uses is that of urging Walther to marry and offering to confer large estates upon him. Walther, who secretly intends to return to his own land, has to find convincing reasons for rejecting Attila's offer without arousing suspicion:

> Si nuptam accipiam domini praecepta secundum,
> Vinciar inprimis curis et amore puellae
> Atque a servitio regis plerumque retardor,
> Aedificare domos cultumque intendere ruris
> Cogor, ...
> Nil tam dulce mihi, quam semper inesse fideli
> Obsequio domini; quare, precor, absque iugali
> Me vinclo permitte meam iam ducere vitam![18]

In effect Walther says that, if he marries, the mingled pleasures and cares of being both husband and landlord will distract him from single-minded service to his king and that to him such service is sweeter. It may be that in this passage we can already hear an anticipation of the conflicts of loyalty endured by Yvein or of the style of argument used in may medieval dissuasions against marriage. But,

[17] *Asser's Life of King Alfred*, ed. W. H. Stevenson (Oxford, 1904; repr. 1959 with contr. by Dorothy Whitelock), p. 87; cf. p. 337, n.

[18] *Waltharius* (lines 150–4 ad 158–60), ed. Karl Strecker (Berlin, 1947), pp. 30–2. 'If I take a wife according to the command of my lord, I shall first of all be tied down by responsibilities and the love of my young wife and I shall be greatly hindered in the service of my king: I shall be compelled to build a house and look after the cultivation of the land ... To me there is nothing so sweet as to be always faithfully occupied in the service of my lord: wherefore I beg you, allow me to lead my life unfettered by marriage!'

regardless of this, these lines make plain the absolute incompatability between the ideals of Tacitus's *comitatus* and those of a stable Christian society.

It follows from this kind of evidence that, if *The Battle of Maldon* gives the impression that Byrhtnoth and his *heorðwerod* [household retainers] lived the life of a Germanic chieftain and his *comitatus*, this is poetic fiction and not historical reality. It is known, furthermore, that some of the men who fought with Byrhtnoth were of such high birth that they owned bookland in various parts of the country; these may also have held folkland from Byrhtnoth, as would certainly have done those thegns who did not have inherited land. It is inconceivable that such a company of noblemen in reality had their lives materially and emotionally focussed upon Byrhtnoth: this is a moving invention of the poet's. *Maldon* in fact draws attention to the interesting phenomenon that it is late rather than early texts that generally display the clearest descriptions of a leader with his *comitatus*. The fourteenth-century *Hrólfs saga kraka* provides a very good illustration and, if it were not for the Germanic associations, so would the various versions of Arthur and his knights.

Though *Beowulf* is earlier than these examples, it strikingly shows the fictional use of a *comitatus* society and the value of this fiction to the poet. In the first half of *Beowulf* Hrothgar seems to live at Heorot with a *comitatus*. His followers appear to live entirely at court, they are without land or family and they aspire not to land but to treasure. That the poet was here displaying a heroic way of life which did not mirror the society of his times can be inferred from Bede's *Letter to Egbert*. But more interestingly it can also be inferred from the poem itself, for in the second half Beowulf, when king, does not have a *comitatus*. This is plain when he sets out to fight the dragon with a band of eleven men, who, according to Wiglaf, were chosen from the *here*. The latter is an unemotive word and must surely refer to the whole body of fighting men who were in the service of Beowulf rather than to an inner ring of close companions.[19] Furthermore, when

[19] The Old English equivalent to the Latin *comitatus* is usually taken to be *gesiþas*. It may be worth noting that Old English does not appear to have a collective noun regularly used in Tacitus's sense of *comitatus*. A probable equivalent, *gesiþ(þ)*, is recorded at most three times, twice in *Genesis (A)* (2403a and 2808a), where it has the general sense of company, and probably once in *Deor* (3a), where the nuances are unclear. Compounds, of which the second element is *werod* and the first a word for some part of the hall, seem to come nearest to the sense of *comitatus*, i.e. *fletwerod* (*Beowulf* 476b) and *heorðwerod* (*Maldon* 24a). *Heorðwerod*, however, occurs three times in *Genesis (A)* (1605a, 2039b and 2076a), where its meaning is variable.

Wiglaf later proclaims to them the penalty for their cowardice, it is made plain that they will not lose solely the heroic rewards *sincþego ond swyrdgifu* [receiving of treasure and gift of sword], but also their homes and lands, *londriht*, and will thus become exiles with their families.[20] It is characteristic of the method of the *Beowulf* poet that the external world is constructed to reflect his imaginative but temporary purposes. There is a true *comitatus* in Heorot because the ravaging of Grendel will be the more terrible if its object is an isolated, self-contained community; but the corresponding retainers in the second half have lands to lose and families to be dispossessed so that the size of the penalty may fully reflect the magnitude of the crime.

This poetic willingness to depict an unrealistic type of society, anachronistic in its time but reflecting primitive forms, might suggest that the related ideal of a retainer dying with his lord might be preserved in literature long after it had in historical terms become senseless. There is, however, no evidence for this view and some quite strong evidence against it. Some of the most important evidence against this theory is to be found in *Beowulf* itself, and firstly in the Finn episode. Obscure though the tenor of this narrative may be, it is clear that after Hnæf's death his followers make peace with their lord's slayer 'þa him swa geþearfod wæs' [as they were thus forced by necessity]. But they are obviously only so compelled in the sense that the alternative of vainly fighting until all are killed is not an issue for them. The moral implications of the Finn episode are plainly that what is required of a lord's retainer after his death is not that he should die with him as an end in itself but that he should effectively avenge his lord.

In the Finn episode the heroic obligation of a man dying with his lord is flagrantly absent: instead there is the ideal of effective vengeance. That this was the code of loyalty understood by the *Beowulf* poet is strikingly confirmed by the conduct of Beowulf himself. When Hygelac had been killed in the raid against the Franks Beowulf might have said of him as Ælfwine said of Byrhtnoth, 'He waes ægðer min mæg and min hlaford' [He was both my kinsman and my lord]. Nevertheless he returns to the Geatish court where nobody reproaches him that he has returned lordless from the battlefield: on

[20] For comment on this passage (2884–91) and others of interest from various other works see Eric John, *Land Tenure in Early England* (Leicester, 1960), pp. 54–6. In the lines from *Beowulf* the meaning of *londriht* is probably anticipated by that of *eðelwyn* and *lufen* (for the latter, see Johannes Hoops, *Kommentar zum Beowulf* (Heidelberg, 1932), p. 301).

the contrary the queen instantly offers him the throne. It might perhaps be thought that the poet was here contrained by the problem of harmonizing his sources, that perhaps he even tried to divert attention from the moral awkwardness of Beowulf's return by stressing the fabulous feat of Beowulf swimming back whilst carrying thirty suits of armour. But this is an unacceptable explanation, since the poet so evidently intends a contrast between Beowulf's loyalty to Hygelac and the various types of disloyalty hinted at or set out in the so-called digressions. It is inconceivable that Beowulf should be guilty of what poet and audience would agree to be a supreme failure in loyalty and heroism. Furthermore it is clear that the poet was not embarrassed by the narrative necessity of bringing Beowulf back from the raid against the Franks, for he returns to this theme in the sober monologue of reminiscence which Beowulf speaks before the dragon fight. In this Beowulf (who had first been introduced in the poem as *Higelaces þegn*, 194b) recalls the reciprocal relationship that had existed between Hygelac and himself. Hygelac gave him land and he gave Hygelac the treasures that he had won, he always fought before him in battle and, when Hygelac was killed, he himself killed Dæghrefn who had come to despoil the body (and who was therefore by implication the killer). In this speech the poet surely sets out the ideal standards of behaviour of the perfect retainer. What the poet had said of Beowulf earlier stands uncontradicted and indeed reaffirmed: 'Hygelace wæs / niða heardum nefa swyðe hold' [the nephew, fierce in conflicts, was very loyal to Hygelac] (2169b–70).

The evidence of *Beowulf* is obliquely confirmed by the narrative of Cynewulf and Cyneheard in the *Anglo-Saxon Chronicle*, though it is a story that has to be analysed with care, as political stratagems and heroic ideals are entangled within it. Some of the political calculations are clear: Cyneheard is seeking to recover the West Saxon throne from which his brother had been deposed by the decision of the witan: his plan, only partially successful, was to kill the king and bribe his thegns into serving him; to the manifestly outnumbered thegns who were actually with the king he makes a fairly small offer, 'feoh ond feorh' [money and life], whilst the more formidable company of the king's men he tries to entice with the very substantial promise that they shall have 'hiera agenne dom feos ond londes' [money and land on their own judgement], providing that they will acknowledge him as king (a condition that must have applied equally to the first offer). The heroic values are also clear: to a thegn death is preferable to ignobly entering the service of the murderer of his lord. But the point at which political and heroic motives mingle is crucial to the patterning of the story. For what the members of Cynewulf's bodyguard courageously reject is not a strategic withdrawal from the fight coupled with the hope of fighting another day (as, by implication, is the case in *Maldon*[21]) but an agreement to serve as king the man who has just killed their lord. It is probably this point that also accounts for the difference of behaviour in the followers of Hnæf and the followers of Cynewulf. When Hnæf's men enter the service of Finn it is a temporary arrangement designed to provide for them during the winter and it confers no political advantage on Finn; if Cynewulf's men had acted similarly, their new allegiance would have been permanent and they would have enabled Cyneheard to secure the throne.

This political purpose, however heroically achieved, is very important and divides this story sharply from both the *Germania* and *The Battle of Maldon*. Any king would wish to have followers such as Cynewulf had: without such loyalty a king would be extremely vulnerable to assassination by a contender to the throne. But no king would wish his ealdormen to have followers such as Byrhtnoth had, for, if whenever an ealdorman was killed all his best and bravest men were also morally compelled to die, the king's army would be intolerably weakened. This was surely not the way that Alfred drove the Danes out of his kingdom during the campaigns of 891–4. The ideals of the *Germania* have of course been read into the story of Cynewulf and Cyneheard,[22] but if one approaches the *Chronicle* entry with an open mind one is struck more by the absence of this theme than by its presence. The first stage of the resistance of

[21] It has been suggested that the driving away of the horses was to prevent flight (cf. M. J. Swanton, '*The Battle of Maldon*: a Literary Caveat', JEGP 67 (1968), 448). If this were so, the gesture might be understood realistically (as Swanton takes it) or it might be reminiscent of famous stories such as that of how Hagen destroyed both boat and boatman which had carried the Burgundians across the Rhine or that of Stýr-Bjorn who burned his ship before his battle on the plains before Upsala. But the driving away of the horses in *Maldon* cannot be so interpreted, for the possibility of retreat on foot to the safety of the wood is made clear by desertion of the cowards: the decision to stay and fight is manifestly one that is freely taken.

[22] Earle and Plummer, for instance, in their note to the phrase *oþ hie alle lægon* (*Two of the Saxon Chronicles Parallel* (Oxford, 1892; repr. 1952 with contr. by Dorothy Whitelock), II, 46), argue that the disgrace of a member of a *comitatus* surviving his lord is implied by the excuses made for the sole survivor. These excuses, however, imply only the shame that attaches itself to cowardice and disloyalty but not the precise moral precept that should have been obeyed. The idea of a sole survivor, which occurs twice in this story (perhaps with different implications on the second occasion), may be a traditional heroic theme; there is, for instance, a sole survivor in one version of *The Gododdin* (trans. K. H. Jackson (Edinburgh, 1969), p. 4).

Cynewulf's men, in which all die save one, could readily have been interpreted as an illustration of a retainer's loving determination to die with his lord, but that does not seem to be the way that the chronicler understood it.

Whilst the only positive evidence for the view that a man could honourably retreat from the battlefield, though his lord lay dead upon it, comes from *Beowulf*, there is much confirmatory evidence for this from the total absence of stories about the semi-suicidal death of a leader's retainers in works that might have been expected to contain such stories had they been current. There are no stories of this kind in the work of Latin historians who may from time to time have drawn upon heroic lays or popular native traditions: in England, Bede (though attempts have been made to find them in his work[23]) and some post-Conquest historians such as William of Malmesbury have none; nor, on the continent, have Jordanes, Gregory of Tours and Paul the Deacon. It is an ideal uncharacteristic of Old Norse literature (though there is a notable exception here to which we shall return), it is notably absent from Welsh heroic poems such as the *Gododdin* and there are no echoes of it in early medieval Latin epics or in *chansons de geste*. It may be objected that such silence signified nothing, since it would be in early lost Germanic lays that such stories might be expected, not in works which are too learned or too late. This objection, however, does not make the evidence worthless, for to a greater or lesser extent all the works enumerated contain splendid instances of other heroic acts of loyalty. Indeed a consideration of them suggests that the ethical code of *The Battle of Maldon* should be sharply distinguished from that governing the behaviour of the ideal retainer which is regularly observable in other works.

The ties of loyalty that bound a retainer to his lord might require

[23] This generalization stands, altough it has not been uncommon for scholars to associate *Germania* XIV with some passages in Bede; cf. *Bede's Ecclesiastical History of the English People*, ed. Bertram Colgrave and R. A. B. Mynors (Oxford, 1969), p. 164, where, in the note to the story of Lilla, this and two other stories (one of them in the 'Life of Cuthbert') are connected with Tacitus. The stoy of Lilla itself is of a distinctive type and is discussed below, p. 74. That of Æthelhere (*ibid.* p. 290) has only superficial affinities: 'Inito ergo certamine fugati sunt et caesi pagani, duces regii XXX, qui ad auxilium uenerant, pene omnes interfecti; in quibus Aedilheri ... auctor ipse belli, perditis militibus siue auxiliis interemtus.' The emphasis in this passage seems to be on the number of enemy destroyed, but, more importantly, the Latin construction makes it plain that the *milites siue auxilia* were killed either before or at the same time as Æthelhere himself: they were not killed after him. The same comments apply to the description of the death of Ecgfrith and his followers in Bede's 'Life of Cuthbert' (*Two Lives of Saint Cuthbert*, ed. Bertram Colgrave (Cambridge, 1940), p. 248; the translation there given is misleading).

him to endure voluntarily all degrees of self-sacrifice, ranging from physical hardship to death. A retainer should share disaster as willingly as share prosperity with his lord; if, for instance, his lord is exiled he should go into exile with him. A retainer should protect his lord from attack even if he has to risk death or die in order to accomplish this successfully. If his lord is killed, the retainer should take vengeance on the killer, again if need be at the cost of his own life, and such vengeance is particularly compelling if the alternative is to give aid to the killer by entering his service. This code of behaviour is not always stated explicitly but, when not, is unmistakably implicit as the following examples will show.

There is a well-known statement about a retainer's obligation to go into exile with his lord in a letter from Aldhelm to the clergy of Bishop Wilfrid, written in about 650. In it he rebukes those clerics who failed to follow Wilfrid into exile, and the portion of it that William of Malmesbury preserved ends with the following comparison:

> Ecce! seculares divinæ scientiæ extorres, si devotum dominum, quem in prosperitate, dilexerunt, cessante felicitatis opulentia, et ingruente calamitatis adversitate, deseruerint, ac secura dulcis patriæ otia exulantis domini pressuræ prætulerint; nonne execrabilis cachinni ridiculo et gannaturæ strepitu ab omnibus ducuntur? Quid ergo de vobis dicetur, si pontificem, qui vos nutrivit et extulit, in exilio solum dimiseritis?[24]

The style is elaborate, the tone vehement and general meaning abundantly clear; but the precise meaning is slightly conjectural. As scholars have suggested, however, there is surely a resemblance between this passage and the one in *Beowulf* in which Wiglaf denounces the cowards who will become exiles:

syðđan æðelingas
feorran gefricgean fleam eowerne,
domleasan dæd. Deađ bið sella
eorla gehwylcum þonne edwitlif.

(2888b–91)[25]

[24] *De Gestis Pontificum Anglorum*, ed. N. E. S. A. Hamilton, Rolls Series (1870), p. 339. 'Consider this: if laymen, wholly ignorant of divine learning, desert a gracious lord, dear to them in his days of prosperity, when he is no longer fortunate and rich but overtaken by calamity and adversity—if these men prefer the security and ease of their native land to sharing the burdens of exile with their lord, will not everyone think them worthy of execration, mocking laughter, ridicule and loud jeering? What then will be said of you, if you abandon the priest who cherished and raised you to the loneliness of exile?'

[25] Cf. P. F. Jones, 'Aldhelm and the Comitatus-Ideal', *MLN* 47 (1932), 378. 'When princes far away hear of your flight, that inglorious deed. For every earl, death is better than a life of dishonour.'

It is a commonplace of Old English poetry that loyalty to a lord in the face of hardship or danger wins a good name whilst cowardly desertion brings ignominy. Religious poetry provides examples. The companions of Andrew, for instance, say of their future reputation if they abandon him, 'We bioð laðe on landa gehwam, / folcum fracoðe' [We are hated in every land, despised by nations],[26] and in the *Heliand* (which may be taken to represent the English tradition) Thomas speaks of the good name that the apostles will gain if they accompany Christ to Jerusalem:

ac uuita im uuonian mid,
thuoloian mid ûsson thiodne: that ist thegnes cust,
that hie mid if frâhon samad fasto gistande,
dōie mid im thar an duome. Duan ûs alla sô,
folgon im te thero ferdi: ni lâtan ûse fera uuið thiu
uuihtes uuirðig, neƀa uui an them uuerode mid im,
dôian mid ûson drohtine. Than lêƀot ûs thoh duom after,
guod uuord for gumon.[27]

Examples such as these suggest that what Aldhelm was holding up for comparison may not have been thegns gossiping about the cowardice of some of their comrades but the reactions of hearers to some seventh-century poem which described how an exiled lord was deserted by his followers. It is impossible to make even a guess at the subject of this lost poem since there are too many candidates for the rôle of exiled lord: the line of literary exils stretches from Theodoric to Beowulf's father. As it happens, extant Old English literature preserves no signal instance of a retainer either abandoning or accompanying his master when sent into exile.[28] But there is a splendid example of the latter in the *Historia Langobardorum* of Paul the Deacon. According to this story Grimwaldus asked the two faithful followers of the banished Perctarit whether they would prefer to stay at his court or join their lord; the first to be addressed replied

[26] *Andreas* 408–9a; *Andreas and the Fates of the Apostles*, ed. Kenneth R. Brooks (Oxford, 1961), p. 14.

[27] *Heliand* (3995b–4002a), ed. Otto Behaghel, 6th ed. (Halle, 1948), p. 139. 'Let us stand fast with him and endure with our lord. That is the chosen duty of a thegn that he should stand firm together with his lord and die there in the hour of decision. Let us act then and adhere to him on his road; let us value our life as nothing as long as we die with our lord in the following. Then our honour will live after us, a good reputation amongst men.'

[28] I do not include here the various references to exile in the *Ecclesiastical History* (cf. *English Historical Documents* c. *500–1042*, ed. Dorothy Whitelock (London, 1955), p. 55), since they are related neutrally, and, if interpreted in terms of historical realism, a man's decision to go into exile with his banished lord is as likely to reflect prudent self-interest as self-sacrificial loyalty.

'prius se vellet cum Perctarit mori, quam usquam alibi in summis deliciis vivere', and the second replies in the same vein.[29]

This story at an earlier stage also notably sets forth the duty of a retainer to save his lord's life even at the cost of his own. The life of Perctarit is saved by his two followers, who, knowing that Grimwaldus plans to kill him, help him to escape in disguise the night before. This stratagem is so devised that, once the escape of Perctarit is discovered, the complicity of his followers (and in particular of his *vestiarius* [valet]) will also be clear. After the escape Grimwaldus asks those around him how he should treat the *vestiarius* and all agree that he should be put to death. The magnanimous Grimwaldus, however, replies that the *vestiarius* foresaw that this was the penalty due to him, and 'dignus est homo iste bene habere, qui se pro fide sui domini morti tradere non recusavit'.[30] It is not, however, only on the continent or in semi-legendary stories that examples of such loyalty are to be found. Bede, for instance, tells of an attempt to assassinate King Edwin of Northumbria. The assassin, feigning to be a messenger, gains access to the king and then suddenly strikes at him with a poison-pointed sword. The king's thegn Lilla, being unarmed, uses his own body as a shield and is pierced through by the sword as he saves the king's life. Bede praises Lilla's loyalty and courage in one moving appellation, 'minister regi amicissimus'.[31]

For stories of how a man avenged the death of his lord at the cost of his own life it is necessary to turn once more to continental stories.[32] There are two well-known examples. One is again in the *Historia* of Paul the Deacon, where in a somewhat gothic story Paul tells of the vengeance that a dwarf took for the killing of his master Godebertus. On an Easter Sunday the dwarf lodges himself on the font in the baptistry of a church, and, as Garibaldus, the betrayer of his lord, passes through the church, he reaches down and cuts off his head. Inevitably the dwarf was himself killed, but, as Paul says, 'Godeperti sui domini iniuriam insigniter ultus est'.[33] The other notable act of

[29] *Pauli Historia Langobardorum*, ed. L. Bethmann and G. Waitz, Monumenta Germaniae Historica, Script. Rer. Lang., p. 145; 'that he would prefer to die with Perctarit than live anywhere else amongst the greatest delights'.

[30] *Ibid.*; 'this man deserves to fare well who out of loyalty to his lord did not refuse to deliver himself to death'.

[31] *Ecclesiastical History*, ed. Colgrave and Mynors, p. 164; 'a thegn who was the truest friend of his lord'.

[32] The much referred to story of Torhtmund, who avenged the death of Æthelred of Northumbria (cf. *EHD*, ed. Whitelock, pp. 250 and 794–5), is not included here, since Torhtmund survived, though he had to go into exile.

[33] *Historia Langobardorum*, ed. Bethmann and Waitz, p. 139; 'he outstandingly

vengeance is told by Saxo immediately after his paraphrase of the *Bjarkamál*. According to this story the death of Hrólfr Kraki is avenged by the slightly buffoonish retainer, Wiggo, who, in the course of pretending to take an oath of allegiance to Hiartuarus, drives the sword into him. Again inevitably he is killed and Saxo exclaims, 'Clarum ac semper memorabilem uirum, qui uoto fortiter expleto, mortem sponte complexus suo ministerio mensas tyranni sanguine maculauit.'[34] Slightly less well-known, but similar, is the account in the *Heimskringla* of the man who, when he sees the body of his lord, King Eystein, carried in before his slayer, King Magnus, attempts to kill Magnus and is in turn killed: of him the saga says, 'ok er þess mannz hreysti allmjǫk lofuð'.[35]

The stories cited above clearly provide the heroic-moral ambience of *The Battle of Maldon* without furnishing precise analogues. The duty closest to that of dying with one's lord is obviously that of sacrificing one's life with the purpose either of refusing to give needed support to the killer by entering his service or of avenging the dead lord. The first of these bears no relationship to *Maldon*, but the second requires further definition in order that it may be distinguished from the ideals of *Maldon*. It is important to notice that in known stories of this type the nature of due vengeance is closely defined and is in consequence usually (though not invariably) attainable. Vengeance does not consist of victory over a body of attackers, but rather of killing a single man who bears the chief moral responsibility for the death of the retainer's lord—the killer himself (Beowulf and Dæghrefn) or the betrayer (Godebert's dwarf and Garibaldus) or the leader responsible for the attack (Wiggo and Hiartuarus). In particular contrast to *Beowulf*, where the poet has contrived to emphasize Beowulf's successful act of vengeance by the sudden bestowal of a name upon the killer of Hygelac,[36] the poet of

avenged the wrong done to his lord Godebertus'.

[34] Saxo Grammaticus, *Gesta Danorum*, ed. Alfred Holder (Strassburg, 1886), p. 67. 'Famous and memorable man, who valiantly fulfilled his vow, and willingly embracing death in service [to his lord] stained with his blood the tables of the usurper.'

[35] *Heimskringla*, ed. Finnur Jónsson IV (Copenhagen, 1900–1), p. 490; 'and the courage of this man is much praised'.

[36] Whilst this suddenness is very apparent to the modern reader it would have been less so to an Anglo-Saxon audience who knew a lay of the fall of Hygelac. Scholars agree that the name Dæghrefn is Frankish (cf. *Beowulf*, ed. Fr. Klaeber (Boston, 1922), n. to 2501 ff.) and the *Beowulf* poet therefore probably derived it from a heroic lay; for the argument that the poet knew a lay of the death of Hygelac see Alistair Campbell, 'The Use in *Beowulf* of Earlier Heroic Verse', *England Before the Conquest: Studies in Primary Sources presented to Dorothy Whitelock*, ed. Peter Clemoes and Kathleen Hughes (Cambridge, 1971), p. 290.

Maldon has contrived his poem in such a way that this kind of limited, effective vegeance is impossible. Byrhtnoth's retainers cannot kill the Viking leader because no Viking leader is identified; though the actual dealer of the death-wound is killed, this is rendered insufficient by the fact that others, unnamed and unspecified in numbers, cut him down: 'Đa hine heowon hæðene scealcas' [Then heathen warriors hewed him] (181). The depiction of the Vikings as an anonymous horde may owe something to the contempt for the opponent characteristic of hagiography rather than of heroic poetry; but unless the poet was inept, it must be assumed that he intended the effect which he produced, namely that the Viking army was corporately to blame for Byrhtnoth's death and therefore that, exceptionally in this poem, defeat and effective vengeance were mutually exclusive. That this was indeed the poet's intention is made the more likely by the observation that he has blurred the historically distinct aims of vengeance and dying with one's lord. On the one hand some of the retainers, Byrhtwold, Ælfwine and Offa, talk either of their desire to die with their lord or of their refusal to leave the battlefield lordless. On the other hand others, including Leofsunu and Dunnere, talk of avenging Byrhtnoth. But the issues are confused; Leofsunu, for instance, though he delcares his intention of avenging his lord also says that he will not bear the reproach of leaving the battlefield lordless; Edward proclaims that he will not retreat now that his lord lies dead, but the poet speaks of him avenging his lord. Since in this poem the aim of vengeance is a hopeless one,[37] it merges readily with that of dying with one's lord. But if the latter aim was not part of the common heroic currency, then it may be suspected that the poet has skilfully sought to naturalize an alien and unfamiliar ideal by blending it with a familiar one.

Since all extant evidence shows that the agreement between the *Germania* and *Maldon* on the obligation of man to die with his lord cannot be explained in terms of a pervasive historical or literary tradition, the explanation to be sought is that the *Maldon* poet drew upon some single uncharacteristic work. In the first place it is to be asked whether this work was indeed the *Germania* itself. Manuscript and circumstantial evidence for this is not strong but is by no means so weak that the possibility has to be excluded. No complete early manuscript of the *Germania* survives, but in the fifteenth century

[37] In lines 207–8 a possibility of avenging Byrhtnoth and, by implication, of living is briefly stated but with insufficient force to disturb the dominant theme of inevitable death.

Italian humanists knew one which had been preserved in the monastery at Hersfeld, and this may in the ninth century have been in the library of the neighbouring and more famous monastery of Fulda (twin manuscripts of the *Historiae* of Ammianus Marcellinus come respectively from Hersfeld and Fulda).[38] In view of the Anglo-Saxon origins of both these monasteries (Fulda was founded by Boniface and Hersfeld by Lull, when he was bishop of Mainz), it is possible to hold with Levison that the *Germania* could have been one of the Italian texts that reached Germany by way of England, and, if this were so, a copy might have remained in England.[39] But there is no evidence of a knowledge of the *Germania* in England, unless *Maldon* itself were taken as evidence, whereas there are some indications of a north German monastic interest in the works of Tacitus, including the *Germania*, over a period of 200 to 250 years. In the ninth century the centre of this interest was at Fulda. Einhard, the biographer of Charlemagne, who was trained there, echoes the *Germania*; some decades later Rudolf of Fulda quoted copiously from it in his *Translatio sancti Alexandri*; and as late as about 1075 Adam of Bremen echoed the *Germania* in his *Gesta Hammaburgensis Ecclesiae Pontificum*.[40] The possibility therefore exists that in the tenth century an Anglo-Saxon, who might have been, but was not necessarily, the author of *Maldon*, travelled to Fulda and was there shown the manuscript of the *Germania*; since it fairly certainly also contained the *Agricola*, it might well have been thought of interest to him.

Nor is it impossible, even if it is difficult, to recover the imaginative process by which a poet might think it apt to attribute to Byrhtnoth's men an unfamiliar heroic ideal of which he had learned from a Latin historical treatise on Germanic tribes, if we consider *Maldon* an occasional poem in which the poet was called upon to commemorate men who had died defeated by the Vikings. The enumeration of the dead in the annals of the *Anglo-Saxon Chronicle* always indicates the measure of the Vikings' strength, even when the outcome of the battle has been a victory for the Anglo-Saxons. An ingenious poet might

[38] On the manuscripts of the *Germania*, see *The Germania of Tacitus*, ed. R. P. Robinson (Middletown, Connecticut, 1935), p. 1, n. 1; for the manuscripts of Ammianus, see Rodney P. Robinson, *The Hersfeldensis and the Fuldensis of Ammianus Marcellinus*, Univ. of Missouri Stud. 11.3 (1936), 118–40, and Wolfgang Seyfarth, *Der Codex Fuldensis und der Codex E des Ammianus Marcellinus*, Abhandlungen der deutschen Akademie der Wissenschaften zu Berlin, Kl. f. Sprachen, Lit. u. Kunst, 1962 (2).

[39] Wilhelm Levison, *England and the Continent in the Eighth Century* (Oxford, 1946), pp. 141–4.

[40] For these references see Robinson (ed.), *Germania*, p. 1, n. 1.

have seen how the code of the *Germania* would enable him to provide a roll-call of the noble dead which would not be a melancholy reminder that the Vikings were stronger than they: to the imagination at least, those who choose to die are the victors not the vanquished. All in all, it is not out of the question that the *Germania* itself was the poet's source.[41]

Another possibility, however, presents itself. The source might have been a narrative lay, which, it may be conjectured, had as its theme a heroic last stand in which, contrary to the most famous examples, such as the *Chanson de Roland* and the *Niebelungenlied*, the leaders did not live to die last. It is perhaps unlikely that this would have been an Old English lay, for, though it would be possible to reconstruct famous stories, such as that of Ingeld, so that they fitted this pattern, it is hardly to be expected that such a lay would co-exist with the lay of Finn known to the *Beowulf* poet. Widely different moral ideals can of course live side by side in literature but normally within different genres (Edmund the pacific beside Byrhtnoth the exultant fighter). The most likely source is therefore one which has a similar narrative pattern to that of *Maldon* and which became known to Old English poets after the period of *Beowulf* and of the lays that preceded it.[42]

[41] It would be more probable if any significance could be attached to the description of Wulfmær as Byrhtnoth's *swustersunu*. The importance of the sister's son in medieval English and French literature has been examined respectively by Francis B. Gummere, 'The Sister's Son', *An English Miscellany presented to Dr Furnivall* (Oxford, 1901), pp. 133–49, and W. O. Farnsworth, *Uncle and Nephew in Old French Chansons de Geste* (New York, 1913). The evidence presented in these two works needs a fresh and rigorous reconsideration. Linguistic evidence of course makes plain that at an early stage of European history a distinction was seen between a brother's son and a sister's son (cf. Émile Benviste, *Le Vocabulaire des Institutions Indo-Européennes* I (Paris, 1969), 223–37). But whether an emphasis on this bond of kinship is part of the poetic heroic tradition (and therefore unsurprising in *Maldon*) is uncertain. Beowulf and Roland are admittedly sisters' sons by implication; but the lack of explicit interest in this might suggest that the reason for the invention of this relationship was not a poetic concern with the emotional priority which this relationship took over that of paternal uncle and nephew but the convenience of inserting a legendary figure into an historical genealogy through the female line.

[42] Since we lack the evidence to know whether the author of *Maldon* was the only Old English poet to use this conjectured foreign source, I leave out of account the possibility that its influence on *Maldon* was an indirect one through another Old English heroic poem. The only suggestion of the theme in question in extant works of English origin other than *Maldon* is in the probably slightly later *Vita Sancti Oswaldi*, where it is said of Stremwold and the thegns of Devon: 'Nam occisus est ex nostris miles fortissimus, nomine Stremwold, cum aliis nonnullis, qui bellica morte magis elegerunt vitam finire, quam ignobiliter vivere' ('For among our men was killed a very brave warrior, Stremwold, with many others, who preferred ending their life in warlike death to living ignobly'); (*The Historians of the Church of York and its Archbishops*, ed. J.

The only identifiable possibility is the one suggested more than forty years ago by Bertha Phillpotts, namely the *Bjarkamál*.[43] There was even at the time much that was attractive in the argument that the *Maldon* poet knew the *Bjarkamál*; but, as Bertha Phillpotts stated it, there was the serious weakness that many of the resemblances that she noted between the two poems were also shared to a greater or lesser extent by *Beowulf*. She was therefore driven to accepting two assumptions that together made an improbable pair: one was that it was unlikely that the *Maldon* poet knew *Beowulf*, the other that the *Beowulf* poet knew a lost lay of the fall of Hrólfr Kraki. The theory had thus become too elaborate and E. V. Gordon's curt, authoritative rejection of it was perhaps harsh in its brevity, but just, for, if all the resemblances that Bertha Phillpotts found between the three poems are dismissed, the residue of small and mainly stylistic resemblances is insufficient to carry the full weight of the argument. If it now appears, however, that *Maldon* expresses a heroic ideal unknown to *Beowulf* and that in extant narrative it shares this ideal exclusively with the *Bjarkamál*, there will be a strong case for accepting Bertha Phillpott's suggestion that the *Bjarkamál* became known in England in the tenth century through the Danish settlers and that the author of *Maldon* drew upon it: indeed that he was deeply impressed by it and borrowed from it the major theme and mood of his poem.

No close comparison between *Maldon* and the *Bjarkamál* is possible, since the latter is known only from Saxo's translation of it into Latin hexameters. Nevertheless the broad lines of resemblance are plain. The main theme of the *Bjarkamál* is how after the death of Hrólfr Kraki, Bjarki and Hjalti, his two great followers, together with other unnamed companions, make a last stand, seeing the alternatives to be cowardly escape or vengeance for the slaying of their king which must inevitably lead to death. In a long speech that spans the time in which Hrólfr is killed, Hjalti says:

> Illuxit suprema dies, nisi forte quis assit
> Tam mollis, qui se plagis prebere timescat,

Raine, RS, I (1879), 456). Though it is not said explicitly here that the thegns refused to outlive their lord, the placing of this story immediately before a recast version of the Battle of Maldon, shorn of the retainers' last stand, makes it reasonable to suppose that the author was influenced by *Maldon* itself. On Byrhtferth of Ramsey as the author of the *Vita*, see Michael Lapidge, 'The Hermeneutic Style in Tenth-Century Anglo-Latin Literature', *ASE* 4 (1975), 67–111, at 91–3.

[43] B. S. Phillpotts, '*The Battle of Maldon*: some Danish Affinities', *MLR* 24 (1929), 172–90.

Aut imbellis ita ut domini non audeat ultor
Esse sui, dignosque animo proscribat honores.[44]

It is notable that in the *Bjarkamál*, as in *Maldon*, vengeance is equated with a doomed attack upon the enemy, and furthermore, as in *Maldon*, this identification of vengeance with a victory that is known to be unobtainable is inextricably entwined with the retainer's duty and desire to die with his lord. Saxo's comment upon the poem makes this point explicit: 'Tantum enim excellentissimis regis meritis ea pugna a militibus tributum est, ut ipsius cedes omnibus oppetende mortis cupiditatem ingeneraret, eique morte iungi uita iocundius duceretur.'[45] Whilst this idea is not stated so roundly in Saxo's actual version of the poem, it is unmistakably implicit in the tone and structure of the work and more particularly it is stated very movingly in the theme that the *Bjarkamál* also shares with *Maldon*, namely that there is a profound fittingness in the body of a thegn lying beside that of his dead lord. In the *Bjarkamál* Bjarki and Hjalti resolve to lie respectively at the head and foot of Hrólfr:

Ad caput extincti moriar ducis obrutus, ac tu
Eiusdem pedibus moriendo allabere pronus,
Vt uideat, quisquis congesta cadauera lustrat,
Qualiter acceptum domino pensauimus aurum ...
Sic belli intrepidos proceres occumbere par est,
Illustrem socio complexos funere regem.[46]

Saxo's style is ponderous, but the thought is the same as that which is expressed in *Maldon* in one dignified and tranquil line summarizing the death of Offa, 'He læg ðegenlice ðeodne gehende' (294) [He lay as befits a thegn by his Lord's side] and in the elegiac vow of Byrhtwold:

Fram ic ne wille,
ac ic me be healfe minum hlaforde
be swa leofan men licgan þence.
(317b–19)[47]

[44] *Gesta Danorum*, ed. Holder, p. 61. 'The last day for all of us has dawned unless there should be anyone here so soft that he fears to expose himself to wounds or so cowardly that he dare not be the avenger of his lord and refuses to give fitting honours to his spirit.'

[45] *Ibid.* p. 67; 'For so great a tribute was paid by the warriors to the most noble virtues of the king that his death inspired in all the desire to seek death, and to join him in death was held more pleasing than life.'

[46] *Ibid.* p. 66; 'By the head of my dead leader I will die overpowered and at his feet you also shall sink forwards in death so that whosoever gazes upon the pile of corpses may see how we repaid our lord for the gold we received from him. ... Thus it is fitting that leading warriors undismayed should fall, embracing their illustrious king in the companionship of death.'

[47] 'I will not go from here, but mean to lie by the side of my lord, the man so dear to me.'

In later medieval literature there is of course a strong awareness that it is fitting that those who had loved each other in life should lie together in death: it is a symbolic ordering that seems to confer a true immortality upon what lies beneath the surface transience of life, but in later literature it is of course lovers, husband and wife or lover and mistress, who are thus united. The epitomizing of the loyalty and love or the lord-retainer relationship by this poignant means belongs only to the *Bjarkamál* and *Maldon*.

The supposition that the author of *Maldon* learnt of this motif from the *Bjarkamál* provides not only a satisfactory literary explanation of the resemblance but also a satisfactory historical one, for it was in the long unconverted Scandinavian countries that highly primitive traditions survived into the Christian literary era. In particular it is worth noting that, whilst in Old Norse literature the idea of a retainer's semi-suicidal resolve not to outlive his lord is peculiar to the *Bjarkamál* and later poems closely influenced by it,[48] cognate ideas are found elsewhere, as, for instance, in the *Volsunga saga*, where Brynhild throws herself upon the funeral pyre of Sigmund, or in the story told in both *Egils saga* and the *Jómsvíkinga saga* of how King Herlaugr and eleven followers chose to immure themselves in a howe rather than submit to an invader.[49] Nevertheless, of course, the theory inevitably falls well short of proof.

Fortunately for a reading of *Maldon* it is not essential to know the poet's exact source for the ideal of a man dying with his lord, satisfactory as this would be; it is necessary only to know that this idea was not an ancient and traditional commonplace of Old English heroic poetry but was new and strange, so that the poet had to use contrivance to make it seem familiar. Liberated from the view that it illustrates a central tenet of the heroic code *The Battle of Maldon* becomes more moving. In the first place, the poet's reiteration of the retainers' ideal through a succession of speeches takes point if he is seeking to persuade his audience to suspend disbelief rather than repeating a well-worn heroic theme without care for the danger of monotony. In the second place, the isolation of the retainers' ideal from the poem and from the characterization of it as an established moral precept allows the modern reader to estimate the value of the ideal itself without reference to its presentation in the poem. But of all the heroic ideals of loyalty it alone is alien to a literary taste formed by

[48] See Olrik, *Heroic Legends*, pp. 169–99.

[49] For references see Gilbert Trathnigg, 'Über Selbstmord den Germanen', *ZDA* 72 (1936), 99–102.

the reading of later English literature and therefore seems repugnant—not noble and courageous but primitive and barbaric.

But once the ideal of a retainer refusing to outlive his lord is allowed to subside into the substance of the poem it ceases to be an appropriate object of moral scrutiny. As a general precept it may be imaginatively unattractive, but as the poet presents it, namely as a decision of a certain group of men of high courage, who on one occasion thus resolved to die, it transcends such evaluation. There are some scenes in literature, such as the defence of the Burgundians at the court of Attila in the *Niebelungenlied* or of Roland and the men of the rearguard in the Pyrenees in the *Chanson de Roland*, which neither exemplify nor deny a moral commandment but rather illustrate the heroic dimensions of the human will. The last stand of Byrhtnoth's men, despite the moral articulacy that the poet has conferred upon them, surely belongs with such legendary scenes. The poet has apparently taken a local defeat—Byrhtnoth was killed and the English paid tribute—and transposed it from the historical world into one of heroic story in which paradoxically it is better to lose than to win. By cunning strategy and superior numbers victory can belong to anyone, but it is a prerogative of the truly noble to lose in so magnificent a way. The decision to die taken by Byrthnoth's retainers is therefore not a matter of adherence to a traditional code of duty but rather an individual insight into the nature of loyalty which reflects their own peculiar greatness.

XIII

MORAL CHAUCER AND KINDLY GOWER

CHAUCER's apostrophe to Gower as 'moral'[1] and Coleridge's reference to the 'innate kindliness' of Chaucer's nature[2] have had a distorting effect upon much modern criticism of these two authors. It is known, but too often ignored, that when Chaucer saluted Gower as 'moral' he was thinking of him as the author of the versified moral handbook, the *Mirour de l'omme*, and probably also of the *Vox clamantis*, a lengthy complaint against the times; the *Confessio amantis* was as yet unwritten. Chaucer therefore did not mean that Gower was 'moral' in the modern sense any more than that Strode (a then well-known Thomist philosopher and logician) was 'philosophical' in the sense that this epithet now has when applied to people. Nevertheless, the term 'moral' has been reserved for Gower both by his admirers and by his detractors. The latter find in it a good reason for describing the *Confessio amantis* as dull, whilst the former have breathed new life into the term 'moral' by associating it with the recognition that Gower's ideal of love in the *Confessio* was happy married love not the supposed courtly love code.

Coleridge's emphasis upon the kindliness of Chaucer probably arose from a blindness to Chaucer's use of irony, particularly perhaps in the Prologue to *The Canterbury Tales*; but its propriety has also to be considered in a historical context. When the most recent and the most eminent satirist known to Coleridge was Pope, it might seem appropriate to him that a poet, who was so notably free from asperity and personal malice, should be described as having a kindly nature.

[1] *Troilus and Criseyde*, V.1856, Geoffrey Chaucer, *The Works of Geoffrey Chaucer*, ed. F. N. Robinson, 2nd ed. (London, 1966), p. 479. Unless otherwise stated this is the edition used throughout for references to Chaucer's works or for quotations from them.

[2] S. T. Coleridge, *The Table Talk and Omniana* (London, 1917), p. 294. It is worth noting that this view of Chaucer was repeated by Matthew Arnold, who referred to Chaucer's 'large, free, simple, clear yet kindly view of human life' ('The Study of Poetry' in *The Complete Prose Works of Matthew Arnold*, IX, ed. R. H. Super (Ann Arbor, 1973), 174, and this characterisation of Chaucer is at least to some extent related to Arnold's famous charge that Chaucer was lacking in 'high seriousness'.

The danger to criticism arises only when this view is perpetuated as a truism amongst critics, and furthermore when an overt contrast is made between kindly and tolerant Chaucer and moral Gower.

Gower, as the author of the *Confessio amantis*, has of course some claim to be called moral in the Chaucerian sense. Some of the stories told in the *Confessio* are not feigned exempla (in the sense that the stories in *The Legend of Good Women* are feigned saints' lives) but genuine exempla, deriving from a well-established didactic tradition, and exceptionally well-told: good examples are *The Trump of Death* and *The Three Questions*, both of which bear upon the levelling power of death, a subject that always moved Gower imaginatively.[3] Similarly, though less certainly, Chaucer has some claim to demonstrating a kindly nature in his works in that some of his insights into human behaviour are perceptively tender rather than ironically acute: indeed, if Chaucer were being contrasted with another of his great contemporaries, Langland, kindliness might well be distinguished in him, though even then only as one of many traits. However, despite the possibility of these claims, it is not at all certain that Chaucer and Gower, who knew each other well and must have benefited from each other's comments on the art of poetry, should be isolated as a historical pair, one kindly the other moral. Indeed, when they are considered as a pair, it may be more illuminating to reverse the labels and call them kindly Gower and moral Chaucer.

That a narrative writer should display a keen moral sense may in literary terms be either good or bad. Gower's willingness to absent himself from didacticism in the *Confessio* is obviously at an elementary level of criticism good in that it allows him to tell powerful stories, such as those, for instance, of Albinus and Rosamund or of Horestes, without care for their lack of didactic value. But more interesting than these tales of appalling crimes and appalling acts of revenge, which would shatter the penitential framework if too closely attached to it, are the stories where Gower could have adhered to the traditional moral views which he expounds elsewhere, but has chosen to eschew them. At times this suspension of moral judgment works well, liberating a fresh and illuminating sympathy for his characters; at other times it leaves the story flaccid, the controlling moral pattern of the source being disregarded. All the stories to be examined are concerned with love and in a true penitential work most of them would therefore find a place under the various subheadings of lust.

[3] For lists of analogues to these exempla see *Gesta Romanorum*, ed. Hermann Oesterley (Berlin, 1872), s.v. *Drei Fragen*, p. 723, and *Todestrompete*, p. 736.

But, as has often been noticed, Gower, when he reached the last of the seven deadly sins, abandoned his traditional method of dividing each sin into five branches (each illustrated by one or more exempla), and instead confined himself to the sin of incest, chiefly illustrated by the inordinately long story of Apollonius of Tyre. Stories which could have served to illustrate all five branches are, however, scattered through the work, attached to the moral frame in a variety of ingenious ways. By a tradition commonly (though not invariably) followed, lust was divided into the following branches of sin, arranged in order of gravity: sexual acts against nature (i.e. those that could not lead to procreation); incest, which had an element of the unnatural since it violated the reverence due between father and child and by extension between other members of the family; rape; adultery; fornication.[4] It is worth bearing this medieval classification in mind because it does not necessarily correspond with the views of modern readers and certainly does not accord with the modern criminal law.

Gower seems to be alone among medieval vernacular narrative writers in his willingness to deal with or touch upon the subject of homosexuality (which of course comes under the first heading) and equally remarkably to do so with sympathy. It is worth noting first of all a surprising but imaginative touch that Gower has invented in the story of Achilles and Deidamia. In the original, which is part of the *Achilleid* of Statius,[5] Achilles feels repugnance when compelled by his mother to dress in women's clothes and to adopt a womanly manner. He becomes manifestly satisfied with this attire only when he finds that the disguise will serve as a stratagem to bring him close to Deidamia, with whom he has fallen in love. Gower makes his Achilles more youthful and less consciously a man. Initially, dressed as a girl, he pays no attention, 'And he was yong and tok non hiede'; later, taught feminine graces, he becomes positively pleased:

> Achilles, which that ilke while
> Was yong, upon himself to smyle
> Began, whan he was so besein.[6]

[4] For this order and its justification see Thomas Aquinas, *Summa Theologica* II.ii, q. 154, a. 12.

[5] Statius, *Achilleid*, ed. O. A. W. Dilke (Cambridge, 1954), pp. 41–43. For knowledge of the *Achilleid* in the Middle Ages see Paul M. Clogan, *The Medieval Achilleid of Statius* (Leiden, 1968).

[6] Book V, ll. 3011–13, John Gower, *English Works*, ed. G. C. Macaulay, Early English Text Society (hereafter EETS), 81, 82 (London, 1899–1902), III, 29. This edition is used throughout for references to and quotations from the *Confessio amantis*.

It was of course not Gower's intention to portray Achilles as a homosexual: shortly afterwards he shows Achilles's masculinity asserting itself in both amatory and martial instincts. But he has created for Achilles a moment of sexual indeterminacy which is much more psychologically striking than the straight-forward conventional responses described by Statius.

Gower also borrowed a full-length story of homosexuality from the *Metamorphoses*.[7] The outline of the plot is the same in both works: Iphis, daughter of Telethusa, is brought up as a boy, because her father had ordered that if a girl was born she must be put to death; when grown, Iphis is betrothed to Ianthe and the dilemma is resolved when the gods transform Iphis into a man. The later stages of the story are recast by Gower in order to achieve a different moral patterning. In Ovid, Iphis at the age of thirteen finds the marriage arranged and her proposed bride Ianthe in love with her (believing her to be a man). To her horror Iphis is aware that she returns this love and in an eloquent monologue she laments this strange passion, one alien to animals and worse than the monstrous love of Pasiphaê for the bull. Iphis is appalled at what has befallen her, and the reader is correspondingly appalled.

By contrast Gower denies to Iphis any recognition of her predicament. The age of the arranged marriage is lowered from thirteen to ten[8] and in this child-marriage the two for a time remain loving but unaware that their marriage cannot be a normal one. When their period of innocence was about to end, Cupid took pity on them and, in order that they might continue to love but within the natural law, transformed Iphis into a man. By removing conscious moral responsibility from the protagonist Gower has obscured the moral issue, and by some unclear generalisations (nature, it would seem, can constrain to unnatural acts), he further absolves from blame. His one explicit acknowledgement of the sin in his statement that Cupid hates that which is against nature carries far less moral weight than does Iphis's understanding of her own situation in Ovid. Both in terms of narrative and moral strength the story has become much more lightweight in Gower's hands: the potentiality for tragedy is lost; in place there is a certain delicacy and tenderness.

[7] *Confessio amantis* IV.451–505; *Metamorphoses* IX.666–797.

[8] The usual minimum age given by the canonists for marriage was fourteen for a boy and twelve for a girl; on English custom cf. William Lyndwood, *Provinciale* (Oxford, 1679), p. 272. For further discussion and references cf. H. A. Kelly, *Love and Marriage in the Age of Chaucer* (Ithaca and London, 1975), p. 182 and n. 17.

In telling stories about incest Gower is of course not alone in the Middle Ages: indeed incest, whether committed, threatened, or narrowly avoided is a common medieval theme. It is to be found, not only in the re-telling of stories of classical origin, but also (perhaps often borrowed from these prototypes) in some of the most widespread of medieval tales, such as that of the legend of Pope Gregory[9] and in some versions of the Constance story (though not in Trivet's account followed by both Chaucer and Gower). Where Gower is remarkable therefore is not that he tells the story of Apollonius of Tyre in Book VIII,[10] but that earlier he had related the tale of Canace and Macareus with compassion, achieving this end by recasting his source in the *Heroides*.[11] Some changes were of course inevitable in the adaptation of Canace's letter to her brother (after their incestuous relationship has been discovered) into a continuous narrative, but it is clear that Gower used these opportunities to invest the whole tale with a sense of pathos, which in Ovid had been reserved for one part of it only, namely the murder of the baby.

Though Gower on this occasion says nothing about the age of the lovers, he manifestly intends to convey the same impression of innocent youthfulness as he had done in the tale of Iphis. In Ovid, Canace fully understands and powerfully laments the relationship that there had been between her and her brother:

> Cur umquam plus me, frater, quam frater amasti,
> et tibi, non debet quod soror esse, fui?[12]

In the *Confessio* Canace pleads her innocent unawareness to her father: 'That I misdede yowthe it made.' To justify this plea Gower had invented a past for the brother and sister in which they grew up in isolated companionship, childish love thus turning into sexual love

[9] Cf. *Die mittelenglische Gregoriuslegende*, ed. Carl Keller (Heidelberg, 1914), and Margaret Schlauch, *Chaucer's Constance and Accused Queens* (New York, 1927). The theme of unintended incest between mother and son whether committed as in the story of Pope Gregory or narrowly avoided as in *Sir Degarré* probably derives from the story of Oedipus known in the Middle Ages from the beginning of the *Thebaid* of Statius and of its romance derivative the *Roman de Thèbes*, ed. Léopold Constans, I, Société d'anciens textes français (Paris, 1890).

[10] In his history of the pagan gods in Book V Gower also tells a brief story (of at present unknown origin) of how Cupid lay with his mother Venus, he being blind and she 'unwis'. This is part of a generally censorious summary of classical mythology.

[11] *Confessio amantis* III.143–336; *Heroides, Epistle* xi.

[12] *Heroides*, ed. Grant Showerman, Loeb Classical library reprints (Cambridge, Mass., 1963) p. 134. 'Why brother, did you ever love me with more than brotherly love? And why was I to you what a sister ought not to be?'

without their recognising the change. Again Gower is obscure in his extenuating generalisations: in this instance 'kinde' and love overrule 'the lawes of nature' (since 'kinde' and 'nature' are synonymous, it would seem that nature here has a part in overruling nature).[13] In Ovid incest remains an abominable sin and therefore Aeolus in commanding his daughter to commit suicide appears to impose a harsh but inevitable penalty. It is only in ordering that the baby be cast out to be devoured by animals that Aeolus inhumanly exceeds the laws of tragic justice, and it is for the innocent baby that Ovid contrives that the reader shall feel pity. In the *Confessio*, however, the killing of the baby is postponed in time and entirely subordinated to the fate of Canace. It is she who is seen primarily as the pathetic and helpless victim of her father's fury and her own sin thus becomes trivial in comparison with the savagery of Aeolus (indeed the tale is told as an exemplum against wrath). In this story, as in that of Iphis, Gower has skilfully and deliberately worked against the moral pattern of his original, worked against the didactic teaching of his age, and furthermore worked against the moral assumptions of all other medieval stories on the same type of subject.

It will be apparent from the story of Canace and Macareus that Gower is skilful and agile in manipulating the seeming rigidity of his moral framework. Had Gower attached the tale to the frame by its primary theme, he would have been compelled to place it in Book VIII alongside that of Apollonius, and he would then have been compelled to condemn the lovers. By fastening it through a subordinate element he achieves an ingeniously won moral freedom for himself. This device is even more noticeable in Gower's numerous tales of rape, which are scattered through at least four of the books (excluding Book VIII on lust). This arrangement was clearly dictated primarily by the requirement of diversity rather than by the intention to effect an unexpected distribution of sympathies: thus the story of Lucretia is included in Book VII under the heading of chastity as a virtue in princes, whilst that of Tereus and Progne appears in the book on avarice, rape here being classified as a vice of lovers who take by strength that which is withheld from them. But stories of rape, which are less horrific than that of Tereus, are fastened to the frame in a neutral way. The much-told story, for instance, of the begetting of Alexander by Nectanebus is told as an illustration of sorcery as a

[13] Macaulay's comments on the relationship between *kinde* and the *lawe positif* (Gower, *English Works*, note to III, 172) are superseded by the discussion of this point by Kelly, *Love and Marriage*, pp. 141–44.

branch of gluttony, and the emphasis of the story is correspondingly more upon the marvellous than the wicked; similarly the story of Mundus and Paulina is related in Book I under the heading of hypocrisy (in this context deceptive disguise) as a branch of pride.[14] In this tale Gower shows an unexpected sympathy for Mundus, but he has not had to recast his source in order to justify this sympathy for a mitigating reference to the irresistibility of love was included in it. This dependence upon a source perhaps explains why Gower's sympathetic extenuation of Mundus's behaviour does not carry conviction in the way that his sympathy for the potentially homosexual and the incestuous lovers had done.

The origin of the story is in the *Antiquities* of Josephus.[15] In this version the explanation at the end that Mundus was given a more lenient sentence than the others involved in the stratagem, 'quod amoris vehementia deliquisset' [because he would have melted with the fire of love], makes sense, for Mundus is no more than a helpless and lovesick youth, and the ruse of his disguising himself as the god Anubis is devised by the freedwoman Ida in order to save his life: it is she therefore and the conniving priests, who had allowed the temple to be desecrated, that are sentenced to death; Mundus fittingly is merely banished. In subsequent versions, however, including that in the *Speculum historiale* of Vincent of Beauvais (in all probability Gower's source),[16] the figure of Ida and all other mitigating circumstances have vanished though the milder penalty and the reason for it remain. The moral patterning of the story thus becomes distorted, particularly if one considers it alongside that of Lucretia, for instance, in which Tarquin is traditionally villainous, and it is therefore not surprising that Godfrey of Viterbo in his *Pantheon* (a work known to Gower) recast the story, omitting the reference to the compelling power of love and having Paulina commit suicide.[17] Gower, however, follows the gentler ending: Paulina, having lamented her defilement, is comforted by her husband, and Mundus, unlike the priests, has his life spared, 'For Love put reson aweie / And can noght se the rihte weie.' Until

[14] *Confessio amantis* I.761–1059.

[15] *Antiquitates Iudaicae* XVIII.7 (Cologne, 1534), p. 190.

[16] *Speculum maior* IV.4 (Venice, 1591), p. 75. Macaulay's note on the sources of this story has been corrected in the Oxford D. Phil. thesis of H. C. Mainzer, 'A Study of the Sources of Confessio amantis of John Gower' (1967; Bodley MS d.Phil.d. 4209), pp. 93–96.

[17] Ed. G. Waitz, MGH, *Scriptorum*, XXII (1872), 153. Gower refers to the *Pantheon* in Book VIII, 1.272.

that moment, however, Mundus's coldblooded stratagem and his subsequent taunting of Paulina had seemed morally repugnant, and it is difficult for the reader to see why the passions that overcame Mundus should be so much more simply and gently described than those that moved Tarquin (cf. V.3998–4900). The explanation undoubtedly lies in the respective sources, but, though Vincent had referred to the *vis amoris* [power of love], Gower would have done better not to repeat him. In his efforts to penetrate with an unscolding eye into the depths and ramifications of human weakness, Gower from time to time accidentally debases some of the key terms of his poem. 'Love' in the story of Mundus seems to be equivalent to 'kinde' in other contexts, and in some of these other contexts 'kinde' is apparently reduced to its most restrictive meaning of sexual instincts. This debasement is undoubtedly not intended but it represents a serious flaw in the poem. Chaucer (as we shall see) at times also debases some of his recurring terms but he does so with sharp awareness and for a moral purpose.

It would be tediously time-consuming to investigate all the stories in the *Confessio* in which Gower related either neutrally or sympathetically stories that in Christian terms involve the sins of either adultery or fornication; but there is one in each category that may be briefly mentioned. The first is the tale of the king and his steward's wife, borrowed from the *Roman des sept sages*.[18] The story is told as an exemplum against avarice in love and serves this purpose very well, for the steward, who is indignantly banished by the king, firstly has married his wife for her wealth and secondly procures her for the king's bed on payment of a hundred pounds. What is curious is that a happy ending is contrived by the king adulterously—indeed bigamously—marrying the steward's wife. The moral presuppositions of the story resemble the sentimental conventions of some of the best French or Anglo-Norman romances of the twelfth century, wherein there might be a rightness in mutual, requited love that annulled the obligations of a marriage that was wretched and loveless. Careful and sensitive writers, however, such as Chrétien de Troyes in *Cligés* and Marie de France in *Guigemar*, delay the marriage of the lovers, which provides the happy ending, until the first husband has died. Gower, concerned for the happiness of the

[18] *Confessio amantis* V.2643–2825; *Le Roman des sept Sages de Rome*, ed. Leroux de Lincy (Paris, 1838), pp. 51–54. Mainzer, 'Study', pp. 204–7, notes that Gower probably drew also upon English versions of this work. .

well-meaning king and unhappy wife, provides a bigamous marriage to expunge the ugliness of the steward's actions. Sensitive moral judgment has manifestly deserted Gower at this point.

Yet more curious from the moral point of view is the story of Iphis and Anaxarete, borrowed from the *Metamorphoses* and told under the heading of sloth in love.[19] Despite its theoretical appropriateness as an exemplum, both Gower's choice of the story and his treatment are remarkable. According to Ovid, Anaxerete was a young man of low birth who fell irresistibly in love with Iphis, a princess. Unable to refrain, he made known his love, and Iphis, who was more cruel than the sea and more hard than iron or rock, did nothing but scorn and mock him. Anaxarete in despair committed suicide, and, as Iphis unemotionally watched the funeral procession, the gods turned her into a statue, so that she who in life had been stony-hearted, fittingly became all stone. This unimpressive story is given point in the *Metamorphoses* in that it is related by the god Vertumnus (disguised as an old woman) to Pomona, whose love he wishes to gain. As part of a seductor's persuasions the tale falls into place. Robbed of its cynical context and told as a warning against despondency in love, the story underwent radical changes.

In Gower's version the social positions of the protagonists are reversed: Iphis is now a maiden of humble birth, Anaxarete a prince. Though Iphis no longer has any arrogant reasons to reject his love, she does so 'to save and kepe hir wommanhiede'; nevertheless after Anaxarete has committed suicide she distractedly reproaches herself for being the cause of his death and for not having shown *pite*, and the gods transform her into a statue out of compassion for her grief. The epitaph engraved upon the marble tablet at the sepulchre, however, points the Ovidian moral: women should take warning from this statue, which was once of flesh and blood and showed no pity. Gower tells the story with feeling but its moral outlines are extraordinarily fuzzy: his one attempt to sum up and strike a balance, 'He was to neysshe and sche to hard,' is inadequate. Gower's attempt here to sentimentalise the cynical, to sympathise with characters for whom the plot forbids sympathy, is a failure. 'Moral' Gower would surely have recognised the material as intractable and would not have sought to transform it.

Gower's abstentions from received morality and his observations of human weakness which are often uncritically kind may reasonably

[19] *Confessio amantis* IV.3515–3684; *Metamorphoses* XIV.698–761.

be demonstrated by choosing appropriate examples. To attempt to prove the strength and subtlety of Chaucer's moral imagination within a short space is difficult, for one of the most striking characteristics of his narrative technique is the effect of continuous moral probing and of a sure and delicate sense of decorum, which never fail unless Chaucer contrives a deliberate breach. It is only in his overt classical imitations, notably *The Legend of Good Women* and the Physician's tale and the Manciple's tale in *The Canterbury Tales*, that Chaucer tells stories that conflict with Christian moral principles in what is on the whole a serious, unquestioning way. But even in these he shows a moral awareness and moral scruples alien to Gower. In the telling of these tales he has in the first place a moral advantage over Gower. Since he is a poet highly conscious of genres and consequently of the different moral codes appropriate to them, he can suspend ordinary moral judgment simply by indicating a classical setting for his tales. The reference to Titus Livius as a source in the first line of the Physician's tale, for instance, inhibits us from asking whether a father had the right to kill his daughter. But so many genuine exempla had acquired the trappings of a Roman setting that this kind of moral indicator was not available in the *Confessio*.

In the second place in *The Legend of Good Women* Chaucer spatters the stories with oblique allusions and ironic hints which undercut the surface morality.[20] Two examples will illustrate this. Through their re-telling of classical stories Chaucer and Gower are committed to the non-Christian view that in some situations (particularly those in which a woman has been betrayed or violated) suicide is either apt or admirable. Though Gower ostensibly tells the story of Pyramus and Thisbe as a warning against suicide (as a part of homicide), the matter is lightly treated, and it would appear to be the hasty imprudence of a lover's suicide that is at issue. Other stories of suicide, including that of Lucretia, are manifestly untouched by the moral so faintly drawn and applied only to the suicide of unhappy lovers. When Chaucer, however, tells the story of Lucretia, the only example of suicide in *The Legend* which might seem legitimate in

[20] It has been plausibly argued that there are many odd, deflationary touches in *The Legend of Good Women* which reflect Chaucer's awareness of his own presentation of the characters as Love's martyrs with the traditional view of the *accessus* and *scholia* that it was Ovid's intention to blame 'foolish love'; for this argument see M. C. Edwards, 'A Study of Six Characters in Chaucer's *Legend of Good Women* with reference to Medieval Scholia on Ovid's *Heroides*' (Oxford thesis, 1970; Bodley MS B.Litt.d. 1589).

Christian terms (Jerome, for instance, had considered it so), Chaucer allusively hints that it was wrong:

Nat only that these payens hire comende,
But he that cleped is in oure legende
The grete Austyn, hath gret compassioun
Of this Lucresse, that starf at Rome toun.

Chaucer in other words slyly goes out of his way to refer us to the *De Civitate Dei* which furnished a *locus classicus* for the view that neither virgins nor wives should commit suicide after rape, with specific reference to the story of Lucretia.[21] Many or most of Chaucer's audience would of course not have recognised the significance of the mention of Augustine's name; but to anyone attuned to Chaucer's style his statement that pagans praised Lucretia and Augustine felt pity for her would rightly arouse the suspicion that Augustine pitied but did not approve. There is a more subtle moral conscience at work here than in Gower.

A slightly different example is that of Chaucer's moral good taste in his treatment of the story of Tereus and Progne. This story of horror had first been told by Ovid and then in twelfth-century romance style by Chrétien de Troyes.[22] Chaucer, recognising that this story could not be told with lightness of touch and as an illustration of the sufferings of helpless women adopts the clever strategy of lapsing into a kind of mumbling reluctance to tell it and indeed stops short. Gower, however, persists to the end, unaware that some softening of detail will scarcely make Ovid's account of Philomela's vengeance (she kills her son and feeds his flesh to Tereus) any the less appalling, whilst his excusing of her in that she was 'as who seith, mad / Of wo,' is a pathetically insufficient moral reaction. Milton was later to use a

[21] Robert W. Frank, Jr., *Chaucer and the Legend of Good Women* (Cambridge, Mass., 1972), p. 97 and notes 7 and 8, has argued strongly for Chaucer's entirely eulogistic presentation of Lucretia. Whilst the evidence of note 8 is important, however, the argument of note 7, i.e. that Chaucer derived Augustine's name from the *Gesta Romanorum*, is unconvincing. *Oure legende* is undoubtedly the *Legenda aurea*, in which as part of an etymological exposition of the name the term *magnificus* is used (cf. edition of Th. Graesse [Leipzig, 1850], p. 549). Either *grete* is a translation of *magnificus* (it appears in Caxton's translation) or *magnus* may be a manuscript variant. Like the appellation 'the grete' the statement that Augustine had 'gret compassioun' of Lucretia is not to be found in the *Gesta Romanorum*. The *De Civitate Dei* does, however, provide a source in that two chapters before that on Lucretia, Augustine says of virgins who committed suicide after being raped, 'Ac per hoc et quae se occiderunt, ne quicquam huius modi paterentur, quis humanus affectus eis nolit ignosci?', I.xvii, CCSL, XLVII, p. 18.

[22] Chrétien de Troyes, *Philomena*, ed. C. de Boer (Paris, 1909).

comparable story, that of the vengeance that Atreus took upon Thyestes, as a metaphor for the Fall: the eating of the fruit was a 'Thyestean banquet.' The morally horrific was of course within Milton's range; it was beyond Chaucer's, but he knew it and through mock contortions of authorial boredom evaded the issue; only Gower, unaware of the morally perilous nature of his material, stolidly and weakly completed the story.

Chaucer's serious treatment of love and of its sinful complement lust can best be illustrated from three of the most famous parts of *The Canterbury Tales*, the Merchant's tale, the Franklin's tale and the Wife of Bath's prologue. The depiction of lust in the Merchant's tale is extraordinarily forceful and for Chaucer forthright. In the Middle Ages it was an accepted view of canon lawyers and other moralists that a husband could commit adultery with his wife. This is a view unlikely to command immediate acceptance in the present age and it is therefore the more remarkable that the Merchant's tale can instantly persuade one of the truth of this. The story normally used by medieval writers to illustrate this doctrine was that of Tobit: Gower tells it as an illustration of the virtue of chastity as a point of policy for princes.[23] But the biblical narrative of how Sarah's first six husbands had their necks wrung by the demon Asmodaeus because on the wedding night they approached Sarah lecherously is too bizarre to be morally convincing. But the union of January and May is plainly an instance of this teaching, and that this point was in Chaucer's mind can be seen from the way in which he makes January deny it, 'A man may do no synne with his wyf,' adding a preposterous reversal of the persuasive image, used in the Parson's tale, that a man can sin with his wife just as he can harm himself with his own knife.[24] When January asserts this to be impossible his folly is unmistakable: there are few commoner accidents.

In the first part of the tale in which Chaucer draws eclectically from many works for arguments for and against marriage a dominant source for the praise of marriage is the wedding service itself. The service is concerned to assert the dignity and significance of the sacrament: marriage was the first sacrament instituted for man and it was instituted by God himself; it makes man and wife one flesh; above all, as the special nuptial blessing (reserved for first marriages only)

[23] *Confessio amantis* VII.5307–81: for discussion cf. Kelly, *Love and Marriage*, pp. 275–78.

[24] Robinson, ed., *Works*, p. 256.

describes, it is a figure of the relationship between Christ and the church.[25] The marriage between January and May, however, is clearly an outrageous travesty of the meaning of the sacrament. Contrary to Chaucer's narrative custom, the religious ceremony is itself described though the contemptuous style draws attention to the discrepancy between the mysterious meaning of the service and the intentions of the participants. The marriage feast too is described and also mocked by the apparently auspicious presence of Venus, though its inauspiciousness is also indicated by the casual manner in which Venus, lyrically dancing before the married couple, wounds another man with passion for the bride.

This lengthy description of Christian rite, secular pomp, and pagan allegory focuses the reader's attention upon the idea of marriage. That January is a lecherous old man who degrades this idea by using the sacrament as a means of buying himself a young wife is entirely plain. It may not, however, be quite so evident that May enters into the marriage in almost as tarnished a state: it is only gradually that one becomes aware of a conspicuous omission in the narrative, namely the lack of a statement that May was married against her will. Parental compulsion is of course a stock theme in the *chansons de mal mariées*, whilst in one of Chaucer's immediate sources for the earlier part of the tale, Boccaccio's *Ameto*, the nymph is married against her will to an old man though she longs for (and later obtains) a young and beautiful husband.[26] In such a highly-wrought work it is exceptionally unlikely that Chaucer intended this meaning but forgot to insert the required mention of it. This understanding is confirmed by the narrator's twice-repeated refusal to tell us what May thought. This rejection of authorial omniscience seems heavy-handed if its only point is to indicate May's maidenly revulsion at January's obscene embraces: but it is sinisterly acute if intended to suggest that May had cold-bloodedly made a bargain and that what she felt was a

[25] *Sarum Manuale*, ed. A. Jefferies Collins, Henry Bradshaw Society 91 (1958), 44–59; *Manuale et processionale ad usum insignis Ecclesiae Eboracensis*, Surtees Society 63 (1875), 24–40.

[26] *Sources and Analogues of Chaucer's Canterbury Tales*, ed. W. F. Bryan and Germaine Dempster (London, 1941), p. 339; for the full story see the same work published under the title *La Comedia delle ninfe fiorentine* in Giovanni Boccaccio, *Tutte le opere*, ed. Vittore Branca, II (Milan, 1964), 772–81.

[27] Cf. Kenneth Kee, 'Two Chaucerian Gardens', *Mediaeval Studies* 23 (1961), 154–62. An association has also been made with Susannah's garden (Alfred L. Kellogg, 'Susannah and the *Merchant's Tale*', *Speculum* 35 [1960]), 275–79, but this is less likely.

calculated acquiescence in the price she had to pay for all the legal documents conferring January's property upon her, documents so abundant that it would have taken the narrator too long to enumerate them. It may be worth noting that the first time that the narrator reveals May's feelings is when she is said to feel 'pitee' for Damian, in a context where the word can be nothing but a euphemism, and where it is almost instantly repeated in one of Chaucer's most beautiful recurring lines, 'Lo, pitee renneth soone in gentil herte,' but this time occurring in a conjunction which makes the whole passage a shady *double entendre*.

Whilst the nastiness of the relationship of January and May and its almost sacrilegious violation of the significance of Christian marriage is exposed in a variety of ways in the Merchant's tale, its most brilliant expression is through the much-discussed image of the enclosed garden. This garden has often been associated with the Garden of Eden, the *hortus conclusus* [enclosed garden] of the *Song of Songs*, and the garden of love described in many medieval romances.[27] Whilst none of these associations can be excluded it is the last two that are the most telling. That January's garden is intended to recall the *hortus conclusus* is made clear by January's invitation to May to come forth ('The gardyn is enclosed al aboute') in a speech redolent of the erotic imagery of the *Song of Songs*. But in the Middle Ages this was reserved for its mystical meanings, the love between Christ and the church or the love between Christ and the Blessed Virgin. January's use of it therefore once more indicates that which his marriage so vilely presumes to be a figure of, whilst at the same time stressing that this garden is also a travesty of the enclosed garden of the Blessed Virgin's virginity. The reversal of the allegorical significance of the garden of the *Song of Songs* is made addedly obscene by the adjunct of 'the smale wyket', naturalistically required of course, but recalling an image often associated with the *hortus conclusus*, that of the *porta clausa* [closed gate] of *Ezekiel*, 41.2 through which no man will pass, but the Lord has passed through it.[28] Through this gate pass both January and Damian.

The blasphemous parody of marriage is thus symbolised by the blasphemously obscene garden. But the garden could also be called obscene without reference to religious imagery. It disagreeableness is at first hinted at in the superficially innocuously rhetorical statement

[28] For these images and their association see Yrjö Hirn, *The Sacred Shrine* (London, 1958), pp. 311–12, and Anselm Salzer, *Die Sinnbilder und Beiworte Mariens* (reprint, Darmstadt, 1967), pp. 15–16 and 26–28.

that Priapus, though he was god of gardens, could not have described its beauty. Priapus, however, was also the ithyphallic deity whose statue had a prominent place in the temple of Venus in *The Parlement of Foules*.[29] That it is this suppressed aspect of Priapus that is paramount in the Merchant's tale becomes plain a few lines further on where it is revealed that January had devised this garden as a place for love-making. This transference of the conjugal relationship from the marriage-bed to the garden again emphasises its unnaturalness: unnatural, not because medieval poets invariably restrained the union of lovers to the bedchamber, but because the garden setting was reserved for love which was most natural, tender, and beautiful. The scene in *Cligés*, for instance, where Cligés and Fenice make their couch in a walled garden, lying on the sward beneath a tree in full leaf and blossom, is an idyllic scene of romance. The sweetness and living naturalness of the garden reflects the quality of their love.[30] The arrangement in the Merchant's tale is the exact reverse of this, and to emphasise the point Chaucer gives little description of the garden. What the reader chiefly remembers of it are the two necessary props for the action: the bush behind which Damian lurks and the pear-tree into which May and Damian so grotesquely climb.

Whilst the emphasis in the Merchant's tale is upon the corrupt nature of the marriage, it is equally shown that the supposedly courtly affair between May and Damian is equally vitiated. In contrast, for instance, to some of the lays of Marie de France, such as *Yonec* or *Guigemar*, the presence of an old and jealous husband does not release the young wife into a love that is ardent but innocent.[31] These lays of Marie provide a sure moral backcloth for the relationship between the young lovers in the Merchant's tale for Marie's lays reveal a very sure, delicate, and moral sensitivity whilst not conforming precisely to traditional Christian morality. Marie allows a romantic, aesthetically satisfying escape from the kind of marriage that January procures, but in the Merchant's tale Chaucer

[29] Lines 253–56, and cf. notes p. 795. The association of Priapus with an obscene statue was probably as common in the Middle Ages as it was in antiquity. The tradition could have been transmitted, for instance, by the *Etymologies* of Isidore or by Servius's note on *Georgics* IV.111; for the latter references see Hans Herter, *De Priapo*, Religionsgeschichtliche Versuche und Vorarbeiten 23 (Giessen, 1932) 77.

[30] Cf. 'Les romans de Chrétien de Troyes'. Edités d'après la copie de Quiot. T. 2. *Cligés*, ll. 6305–36, publié par A. Micha, CFMA (Paris, 1957), pp. 192–93.

[31] For the texts see Marie de France, *Lais*, ed. A. Ewart (Oxford, 1952), pp. 82–96 and 3–25, and for illuminating commentary Ernest Hoepffner, *Les Lais de Marie de France* (Paris, 1935), pp. 72–94.

deliberately blocks this escape. The relationship between wife and young lover is as gross and distasteful as the relationship between husband and wife.

There is of course no moral doctrine in the Merchant's tale with which Gower would not have agreed. Not only are passages in praise of marriage scattered through the *Confessio* but Gower's French *Traitié* also praises it in specifically Christian terms. The difference between Gower and Chaucer lies in their illustration of the doctrine. Gower in the *Traitié* summarises briefly many of the tales told at leisure in the *Confessio*;[32] but sensational tales from Ovid, such as that of Tereus, are too outlandish to convince the reader that the dignity of marriage should not be violated. In contrast Chaucer has contrived a notable image of vice, perhaps more notable than any in Spenser.[33] The strong element of comedy in the tale has the effect of purifying it from any prurient effect, but in no way undoes its black analysis of a polluted marriage which no conventions of time or place block off from daily life.

An attempt to demonstrate that Chaucer's narrative poetry is controlled by a very fine, analytical moral imagination is difficult, for Chaucer's best tales do not offer a flat, uncontroversial surface as do Gower's. With the exception of the Pardoner's tale, the Merchant's tale is the only one dealing with vice of which one could firmly assert that it was not formed by an imagination always guided by a kindly understanding of human weakness nor by a sensibility which always preferred to sympathise with the sinner than to condemn the sin.[34] Critical intepretations of the Franklin's tale and of the Wife of Bath's prologue are not likely to yield such consent: an examination of them

[32] 'Traitié pur essampler les amantz marietz', *French Works*, ed. C. C. Macaulay (Oxford, 1899), pp. 379–92. In this poem, stories such as that of Mundus and Paulina (p. 386) are briefly re-told without sympathy.

[33] It is certainly far more morally powerful than Spenser's imitation of it in the episode of Malbecco and Hellenore in the *Faerie Queen* III.xi, where the transformation of Malbecco into some kind of loathsome bird, personifying jealousy, is more melodramatic but not as insidiously horrible an end as January's degraded and deluded exit from the garden.

[34] This is not the first essay to find the Merchant's tale moral in intent; cf. for instance the excellent analysis leading to this conclusion by E. Talbot Donaldson, 'The Effect of the *Merchant's Tale*' reprinted in *Speaking of Chaucer* (London, 1970) pp. 30–45, but it is perhaps the first to do so without some betrayal of astonishment. I have throughout avoided the controversy of whether or not the tale was originally intended for another speaker: this would be relevant only if anyone were to argue that the tale could not be moral because the Merchant was not a moral person: this would seem to me in itself an unacceptable type of argument.

is nevertheless useful in that both of them manifestly turn upon crucial moral issues and in both of them Chaucer made additions which clarify his moral intention.

The Franklin's tale is often seen as an idyllic little narrative, important within the design of *The Canterbury Tales* in that it both resolves the marriage debate (presumably an artificial issue which pre-occupies the pilgrims but would have been taken light-heartedly by Chaucer's audience) and also provides an idealisation of marriage which complements the savage examination of it in the Merchant's tale. In order to achieve these effects Chaucer has handled the story and characterisation in a far more sensitive way than Boccaccio had done in the *Filocolo*. But by his more sensitive telling of the story Chaucer has allowed a host of moral questions to arise: should Arveragus have decided that Dorigen should commit adultery in order to keep her promise? Should Dorigen have made the promise in the first place and in the second place was she bound to keep it? Had Aurelius a right to assume that a promise had been made and to regard it as binding? Since the story in the *Filocolo* is an example in a *demande d'amour* some of these questions are implicit in the tale in order that they may later be extracted and analysed, but the manner of the telling does not permit them to become live issues in the course of the narrative;[35] other questions, such as the rightness of Arveragus's decision, are ignored by Boccaccio, but are unavoidable in a reading of the Franklin's tale.

Obviously the answers to all these questions turn upon the nature of Dorigen's promise. On this issue Flametta in the *Filocolo* argues lucidly: as a married woman the lady had no right to make this promise, and, though she did, it was null since it contradicted her marriage vow; furthermore Tarolfo (Aurelius) was not notably generous, since his generosity consisted solely in restraining his libidinous desires and that a man should do anyway.[36] It may be added that outside the world of romance Dorigen's promise was not binding for another reason, namely that a promise to commit a sinful act should not be kept; this was the common teaching of the church.[37] Chaucer, as he wrote the tale, dealt skilfully with this awkward moral problem, namely that for the sake of the plot Dorigen's promise must

[35] Giovanni Boccaccio, *Tutte le opere*, ed. Vittore Branca, I (Milan, 1967), 396–410.

[36] Ibid., p. 408.

[37] E.g. *Summa Theologica* II.ii, q. 89, a. 7, and Robert Mannyng, *Handlyng Synne*, lines 2805–2902, EETS, 119 (London, 1901–3), 99–102.

be regarded as binding, yet Christianity, commonsense, and his source all indicated that it was not. His revisions show a mind still at work upon the moral problems that he had created by adapting Boccaccio's brief and cynically told story to a gentler, more idealistic moral ambience.

For a modern audience perhaps the most difficult element to accept is Arveragus's decision that his wife keep her word by committing adultery. It is of course possible to see this as part of a pattern in *The Canterbury Tales*. The lecherous and jealous January is horribly possessive of his wife's body; the noble and generous-minded Arveragus is too liberal. Between these two extremes there is an unstated mean which a medieval audience familiar with an Aristotelian ethical scheme would have recognised as existing.[38] Furthermore Chaucer sought to gain sympathy for Arveragus in his decision by having him burst into tears at the moment that he makes it. The agonising cost is plain. Nevertheless the fact that modern misgivings are not an anachronistic reaction is shown by Chaucer's insertion of lines 1493–98, preserved only in Ellesmere and one other manuscript:[39]

Paraventure an heep of yow, ywis,
Wol holden hym a lewed man in this
That he wol putte his wyf in jupartie.
Herkneth the tale er ye upon hire crie.
She may have bettre fortune than yow semeth;
And whan that ye han herd the tale, demeth.

Chaucer here gives his narrator a blustering tone and inconsequential argument: But this dramatically uneasy attempt to deflect judgment reassures the reader that Chaucer is aware of the perilous nature of the material that he is handling.

A similar moral tact is seen in the handling of Dorigen. From the start Chaucer had presented her more sympathetically than Boccaccio had done. Long space—indeed unduly long space—had been given to her thoughts of suicide (in the *Filocolo* these had been

[38] For Chaucer's reference to the mean in *The Legend of Good Women*, F 164–65, and Kelly, *Love and Marriage*, p. 285.

[39] John M. Manly and Edith Rickert, *The Text of the Canterbury Tales* (Chicago and London, reprint 1967) II, 308. Their reference to Ellesmere 'picking up' lines 1493–98 presumably implies a belief that these lines were added in the margin of the exemplar of Ellesmere, and it seems reasonable to suppose that like lines 1541–44 and lines 1000–1006 (on which see following footnotes) this was an addition made by Chaucer.

briefly expressed to her husband) and her condition for accepting Aurelius as a lover had been made to seem more human and natural, less sophisticatedly capricious, than in Boccaccio. Nevertheless Chaucer's revisions show that he was not satisfied that these modifications were sufficient and he therefore made two additions affecting her, both of them slightly misplaced in most manuscripts and therefore in the familiar printed texts. One is lines 1541–44 (which should follow line 1550)[40] in which the narrator by warning other women to be beware by Dorigen's example by implication rebukes her:

> But every wyf be war of hire beheeste!
> On Dorigen remembreth, atte leeste.

Since the tale turns upon the fragile romance convention that an oath must in all circumstances be kept, no specific disavowal of this can be made within the story. Chaucer, however, has taken the opportunity to condemn the initial giving of the promise, as the story permits and morality demands: in the revised text it is only after this that the audience may be given the assurance that Dorigen and Arveragus lived happily ever after.

The other and more remarkable addition consists of lines 1001–5, which should follow line 998:[41]

> For wel I woot that it shal never bityde.
> Lat swiche folies out of youre herte slyde.
> What deyntee sholde a man han in his lyf
> For to go love another mannes wyf,
> That hath hir body whan so that hym liketh?

Even in its present slightly illogical position this passage is remarkable in bluntly laying bare the unromantic aspect of any romanticised adultery. In its proper place, however, it makes yet plainer that the promise was made, as the narrator says, 'in pley,' for instantly after making it, Dorigen demonstrates incontrovertibly that the keeping of it, even from Aurelius's point of view, must be without happiness or decency. This is in effect an explicit statement of what Aurelius is later to learn.

It might seem that this last addition would cast an unpleasing shadow over Aurelius's conduct but Chaucer had already contrived

[40] For the argument that these lines are an addition and misplaced in many manuscripts see Manly and Rickert, *Text*, II, 314.

[41] See previous footnote.

to absolve him from responsibility. In the *Filocolo* Tarolfo recognises the lady's answer as a rebuff, but nevertheless sets off to try to fulfil the condition and resolves neither to rest not to return until he had done so. In the Franklin's tale Aurelius's mind is fixed more upon the impossibility of the task set than of the implied rejection. He falls therefore into a fit of love-sickness, and having elaborately called upon the gods for help, helplessly swoons; his brother (a newly invented character) puts him to bed, where he remains wretchedly for two whole years. It is the brother, distressed by Aurelius's incurable sickness, who devises the plan of seeking help from the Orleans clerk and who accompanies Aurelius upon this quest. Here one can see Chaucer doing simply and on a small scale what he had done intricately and on a large scale in *Troilus and Criseyde*. In the latter he had shifted responsibility for the consummation of the love-affair from Criseyde to Pandarus (and ironically from Pandarus to Fortune). In the Franklin's tale he neatly shifts responsibility from Aurelius to a hitherto non-existent brother: Aurelius himself is too sick with love to take any initiative. Of course there remains a strong moral implication in the tale that adulterous love is wrong. Dorigen rightly shows no *pite* to Aurelius although he appeals for it sincerely, and Aurelius, offered a woman who comes weeping and with her husband's consent, apparently learns to 'unlove.' But though the moral is plain, Chaucer has contrived that the characters should be guilty of nothing except a little foolishness.

The Wife of Bath's Prologue has often been taken to show Chaucer at his most tolerant, genial, and kindly: indeed there is a tendency to talk of the Prologue as though it were the medieval forerunner of Molly Bloom's soliloquy. But the Wife of Bath is not characterised by a vital, spontaneous expression of female sexuality: on the contrary she is made to consider her sexual capacity as a commercial asset. There is evidence elsewhere in medieval literature and also in historical records that a young woman might marry a prosperous old husband, her wealth then enabling her in her almost inevitable widowhood to marry a young husband.[42] Such a situation depicted in literature would normally arouse censure.[43] If the Wife of Bath

[42] This pattern has been observed in the transmission of the land-holdings of peasants, cf. R. J. Faith, 'Peasant Families and Inheritance Customs in Medieval England', *Agricultural History Review* 14 (1966), 91. I am indebted to Miss Barbara Harvey for this reference.

[43] Cf. *Piers Plowman*, ed. W. W. Skeat (reprint, Oxford, 1924), B. IX, lines 160–63, where the abuse of marrying a widow for her property is linked with that of an old man marrying a young woman.

escapes censure, it is not because Chaucer has made such conduct seem a tolerable human failing, but rather because the Wife of Bath has accumulated riches by marrying not one old husband but four. This unrealistic excess turns her into a grotesque figure, far larger than life, and one who therefore eludes any simple moral response. The Wife of Bath's venal use of sex is further accentuated by her demanding of actual payments before rendering the 'marriage debt,' the latter phrase expressing one of the less congenial elements in the medieval view of marriage and one which Chaucer pointedly makes characteristic of the Wife of Bath's apologia for her life. It was Chaucer's first intention to underline the theme of the relationship between sex and money by having the Wife tell a fabliau in which a calculating woman should both cuckold her husband and contrive to make him pay for the cuckolding. In terms of narrative diversity Chaucer's rearrangement whereby this tale was relegated to the Shipman and the Wife of Bath with brilliant unexpectedness provided with a debased romance rather than a fabliau was superb. But it carried with it a danger, namely that one or two touches, such as the passage in which the Wife recalls the past with courageous nostalgia, might seem to colour the whole, and that the reader would carry away with him the remembrance of the beautiful, though in context inapposite line, 'Allas! allas! that evere love was synne!' rather than, for instance, the brutal grossness with which the Wife responded to her husband's reproaches to her for seeking a lover, 'Ye shul have queynte right ynogh et eve.'

That Chaucer was aware of the danger can be seen from his addition of lines 619–26 to the text:[44]

> Yet have I Martes mark upon my face,
> And also in another privee place.
> For God so wys be my savacioun,
> I ne loved nevere by no discrecioun,
> But evere folwede myn appetit,
> Al were he short, or long, or blak, or whit;
> I took no kep, so that he liked me,
> How poore he was, ne eek of what degree.

As we have seen, an inevitable corollary in literature of a young woman marrying an old husband was that she would take a young lover, and that the Wife of Bath had done so even more than once had

[44] Manly and Rickert, *Text*, II, 191–92. Of the five additions there listed this is the only one which substantially changes the moral tenor of the Prologue.

been indicated in the General Prologue, where she had had five husbands, 'Withouten oother compaignye in youthe,' and had been implied throughout her own Prologue. But this explicit statement of total promiscuity has a coarsening and alienating effect. Chaucer has used the same device here as in the Merchant's tale. Even if a woman has married an old husband of her own choice, there may still be some residual sympathy for her if she takes a young lover, but not, as with May, if she copulates with him up a tree, and not, as with the Wife of Bath, if she takes innumerable lovers without discrimination. Within context of course this addition does not make the Wife of Bath a repulsive figure but it does counteract any tendencies to take a romantic or sentimental view of her.

If the Wife of Bath is compared with her (and May's) descendents in Dunbar's *Tua Mariit Women and the Wedow*, one can see why as a literary figure she remains attractive despite the repulsiveness of her actions. For Dunbar's figures have become degraded by their experiences whilst the Wife of Bath remains triumphantly undegenerate. But the explanation is surely not that Chaucer thought that a mercenary or promiscuous use of sex would not degrade but rather that as a poet he had a rare and happy gift, namely that he could touch pitch without being defiled. In the *Tua Mariit Women* the effect of indulgence in repellent detail and the unmistakably prurient tone induce disgust but deflect the reader's judgment from moral precision, whilst in the Wife of Bath's Prologue the generally wholesome tone enables the sin to stand out undisguised. In Gower compassion for the sinner sometimes spills over into a blurring of the sin. This does not happen in Chaucer's poetry, and the Wife of Bath's Prologue in particular would be a lesser achievement if Chaucer had not succeeded in combining an amused sympathy for this highly literary though seemingly lifelike figure with a recognition that she exemplifies to a heightened and grotesque degree a misuse of female sexuality and marriage.

XIV

SAINTS' LIVES

THE Anglo-Saxons, on their conversion to Christianity, acquired a spiritual heroic past in the lives of the apostles, martyrs and confessors. The Roman missionaries fostered Anglo-Saxon awareness of their new heroic lineage: Gregory the Great sent relics, and in due course church dedications commemorated not only the apostles but also other famous saints, St. Lawrence, St. Martin, and Gregory the Great himself. But most important of all, during the seventh century, the Roman Church sent manuscripts of saints' lives. Bede was the first scholar to compose a historical martyrology, that is, one which did not merely record names and dates but which also gave a concise summary of the events leading to a martyr's death: for this work he must have had available a large number of passions of the saints. Apart from the saints' lives embedded in the *Ecclesiastical History*, Bede also composed a prose and metrical life of St. Cuthbert as companion pieces and the more historical work of the *Lives of the Abbots*. Slightly earlier, another life of St. Cuthbert had been written by an anonymous monk of Whitby, and the earliest known life of Gregory the Great had been written by an anonymous monk of Lindisfarne. The Whitby Life of St. Cuthbert and those of Bede all show skilled familiarity with the conventions of theme and style which were well established in the Latin tradition. However, this period of Anglo-Saxon hagiographical writing technically stands outside the history of Old English literature, since all the lives were written in Latin. In the Northumbrian Church there was obviously a zealous interest in the saints, and indeed a national pride in the fact that the English Church could contribute holy men such as St. Oswald and St. Cuthbert to the army of saints and martyrs. But the knowledge of these seems to have been largely confined to the monasteries, where Latin was the normal language of learned communication, or, for the native saints, it circulated among the people in informal, popular legend. There seem at this time to have been no saints' lives written in the vernacular, whether in poetry or prose. This inference from the absence of surviving texts is corroborated by Bede's summary of the subject-matter of Cædmon's poetry. From his detailed enumeration it is clear that Bede intended to indicate the exhaustiveness of this, and yet there is no mention of the saints. The monks, whose liturgical year was filled with commemoration of the saints, must have become well acquainted with the kind of Latin lives, now preserved for us in the great Bollandist series of the *Acta Sanctorum*, but the extent to which these were made known to lay audiences is uncertain. If, however, one allows that much of the fabulous element in Bede's account of Oswald derives from popular stories, then one must suppose that the people's expectation of miracles had at least been partly and indirectly fed from Latin sources.

The innovation of composing saints' lives in vernacular poetry seems to belong to Mercia towards the end of the eighth century. Of the six saints' lives in verse, three, *Elene, Juliana* and *Fates of the Apostles*, have conclusively been shown to come from this area by Dr. Sisam, on the grounds of the Anglian spelling of the name Cynewulf in the runic 'signatures'. The two poems on Guthlac (commonly referred to as *Guthlac A* and *Guthlac B*) can also safely be assigned to Mercia on grounds of subject-matter, for Guthlac was a relation of King Æthelbald of Mercia, who in 716 founded Crowland Abbey in his honour. However, the area of composition of the sixth poem, *Andreas*, cannot be established. On the grounds of style and historical tidiness it would be satisfactory to attribute it, not to Cynewulf himself, but to a poet associated with him in a common tradition of writing. But obviously the possibility must remain open that this common style was not restricted to a particular monastery or even to a particular kingdom, and that *Andreas* may, for instance, remain the sole survivor of a Northumbrian school of vernacular hagiography.

It is not at all astonishing that a leap should have been made from Latin prose to Old English poetry. In Anglo-Saxon England there seems to have been no tradition of narrative prose comparable in kind to the later Old Norse sagas. Verse was the vernacular medium for storytelling. At the same time the Anglo-Saxons could have found an authority for the adaption of the conventions of secular writing to hagiography in the *Peristephanon* of the fourth-century Spanish-Latin poet, Prudentius. In this work Prudentius versified the passions of fourteen martyrs in a style and metre designed to please an educated audience, whose standards and taste had been formed by the study of classical poetry. To extend the religious subject-matter of his poetry from Biblical paraphrase to saints' lives may seem such a natural step for an Anglo-Saxon writer to take that a search for a learned explanation in unnecessary. Nevertheless, the work of Prudentius was known in England, and the possibility that it at least encouraged his development is quite plausible.

There is little evidence of an interest in hagiography in Wessex in the late ninth century. The works chosen for translation in the Alfredian programme for a revival of learning are nearly all of a quite different kind. Only the *Dialogues* of Gregory the Great, translated by Alfred's assistant, Bishop Werferth of Worcester, could come under the heading of hagiography, for the second book consists of a life of St. Benedict and the fourth of the deaths of various holy men and of their visions of the other world. It was not until the Benedictine Revival that Anglo-Saxon literature gives evidence of a renewed interest in hagiography, and at this time its purpose again changed. In Northumbria the Latin lives had been designed for a monastic audience. In Mercia, the verse lives, whether intended for a lay or ecclesiastical audience, were obviously primarily intended as edifying substitutes for heroic poetry, and were constructed to please and entertain as well as to give information and instruction; and they could be best appreciated by those familiar with Old English heroic literature. But in the late tenth century hagiography became a part of the remarkable movement to provide sermons in the vernacular for the common people. Ælfric's *Catholic Homilies*, which supply sermons for most of the Sundays and feast-days of the liturgical year, naturally include lives of the apostles, and also of seven other famous martyrs and bishops. Besides these he also wrote a series of homilies on the lives of the lesser saints, including those particularly revered in England, St. Cuthbert, St. Oswald and St. Edmund. Ælfric was not the first to compose a vernacular saint's life in homiletic form. The earliest known is a ninth-century Mercian life of St. Chad, preserved through its inclusion in a twelfth-century manuscript of the *Catholic Homilies*, and perhaps composed for preaching at Lichfield on St. Chad's feast day (2 March), for St. Chad had been bishop of Mercia and it was at Lichfield that he had established his see. The *Blickling Homilies*, which include quite a number of saints' lives, are also slightly earlier than those of Ælfric. Ælfric was not the only writer of saints' lives in the late Old English period. Latin lives continued to be written, such as the almost contemporary life of Edward the Confessor, and Coleman's life of Bishop Wulfstan, which was written at the very end of the eleventh century, and is unfortunately no longer extant, though preserved in translation in the Latin chronicle of

William of Malmesbury.

The saint's life is a highly conventional form, and it must never be measured by the criteria which would be relevant to a modern biography. We should no more look to it for historical or psychological truth than we would to a medieval romance. In origins it is part panegyric, part epic, part romance, part sermon, and historical fact dissolves within the conventions of these forms. A simple comparison may illustrate the difference between the methods of hagiography and history. Ælfric in his Passion of St. Bartholomew describes the conversion of a pagan king, Polymius, and his household. The apostle brings about this change of heart, first by healing the king's daughter of a frenzy and then by compelling a devil, who is concealed within an idol, to confess his identity and to shatter the idol to pieces. With this may be compared Bede's well-known account of Paulinus's conversion of King Edwin: the king summons a council, listens to the advice of Coifi with his image of the sparrow flying through a lighted hall, and after further reflection agrees to the destruction of the pagan shrines. One description has the ring of truth, the other of fiction, but at the same time it is clear what kind of truth the fiction symbolically conveys. Bede describes the scene as an eye-witness might have observed it, but the Passion of St. Bartholomew aims to uncover a Christian truth beneath the surface: that the true Christian is all-powerful, that it is the devil whom idolaters worship, and that conversion is brought about through divine help. It would be a quite practicable exercise to rewrite the story of Polymius's conversion in the manner of the *Ecclesiastical History* or of King Edwin in the manner of the hagiographer. Bede, as has often been pointed out, distinguishes clearly between the methods of the historian and the hagiographer: there is a difference, for instance, between his treatment of material in the highly miraculous *Life of St. Cuthbert* and in the non-miraculous *Lives of the Abbots*; and, though, he uses both methods in the *Ecclesiastical History*, there is reason to think that he was self-consciously aware of when he passed to and fro from one style to the other. It therefore is very important not to confuse what the writers themselves so sharply distinguished, and also to recognise that the garish, spectacular action of most saints' lives is designed to reveal a kind of religious truth which would not stand out so clearly from the confused appearances of everyday life.

In the self-contained world of the saint's life there are two elements which need some further explanation: one is the role of the devil and his relationship to idolatry, the other the importance of miracles. There were two possible explanations of the gods of heathenism. The euhemeristic interpretation was that the pagan gods were originally ordinary human beings. This view is implicit in Anglo-Saxon genealogies and stated explicitly by Ælfric and Wulfstan in their sermons, *De Falsis Deis*: it occurs only very rarely in hagiography (for instance, in Ælfric's sermon on St. Sebastian). The other, propagandist, interpretation was that founded on and summed up in Psalm 96:5, 'All the gods of the heathen are demons'.[1] This view, familiar from *Beowulf*, is a basic presupposition of the saint's life. The fact, therefore, that the Roman pagans are not merely ignorant or foolish in their worship of idols but thereby actually become servants of the devil, gives a kind of dualistic view of the world to the saint's life, in which the soldiers of God are arrayed against the supporters of devil. They are, of course, free from the dualistic heresy in that the opposing forces are so obviously not of equal power. In the face of good, evil becomes blustering, timid and helpless. Nevertheless, within the limits of his ultimate helplessness, the devil was both important and fearful and the chief adversary of the martyr. In the stress upon the devil and the consequent dignity accorded to him there is a close relationship between the theory of martyrdom and the patristic doctrine of the Redemption. According to the theory of the 'devil's rights' the nature of the Redemption consisted of the defeat of the devil by Christ on the Cross, and in literary treatment the devil was therefore represented more seriously than he was in the Middle Ages, when the 'satisfaction' theory reduced him to a subordinate role. For in the scholastic period God was no longer thought to have become man in order to free mankind from the devil who had a just claim to him, but in order to reconcile man to Himself, and therefore, when the devil was no longer a figure whose claims had to be respected even by God, he became reduced to the ludicrous figure of later medieval drama. In the earlier tradition, however, he was not completely lacking in dignity—the Fathers stressed that he was a fallen *angel*—and just as he was the adversary whom Christ came to defeat so also he was the chief enemy of the martyr. The commonest patristic definition of martyrdom was that of a conquest of the devil. For this reason the heroic image is highly appropriate in the saint's life, just as it is in *The Dream of the Rood*, and it was, of course, not

[1] This is a translation of the Vulgate (Ps. 95:5). The Authorised Version has: 'For all the gods of the nations are idols.'

invented by the Anglo-Saxon writers but imitated from their sources. Nowadays it is difficult to think of the Crucifixion or of martyrdom except in terms of love. But in order to understand Anglo-Saxon literature it is essential to exclude this later medieval interpretation.

The Anglo-Saxon also inherited two views of the miraculous: one was that God continued to demonstrate His power by miracles, the other—on the whole held by Augustine and Gregory the Great—that miracles had ceased after the period of the New Testament. But on the subject of miracles, as Delehaye has said, 'there was in each Father, as it were, two men'. Bede, who in different places states both views, was following an authoritative tradition of apparent self-contradiction. Again there is a difference here between the historian and the hagiographer. A Christian historian will only accept a miraculous interpretation of an event if no other seems possible; the hagiographer will prefer a miraculous interpretation unless a naturalistic explanation is inescapable. By definition also the hagiographer cannot allow the working of God's grace to remain secret. Christian credulity is not strained by the idea of God's grace guiding the imagination of a Christian poet, but according to the conventions of hagiography such guidance must be made manifest by a vision of divine origin. Many miracle stories are covered by these generalisations, but there remain a large number in which it is not possible thus to disentangle fact from hagiographical convention. For these another kind of distinction must be made, that is, between those which have a doctrinal foundation and those which are merely fanciful. It has been shown that the miracles in the *Ecclesiastical History* can be divided into clear doctrinal categories which have their prototypes in the *Dialogues* of Gregory the Great. But, while some of the miracles of the saints' lives are of this kind, equally often they are merely fantastic demonstrations of power. St. Peter and St. Paul, for instance, are assisted by God to be yet better magicians than their opponent Simon Magus. In such miracles it is not easy to distinguish popular superstition from literary artifice or edification from delight. Propagandist evidence for God's power can also delight a taste for the marvellous. It must not be thought that such a taste necessarily indicates naiveté. Like the medieval romance, the saint's life as a genre can please by a deliberate and skilful exploitation of the strange, and is designed to arouse a romantic sense of wonder.

One of the most frequent forms of the saint's life is the passion. In this narrative of martyrdom the historical world is heightened and distorted in order to magnify the hero. Every emperor is a persecutor of the Christians and local governors execute imperial edicts with malignant ferocity. Judge and prisoner engage in a verbal theological battle which bears no relationship to the dry and brief investigation which could have been recorded in proconsular acts. No martyr is simply put to death, but undergoes spectacular tortures which are related zealously and in detail. These are borne by the martyrs with insolent contempt. Whereas in the early and historical passions it was stressed that the martyr suffered, though by faith he could see beyond the torment of the body, in the epic passion the martyr is endowed with what seems a superhuman indifference to pain. Most important of all is the emphasis on the miraculous which reflects the pre-eminence of the martyr who is protected at every turn by divine intervention. There is a quite different tone here from that of the more historical passions, where the miraculous is treated in a discreet and dignified way.

This pattern is reflected very clearly in *Juliana*. The widespread slaughter of Christians and destruction of churches as a result of the emperor's edict is described with forceful variation in the opening lines. The consul, Heliseus, has no character apart from that of a torturer of Christians, and Juliana's father is equally evil. Both of these are defeated in verbal battle with the saint. The four separate tortures inflicted upon Juliana are described in detail: naked, she is beaten with rods, for six hours she hangs from a beam by her hair, she is tied to a wheel affixed with swords and enveloped in fire, and she is placed in a vessel of molten lead. In none of these episodes is it suggested that she suffers any pain, and from the last two, which should naturally have ended in death, she is saved by an angel. The poet stresses that she emerges from these whole and unharmed. It is interesting to notice, however, that the Old English *Juliana* is closer to the common pattern of martyr's deaths than the texts of the Latin source which survive. In these, contrary to custom, the consul by his own standards is a reasonable man. He has no devilish hatred for Christians. On the contrary, in order to win Juliana in marriage, he is willing to believe in the Christian faith, though he refuses baptism out of fear for his life. Since it is clear that none of the surviving texts represents that followed by Cynewulf, it cannot be certain that this is Cynewulf's own modification. But the analogous transformation of the character of Holofernes in *Judith* suggests that this may well have been a deliberate Anglo-Saxon return to the stock pattern. The Latin version is, of course, the more subtle: since Heliseus's offer is by one standard so reasonable, Juliana's rejection of it is the more heroic.

There is also a more coherent relationship between Heliseus's tempting offer and the devil's temptation of Juliana disguised as an angel of light (the latter is a recurrent hagiographical motif). The significance of this disguise is repeatedly commented upon in the *Moralia* of Gregory the Great. It is, as it were, an allegorical expression of the insidious way in which the mind can be persuaded that what it wants to do it is also right that it should do. Juliana, of course, is as unmoved by the blandishments and apparent reasonableness of Heliseus as she is by the devil's pretence that God has sent her the message that she should do sacrifice to idols. The moral and psychological parallelism, however, is lost, if from the outset Heliseus acts and speaks from manifest wickedness.

For a long time the passion of Juliana was a comparatively popular story, granted that she was not a famous saint and had no connection with England. It is, therefore, fair to ask why Cynewulf chose to translate it and what kind of people of the early as well as the later Middle Ages enjoyed a story which, however well-told, now seems an uncomfortable mixture of the didactic and spectacular. The early Middle English version with the related texts of the 'Katherine Group' was undoubtedly intended for an audience of religious women, and it is most probable that Cynewulf's version was similarly intended for a convent of nuns. This is very clear in the Middle English text, where, in accordance with twelfth-century thought and the conventions of the 'Wooing Group', Christ is imagined as a more desirable lover than Heliseus. But even in the Anglo-Saxon poem there is an emphasis upon Juliana's dedication of her virginity to God, a point not found in the Latin texts, though it is a commonplace of other lives of virgin martyrs. While no Anglo-Saxon nun need expect to endure such persecutions, there was a model for them in Juliana's rejection of a prosperous lover and committal of her virginity to God. The pleasures to be derived from the text are perhaps equally obvious. In the description of the tortures there was certainly an element of the sensational. In the fact that the martyr is a woman, who resists to the end an unwelcome suitor, there are elements of a plot with popular appeal. It has been suggested that this kind of passion was influenced by the late Greek romances, in which the heroine was often compelled to escape by skill or stratagem from the determined pursuit of a villainous suitor. Though no parallel for this plot can be found in Anglo-Saxon secular literature, it may still be thought that such a plot would not necessarily be unappealing to popular taste in any period. Above all, for a feminine audience there is the pleasure in seeing the principle of heroic magnification applied to a woman. In the later Middle Ages there was a clear distinction between literature psychologically designed to please women and that designed to please men. In the Anglo-Saxon period the particular tastes of the ladies of a noble household seem not to have been considered by the authors of secular poetry, but *Juliana* is unmistakably a religious poem designed for the pleasure and edification of women in a religious community.

The feast of St. Juliana was celebrated on 16 February, but, if the preceding interpretation of the poem is correct, there is no reason to suppose that it was intended primarily for reading or recitation on that day. *Elene*, however, is more probably to be connected with the feast of the Invention of the Cross, a feast of eighth-century Gallican provenance, which could either have reached England directly or by the ninth century could have been adopted here through the authoritative intermediary of Rome. The poem has been given the title of *Elene* from the time of Jacob Grimm's edition of 1840, but it is not a narrative about Elene (Helena, the mother of Constantine) in the sense that *Juliana* is a poem about Juliana. The Latin source is called the *Acta Cyriaci*, in other words the hero of the story is the Jew, who is at first recalcitrant, but later finds the Cross of Helena, and becomes bishop of Jerusalem and a worker of miracles. However, when the feast of the Invention was established, the same *Acta* remained the source for sermons, as, for instance, in the later *Golden Legend*, though Ælfric in his sermon for the Invention leaves out the part played by Judas Cyriacus. It is necessary to stress the inappropriateness of the title, since, if the subject were primarily Helena, the structure of the poem and of its source would be curious. The outlines, however, become clear if the subject is taken to be either the Cross or Judas. In the Latin text followed by Cynewulf there is a prologue describing the vision of Constantine, and the victory and conversion which followed. In *Elene* the substance of this prologue is extended to form a quarter of the whole poem, for these preliminaries give Cynewulf an opportunity for many well-turned amplifications and expansions of his text. This expansion, however, is structurally appropriate, since the stress falls on the Cross and this provides a balance with the glorification of the Cross at the end. The main part of the narrative, however, is given to Judas. Here there is an awkwardness of conception—already present in the source—in that Elene's judicial investigation of Judas and the torturing of him until he submits, is quite obviously modelled upon the outlines of a passion: it is, as it were, an inverted passion, in which the ruler is the Christian and the prisoner the pagan. The reader or hearer who has grown accustomed to the simple distribution of sympathies required of him in the passion may well become confused in *Elene*. The heroic resolve of the martyr, who speaks from physical weakness, sounds false from Elene, surrounded by a strong well-armed company of soldiers, and, though the spiritual blindness of Judas before his conversion is emphasised, his resistance, which is structurally that of the martyr, may arouse an unintended sympathy. None of this is the fault of Cynewulf, who follows fairly closely the outlines of his source: indeed it could only have been eliminated by a radical recasting of the story, which would have been an improper and indeed an inconceivable manner of treating it. However, it is part of Cynewulf's method to embellish and intensify each element of his source. This method, of course, works most satisfactorily when the source is highly consistent, as in *Juliana*, but it also makes inconsistencies stand out with a clarity lacking in the original.

Stylistically, *Elene* is of interest in its demonstration of Anglo-Saxon methods. That Cynewulf inserts set-pieces, such as the description of the sea-voyage from Italy to Jerusalem, has, of course, often been commented upon. Perhaps more remarkable than such inventions are the typical parts in which Cynewulf is closely following his source, but extracts more imaginative meaning from it by the Anglo-Saxon system of variation. A characteristic example may be seen in lines 611–18. The Latin has 'Et quis in solitudine constitutus, panibus sibi appositus, lapides manducat' based on Matthew (7:9) ['And who, finding himself in a desert, when bread is put before him will eat stones?']. In Old English this becomes:

Hu mæg þæm geweorðan þe on westenne
meðe ond meteleas morland trydeð,
hungre gehæfted ond him hlaf ond stan
on gesihðe bu geweorðað
stea[r]c ond hnesce, þæt he þone stan nime
wið hungres hleo, hlafes ne gime,
gewende to wædle ond þa wiste wiðsæce,
beteran wiðhyccge þonne he bega beneah.[2]

[2] 'How could it happen with him who walks the desert and moorland, weary and food-less, and who sees bread and a stone, one hard one soft, that he should take the stone to ward off his hunger and ignore the bread, choose want and reject sustenance, refuse the better when he has both at his disposal.'

The biblical text has already been expanded in the Latin through its association with the first of Christ's temptations in the wilderness, and this Cynewulf again amplifies: the man is weary and hungry, he is in a desert and a wild place, and the actual qualities of bread and stones come to life, one soft, one hard, one representing food, the other want. This passage has not been chosen because it comes from a particular dramatic episode, but rather as a typical illustration of the method used by Cynewulf throughout: that is, that each idea is explored and intensified through a series of well-chosen and controlled variations. Sometimes Cynewulf uses the traditional style mechanically: it is by no means pointedly appropriate that Constantine should return from his vision and defeat of a deadly enemy 'exulting in booty'. But more often he amplifies what is present elegantly and imaginatively. Cynewulf's method reminds one of eighteenth-century theories of poetry. The conception of the story with its structure and episodes is given but the story in its new telling is 'to advantage dressed'. The skill lies, not in fresh thoughts, but in the manipulation of a highly-skilled and polished style. Despite its consistency, the effect of style and treatment in *Juliana* can result in monotony. In *Elene* changes of scene, varieties of action and modulation of tone combine to produce greater brightness and solidity.

The third of the poems of Cynewulf which comes under the heading of hagiography is *The Fates of the Apostles*. This might be called a Christian *Widsith*, though it is not modelled upon this kind of summary of heroic legend but on the Christian tradition of enumerating together the fates of the twelve apostles. The design of the poem, which, despite the absence of dates, is largely mnemonic, gives no opportunity for literary quality. Within such limited compass the brief characterisation of the apostles as heroic and loyal thegns and their persecutors as devil-inspired heathen seems exceptionally mechanical. It is a pity that the highly conventional poetic style and diction of Old English poetry prevented writers from using a plain style for mnemonic verse of the kind that was competently and unpretentiously used in the later Middle Ages.

These three poems, *Elene, Juliana* and *The Fates of the Apostles*, all end with an epilogue not derived from their respective sources. In general tone these epilogues are melancholy and admonitory. The poet, speaking in the person of Everyman, laments the passing of happiness and the terrifying imminence of death and the Last Judgment. These reflections are not autobiographical memories but reflections appropriate to every Christian. The consciousness of sin and the saddened acceptance of old age are not individualised. A possible source for the device of attaching an epilogue of this kind to a saint's life has been found by Miss Gradon in one of the lives of the *Vitae Patrum*. This kind of epilogue would by its sentiments attract an Old English poet, and it is therefore not surprising that, though Cynewulf may have known only one example of this out of hundreds of saints' lives, he nevertheless chose to imitate it. There are obvious affinities between the tone of the epilogue of St. Ephraem and that of parts of *The Wanderer* and *The Seafarer*, and Cynewulf in his variations no doubt drew upon the same kind of sources as did the authors of the elegiac poetry. Poetically, the epilogues of Cynewulf are extremely effective. The semi-symbolical treatment of the action in the saints' lives could suggest a facile judgment of the problems of moral behaviour, and therefore this return to a more recognisable world, in which life is sad and virtue difficult, gives retrospective weight to the confidence and heroism of the saint which had been so emphasised before. From the literary point of view, it is one of the disadvantages of the hagiographical convention that complexities of feeling are impermissible, and therefore the subtlety achieved in *Beowulf* is quite beyond its range. But the epic exaltation of bravery unmodulated by the epic awareness of mortality can appear crudely bright. The epilogues of Cynewulf dissipate this effect of brashness.

The epilogues also serve the further purpose of preserving the poet's name though unfortunately not, for us nowadays, his identity. The author explains that he gives his name in order that his audience may pray for him, but it is fair to infer that this idea indicates a new conception of the poet or at least of the religious poet. This conception—equally clear from the religious motifs in the story of Cædmon—is that the religious poet, like saints and prophets, is inspired and supported by God: it would therefore be fitting that his poems should not be absorbed into a common stock of anonymous verse, but should remain identifiably his own. Cynewulf's use of the runic alphabet may be seen as an ingenious variation of the acrostics and anagrams used in Latin poetry of the ninth century. The use of the runic alphabet for commemorative inscriptions on tombstones might also suggest a particular appropriateness, but it seems unlikely that we should infer from either usage a superstitious trust in the magical efficacy which runes were originally thought to possess. Cynewulf clearly expected an audience capable of understanding this kind of device, for, while graphically the letters stand out clearly, listeners might well miss the double significance of the names of the runic letters, most of which were also common words. Only in one poem, *The Fates of the Apostles*, does Cynewulf draw the hearer's attention to what he must expect: 'The wise man...may here find who composed this poem.' But no such alert is given in the other poems, though it has been suggested that the slightly strained use of some words might also act as a signal. But it is reasonable to assume an audience acquainted with the name of the poet and familiar with such devices, so that probably only a slight emphasis in reading would be necessary in order to draw their attention to the concealed meaning.

With *Elene* and *The Fates of the Apostles* in one manuscript is *Andreas*. The fact that the main contents of this manuscript, the Vercelli Book, consists of sermons suggests that *Andreas* was on this occasion copied for use as a sermon or for monastic reading on St. Andrew's Day (30 November). Originally, however, it probably served a more literary purpose. Andreas may at first sight seem a disconcerting mixture of epic and romance. It derives from one of the earliest collections of hagiographical romances, the apocryphal acts of the apostles, and behind these lies a complicated ancestry which includes the *Odyssey*. But, though much of the detail belongs to the world of romance, the action is far more literally heroic than that of a passion. Nowadays this may seem a hybrid and unsatisfactory mixture: episodes contrived to appeal to the reader's delight in the marvellous might seem to detract from the dignified elevation of thought proper to an epic. This mixture in *Andreas* is particularly interesting because of the poem's relationship to *Beowulf*.

In the poetry of Cynewulf there occur many phrases or half-lines which recall *Beowulf*, but they are unobtrusive, and would perhaps be quite unnoticeable if a larger body of poetry survived. They are obviously used as part of a common poetic stock rather than with direct reference to a precise and previous usage. The author of *Andreas*, however, flaunts his many borrowings from *Beowulf*. Lines or even pairs of lines are repeated for the sake of the allusion rather than for their propriety in the new context. It is clearly part of the author's technique to recall *Beowulf* in the same way as it was Milton's to recall the *Aeneid* by his Latinisms and echoes of it in *Paradise Lost*. An important question about *Andreas* is therefore that of whether the author was well judged in making this marked implicit insistence on a likeness to *Beowulf*.

In the source of *Andreas* the elements of the fabulous and romantic are far stronger than the heroic. The opponents of St. Andrew and St.

Matthew are not people, normal though wicked, but a race with strange customs of the kind commonly described in eastern travellers' tales. It is the world of the fantastic and marvellous, now best known from the much later example of this genre, the *Travels of Sir John Mandeville*. The people to whom St. Matthew goes to preach the gospel are the Anthropophagites, who, as their name indicates, are cannibals. They also possess a magic potion, which, like that of Circe, deprives men of their reason and reduces them to the state of animals. St. Andrew, when relating Christ's works to while away the time on his sea journey, describes a highly apocryphal miracle. Like a magician, Christ brings to life two carved seraphim in the temple and sends them to awaken the patriarchs, Abraham, Isaac and Jacob, from their graves. During the sea voyage also the companions of St. Andrew are granted a vision of heaven: their souls are carried aloft by eagles in a manner which recalls the fate of Ganymede rather than the experience of St. Paul. Only a part of the fabulous elements are here summarised. There can be no doubt that *Andreas* was designed to entertain those who already enjoyed stories of far-fetched wonders such as those of the Alexander legend.

Therefore the value of relating *Andreas* to *Beowulf* in part depends upon the extent to which Beowulf would also have satisfied such a taste for the marvellous. It has been pointed out before that in the extant manuscript *Beowulf* is included with a group of texts consisting of a homily on St. Christopher, *The Marvels of the East* and *The Letter of Alexander*, and that the common element of these four is monsters. It has further been inferred from this that Grendel's ancestry may lie as much in eastern traditions of fabulous monsters as in Germanic mythology. *The Marvels of the East* was certainly known in the eighth century, perhaps with illustrations. The late Anglo-Saxon illuminated manuscript of *The Marvels of the East*[3] shows a monster in human shape, but with bestial characteristics, tearing a man, about a third his size, to pieces. This would be a perfect illustration for Grendel. Though there are no verbal similarities between the description of Grendel devouring a man and that of the habits of the Anthropophagites, there is a strong similarity in tone with the dwelling upon the horrific unnaturalness of cannibalism. It is possible that nowadays, rightly prizing the epic dignity of *Beowulf*, we underestimate the elements of romance, and either

[3] *Marvels of the East*, ed. M. R. James (1929), MS Cotton Tiberius B v, f.81*v*.

ignore them or too readily accept that the Anglo-Saxons would not have found them strange. A poem which contains a giant cannibal, a dragon (also included in *The Marvels of the East*) and a hero with superhuman powers is unlikely to have the same tone of unflagging gravity as the *Aeneid*, and therefore it can be said that the author of *Andreas* was appropriately reminded of *Beowulf* by the romance elements in his source.

It is less certain that the author of *Andreas* was wise to recall so self-consciously the heroic quality of *Beowulf*. Admittedly, he manipulated his source with discretion in order to intensify the heroic tone. For instance, in the source little is made of St. Andrew's arrival at the shore and his finding of the boat, but in *Andreas* he marches down 'brave and resolute, eager for deeds of courage', and finds the sea beating on the sand, the sun glowing and a broad, deep ship. In the source the action is not thus magnified: the only epithets are *beatus* [blessed] for St. Andrew and *parvus* [small] of the ship. Again, the passage in which the companions of St. Andrew refuse to abandon him in danger and imagine themselves as faithless retainers, should they do so ('Where should we go without a lord, sorrowing at heart, ... if we betray you'), is a perfect development from the briefer speech of loyalty in the original, and it would be possible to multiply examples of this kind. Nevertheless the total effect is not quite satisfactory, for *Andreas* falls between two stools. On the one hand, it contains a certain amount of heroic action, particularly in the expedition of St. Andrew to Mermedonia, and therefore the references to martial courage are not unmistakably metaphorical or limited to a spiritual meaning as in the passions of the martyrs. On the other hand, in contrast to *Beowulf*, the heroism in *Andreas* is never fulfilled in actual fighting: St. Andrew, for instance, advances as a 'resolute warrior' to the place where St. Matthew is imprisoned, but as he reaches it, the seven men who are standing guard drop dead. The episode had deliberately recalled *Beowulf*, and therefore there is an inevitable sense of anticlimax. From the modern point of view, therefore, the comparison of *Andreas* and *Beowulf* is unfortunate, and the poet seems imprudent to have demanded it. Compared with *Beowulf, Andreas* seems light-weight, mechanical, even occasionally ludicrous, whereas if we compare the poem with its source, we can see that the author, like Cynewulf, was adept in developing ideas, and judged the tone of his original very well. It is best therefore to enjoy *Andreas* as a good story, without too much solemnity of judgment either from the religious or literary point of view.

In all the poems so far discussed the authors have been closely following a Latin source. The two poems in honour of Guthlac are of particular interest because both style and interpretation are the poets' own. The eighth-century Latin life of Guthlac is modelled in design on the famous Life of St. Anthony translated by Evagrius and this, in turn, like many saints' lives, follows the outline of the Greek panegyric: that is, it begins with the birth of the saint, continues with the marvellous aspects of his childhood and education, his way of life, deeds, etc. In contrast to this, *Guthlac A* begins with the saint already established as a devout ascetic and *Guthlac B* is a poem about the saint's death. The interpretation and tone of both poems are also different from those of Felix's Latin life. While the latter is fiercer and less serene than the Life of Anthony, it nevertheless echoes the sober devotion of its model, and seems designed, like the Life of Anthony, for the instruction of monks, who would see in the respective saints a pattern of holiness, which might be too perfect for their imitation, but was not in kind beyond their aspirations. The Latin life falls roughly into four parts: the early history of Guthlac, his struggle with the devil, his miracles, and death. *Guthlac A*, except for a brief reference at the end of his death, consists entirely of a description of the saint's heroic encounters with the devil: indeed the author of *Guthlac A* has imposed upon his life of an ascetic recluse the pattern of an epic passion. In tone and structure it is far closer to *Juliana* than to any other life of an English solitary, whether in Latin or the vernacular. The structure of both poems is a series of heroic, verbal encounters between the saint and the devil (in *Juliana* also with his servant Heliseus), interspersed with torments and afflictions imposed directly or indirectly by the devil.

In his presentation of the story the author has been influenced by a number of related ideas. That the life of a solitary involved recurrent combat with the devil is, of course, an important theme of the Life of Anthony and of later saints' lives modelled upon it. These attacks of the devil are in part physical and external. The devil, more and more displaced from his old habitations by the spreading of the Church, is particularly angry to be deprived of his desert strongholds. So in *Guthlac* the devils complain that the saint has taken possession of their refuge in the *westenne*, a secret place in which before they had been able to rest. In the Life of Anthony the devils in their efforts to dislodge the saint from his chosen place of retirement at times use physical force, so that on one occasion, for instance, Anthony is found beaten and nearly dying. But more often the attacks of the devil are psychological, such as stirrings to lust or thoughts of duties to relatives necessarily abandoned. There are touches of this kind of temptation in *Guthlac A*, as when the devils, having threatened that the saint will be burnt alive, add that his sufferings will be a source of great distress to his kinsmen. In other words, the temptation psychologically appropriate is represented as the work of the devil. Though this detail does not occur in Felix's Life, most of the attacks in it are of this psychological kind, incitements to despair or to excessive mortification. In *Guthlac A*, however, the main attacks are actually physical or are threats of physical pain, to which the saint replies in speeches of resolution, anger and contempt, highly reminiscent of the style of a passion. In detail it often corresponds to Felix's Life: the difference lies rather in emphasis, that what is briefly mentioned in the Latin becomes important in *Guthlac A*, and that what is analysed at length in the first is scarcely mentioned in the second. It is only in the curious episode of the vision of hell that they truly correspond. Such visions, deriving ultimately from the *Apocalypse of Paul*, were fairly common: Bede, for instance, gives accounts of the visions of Fursey and Drihtelm. But in *Guthlac* the vision is used rather illogically, since its normal and obvious purpose was not as an encouragement to sin but as a deterrent, and therefore the conveyor of the soul was always an angel, not a devil. Among differences of emphasis the most important is that of the heroic idea. The Latin *Guthlac*, like so much hagiographical literature, contains the image of the saint as the *miles Christi*, the warrior of God equipped with the spiritual armour described by St. Paul. But in the Latin this occurs in an isolated passage, while in the poem phrases such as *Cristes cempa* [warrior of Christ] or *eadig oretta* [blessed champion] occur with refrain-like insistence.

This martial imagery is, of course, related to the fact already mentioned, that the author of *Guthlac A* was not interested in the psychological struggles of the ascetic life, and therefore presented the devil as an external persecutor, not as an internal tempter. A double conception of the role of the devil was traditional from the patristic period onwards, and it could, of course, also be combined in the passion. In *Juliana*, for instance, the devil is primarily the external enemy who prompts Heliseus to evil and assists him with advice. But, when he appears to Juliana disguised as an angel of light—a commonplace of hagiographical temptation scenes—and urges her to sacrifice to idols in order to save her life, he has become the psychological tempter. Although this kind of temptation properly belongs to the life of the ascetic, there is far less of it in *Guthlac* than in *Juliana*. The poet conceives the devils' attacks upon *Guthlac* entirely in terms of martyrdom. Here he follows the tradition which developed after the great persecutions of the Christians had ended, when it was held that it was not the shedding of blood alone that constituted martyrdom, but also a holy life entirely devoted to God. St. Jerome, for instance, wrote to Eustochium on the death of her mother Paula: 'It is not only the shedding of blood that is regarded as a confession, but the consecrated life of a devout soul is indeed a daily martyrdom.' For this reason the author of *Guthlac* actually refers to the saint as *se martyre* (line 514).

Guthlac's heroic life of virtue is given a vaster and cosmic significance by being set within the context of the hostility between the devil and the guardian angel. The belief that a guardian angel is assigned to every soul at the moment of is infusion into the body did not become widespread until the later Middle Ages. In the patristic period opinions varied: the author of *Guthlac* quite clearly follows one of the established theories, that is, that the assistance of a guardian angel is a privilege of the saintly. As the poem now stands, it begins with a description of the meeting of the guardian angel with the holy soul after death, but this passage, and perhaps all the lines up to line 108, seem to be an accretion, the stages of which it is no longer possible to distinguish. It has, however, a general relevance through the emphasis that the poet later puts upon the guardian angel; and emphasis which seems to be the poet's own, since the angel does not occur in Felix's Life, where the role of protector is entirely given to St. Bartholomew. The stress upon the conflict of angel and devil fits well with the poet's insistence upon Guthlac as 'the warrior of God'. A life of solitary asceticism is given a heroic magnitude by being enclosed in a supernatural framework.

It is difficult to estimate the quality of *Guthlac A*. The poem is shapeless because there is no story to progress. The basic story which holds together the many long speeches of which *Juliana* chiefly consists is completely lacking in *Guthlac*. This lack of variety in content is reflected in monotony of tone, which is didactic and narrowly heroic, unvaried and unsubtle. It seems limited and inflexible compared with traditional Latin ascetic lives in which courageous struggles were mingled with many passages which described the spiritual serenity of a life devoted to God. In such descriptions the desert retreat of a solitary would seem more like paradise than a field of battle. There is a touch of this kind of sentiment at the end of *Guthlac A*, when Guthlac *sigehreðig* [triumphant] after his final battle against the devils returns, and the birds show by signs their delight at *eadges eftcyme* [return of the blessed man], and feed from his hand. Gentleness and holiness of disposition are most commonly indicated in the eastern saints' lives by this return to a paradisal relationship between man and the animals. This transition into calm comes as a satisfactory conclusion to *Guthlac A*, but the passage is too short and too abruptly introduced for it to carry full weight or to be in proportion to the rest.

The subject of *Guthlac B* is the death of Guthlac, and the saint's life up to this moment is mentioned only in a brief introductory summary. The death of a saint always formed a most important part of his biography. Bede, for instance, gives a long account of the death of Cuthbert and, no doubt influenced by the same hagiographical tradition, devoted a third of the account of Cædmon to his death. Moreover, a commonplace of such death-bed descriptions was the emphasis on the saint's foreknowledge of the time of his death. The concern with Guthlac's death can therefore be explained in terms of well-established tradition, but the idea of making it the subject of an individual poem perhaps again suggests the influence of the passion. But the influence of the passion certainly does not extend beyond form. For, though the death-bed was usually thought of as the moment of supreme struggle against the devil, and therefore *Guthlac B* could easily have been written in the style of *Guthlac A*, the poems are in fact quite different. In *Guthlac B* there is a complexity and range of feeling which make it very unlike *Guthlac A* and indeed quite untypical of hagiography, whether Anglo-Saxon or Latin. In part there is here the serenity of the saintly disposition which belongs to the Antonine tradition: Guthlac's soul passes from his body eager for the joys of eternal blessedness, and this holy contentment is symbolised by the light and sweet perfume which adorn the corpse. Guthlac's attitude could be summed up in the words of St. Paul, 'I desire to die and be with Christ'. But in *Guthlac B* this anticipation and longing for the life of heaven is set very firmly in an elegiac background. Even Guthlac himself sees death as something which saddens the spirit, while the poet's sombre third person narrative and the laments of Guthlac's companion and servant are more reminiscent of the tone of the second half of *Beowulf* than anything else in Old English poetry. Summary or quotation is inadequate to convey this tone: the effect of sadness, profound but highly controlled, can only be appreciated by the reading of the original, where well-established formulas, skilfully used, both impose an artistic pattern on the grief while at the same time suggesting its inevitability. The final elegiac effect derives from the fact that the poem seems to end, not with the joyful description of Guthlac's soul being borne to heaven by angels, but by the lament of his servant, who speaks in the role of the bereaved retainer. The last words of the poem as it now stands are: 'Ic sceal sarigferð, heanmod hweorfan, hyge drusendne' [Sad at heart I must go away, grieving and with mournful spirit]. From the evidence of the manuscript it is clear that either only a few lines are missing or else a large section, which would presumably have followed the Latin Life in describing the burial, the later discovery of the saint's body uncorrupted, etc. It is most tempting to assume the former. Without *Guthlac B* we might well have assumed that the Anglo-Saxon melancholy sensitivity to transience and the Christian confidence in the Resurrection were at least poetically irreconcilable. But *Guthlac B* shows that, on the contrary, the ideas did not need to be kept separate lest they should diminish or obscure each other, but could be combined in such a way that each served to make the other more poignant. The poet of *Guthlac B*, like the poets of *Beowulf* and *The Dream of the Rood*, surely had a perception and sensibility which marked him out from other writers, craftsmanlike but less imaginatively fine. In poetic quality *Guthlac B* stands out very clearly from the rest of Old English saints' lives.

The whole range of Latin hagiography is most completely represented in Ælfric's *Lives of the Saints*, a series of sermons covering many saints whose feasts were not—to use the familiar later terminology—red-letter days; in other words, of saints whom, as Ælfric says in his Preface, 'the monks, not the laity, honour by liturgical offices'. Ælfric, however, also states in his Preface that he intended these lives for the laity, for he explains how he has left on one side the *Vitae Patrum* 'as they contain many subtle points which it is not fitting for the laity to know'. This accounts for the fact that he does not include versions of the lives of any of the desert fathers, not even of Evagrius's translation of the Life of St. Anthony by Athanasius or of St. Jerome's Life of Paul the Hermit. The fact that the complete series with its preface now only survives in one manuscript perhaps suggests that Ælfric's design did not meet any obvious or widespread need. There are, however, two other surviving manuscripts in which a large part of the series has been combined with the saints' lives from the *Catholic Homilies*, and here the intention seems to have been to produce a vernacular passional. This raises the interesting, though perhaps unanswerable, question of whether, in the first part of the eleventh century, sermons to monks could be delivered in the vernacular.

The style and metrical rhythm of the *Lives of the Saints* have been frequently debated. It seems clear that Ælfric in his idea of an adorned prose was influenced by Latin models, but that he drew upon characteristically English rhythms deriving from the alliterative metre. Moreover, however much in places he may use the balance and antithesis of his models, and however constant may be his use of alliteration as a substitute for the rhyme of Latin mannered prose, the effect is nevertheless quite different. The effect of Latin rhymed prose is something highly wrought and artificially contrived, while much of Ælfric's prose, despite its rhythms, at first reading seems simple to the point of artlessness. Whereas the rhetorical and rhythmical devices of the one are flourished, in the work of the other they seem deliberately understated. Ælfric's claim in his Preface to the *Catholic Homilies* to write in a simple style for laymen is not merely a conventional disclaimer of literary pretensions nor relevant only to the *Homilies* themselves. Ælfric's style is smooth, flowing, lucid and succinct: though in rhythm it resembles the alliterative metre, the diction, syntax and literary treatment are those of prose. The deceptive simplicity of this style is matched by the deceptive straightforwardness with which Ælfric tells a story, and clearly both sprang from strong intellectual control and a masterly manipulation of language. It would be almost impossible to infer from the *Lives* the variety of sources which Ælfric had used, sources so varying in both style and length. To tell a story simply and in the best order can be one of the most difficult ways of telling a story. Ælfric's direct, elegant style was achieved by a firm, sensitive resistance to the ornateness and prolixity of most of his originals; what seems the natural order for the narrative has often been achieved by a careful rearrangement of the order of his source. In each one of the *Lives* Ælfric has made to a greater or less extent some alteration which makes it more successful as a story.

The same division into hagiographical kinds which was made with the poems can also be made with the *Lives of the Saints*. The life or passion of the virgin martyr, represented by *Juliana* among the poetry, is one of the commonest kinds of *Lives*, and the homilies on Eugenia, Julian and Basillisia, Agnes, Agatha, Lucy and Eufrasia (Euphrosyne), all fall into this group. At the root of these there lies the traditional and reasonable idealisation of virginity as the virtue upon which the life of the contemplative depended, for, as Cassian emphasised in the *Collations*, tranquillity of heart and mind could not be achieved without chastity. The definition of virginity implicitly present in the lives of the virgin martyrs, however, is nearer to that expressed in the Sacramentary of Leo I, where it is said in the Preface for the Consecration of Virgins that there are a few high souls 'who scorn the union of man and woman in order to love the mystery which it signifies', that is, of course, the union between Christ and the Church. Indeed in many of Ælfric's *Lives* there is already found a use of nuptial imagery: the martyr is often said to have chosen Christ as her *brydguma*, and in the Life of St. Agnes, where Ælfric is following closely a sermon of St. Ambrose, there occurs a long speech echoing the allegory of the Song of Songs. The lives of the virgin martyrs themselves became *exempla* in moral and doctrinal treatises in praise of virginity. In the late seventh century, for instance, Aldhelm, following the example of Fathers such as Ambrose and Augustine, wrote a treatise in praise of virginity designed for the abbess and nuns of Barking, and he included in it summaries of the lives of many of the desert ascetics and of martyrs including Agatha, Lucy, Eugenia and Agnes. This is only one unmistakable example of the invariable fact that the lives of the virgin martyrs are propagandist in their emphasis upon a virtue, which it was thought should be highly prized, and which, in its rejection of the world for the sake of a turning towards God, was thought of as a lesser form of martyrdom.

It is necessary to stress the sober, religious doctrine which underlies these works because otherwise the lives may seem to be no more than sensational novelettes, with a rather crude pattern of the miraculous and the edifying imposed upon them. The sensational elements fall into recurrent patterns. There are the saints, for instance, who disguise themselves as men and enter monasteries: Eugenia, who suffers the same kind of false accusation as did Joseph from Potiphar's wife, and who at last reveals its untruth by baring her breast; or Eufrasia, who remains unrecognised even by her father, and at last discloses her identity on her death-bed. Yet more sensational elements are to be found in the lives of Anges, Agatha, and Lucy, all of whom are destined by their angry and rejected suitors to enter a brothel, though all are miraculously saved from defilement: Agnes, for instance, when she is lodged in the brothel, cannot be approached on account of a dazzling light. Such episodes of course remain unelevated even when the underlying doctrine is remembered.[4] The purpose of calling attention to it is to explain in part how the life of the virgin-martyr developed rather than to justify it as literature. For many elements in it are crude by any standards, whether those of later literature or of *Beowulf*. All these elements, however, were in Ælfric's sources: his own contribution was the elimination of the verbose and a sustained urbanity of style.

The *Lives of the Saints* contain only two of the lives of the apostles, those of St. Mark and St. Thomas: all the apostles had been included in the *Catholic Homilies* save these two, and Ælfric had explained the omission of one, that of St. Thomas, on the grounds that there already existed a life in verse. Unlike the author of the *Andreas*, Ælfric is wary of strangeness and fantastic miracles, and partly for this reason his treatment of this hagiographical form in the *Lives of the Saints* requires no particular comment. Other groups which may be passed over quickly are, on the one hand, those which in the sources are the most legendary, such as the life of St. Eustace which was later to become the romance of *Sir Isumbras*, and on the other hand, the larger group of the more historical lives of famous bishops and abbots, such as St. Martin and St. Mauris. Under the latter heading, however, there is one subsidiary group, which is of particular interest, at least for us nowadays, that is, the lives of Anglo-Saxon saints, Æthelthryth, Oswald, Swithun and Edmund.

In the early Middle Ages there was no question of papal canonisation. Saints were identified by local and popular recognition, and usually no more than this was required. Occasionally a council might order the observance of a feast, as the Council of Clovesho did for St. Augustine of Canterbury, or occasionally a bishop might give his permission, as did Eadberct for the translation of the body of St. Cuthbert. But even such a limited form of authorisation was, at least to begin with, rare, and ecclesiastical authorities tended to intervene only to increase the fame of a saint or to suppress an abuse. The leaders of the Benedictine Revival would have been particularly concerned to propagate the veneration of native saints whose cults had been formed in local tradition. In his life of St. Edmund, in a

[4] It is one of the elements in the underlying doctrine, namely the utter reliance on God's power, which accentuates the sensational effect, for this insistence upon God's protective intervention prevents the authors from approaching the subject from the point of view of the power of virtue itself. It is the latter emphasis which makes the brothel scene in *Pericles* dignified and convincing and provokes the magnificent praise of the power of chastity in the Elder Brother's speech in *Comus*. I am indebted to Professor Stanley for drawing my attention to the comparison with the scene in *Pericles*.

passage not derived from his source, Ælfric displays a strong native pride in the Anglo-Saxons' record for sanctity:

> The Anglo-Saxon people are not deprived of the saints of God, since in England such holy men as this king, and the blessed Cuthbert, and St. Æthelthryth of Ely and her sister [Seaxburg], all lie buried with their bodies uncorrupted for the strengthening of our faith.

Ælfric wrote lives of three of these four (that of St. Cuthbert is in the *Catholic Homilies*), and perhaps he omitted Seaxburg because Bede's account of her is short, and her life so closely duplicates that of her sister.

For the lives of the early saints Ælfric drew upon Bede's *Ecclesiastical History*, following his source fairly closely, though sometimes clarifying the order of events, sometimes stating the moral with the explicitness appropriate to preaching. The story of Æthelthryth is that of a holy woman who, like St. Cecilia and many others, preserved her virginity in marriage, and whose body, like that of so many saints, was found at its translation to be quite undecayed. Here the hagiographical pattern to which the life conforms is quite plain, but there is no such model for the life of Oswald, except for the concluding section consisting of his miracles: for Oswald was a holy king, but his life in the *Ecclesiastical History* is treated primarily historically, and is not shaped to fit any of the well-defined hagiographical kinds.

As Ælfric complains in his *Life*, nothing was then known of the life of St. Swiðun, Bishop of Winchester. Ælfric therefore was only able to follow the Latin account of a monk of Winchester, which described the translation and miracles. There is nothing notable about this. Far more interesting is the account of Edmund. The source, Abbo's *Latin Life*, is in itself interesting in that in it Edmund is transformed into a martyr. Both the *Chronicle* and Asser's *Life of Alfred* relate that Edmund was killed in battle against the Danes, but in Abbo's account Edmund refuses to fight, and is shot to death in a form of martyrdom modelled upon that of St. Sebastian. It is this which gives hagiographical shape to the narrative: without this invention it would have become the same kind of amorphous account as is the *Life of Oswald*. It is interesting to notice, however, the emphasis upon historical truth: Abbo describes a chain of communication by which a private record of what happened could plausibly have extended across a hundred years, and prove the Chronicle entry to be wrong. Ælfric, of course, retains the central fact of the martyrdom, but in his successful attempt to reduce the lengthy and verbose Latin to a short, lucid narrative, he excludes many of the hagiographical motifs of his original. Abbo, for instance, begins in the correct rhetorical way by extolling his hero's country, but Ælfric, as in so many of the *Lives*, begins with an easy narrative introduction and passes quickly to the action of the story; or again Abbo depicts at great length how the raiding leaders are the servants of the devil, a point which Ælfric reduces to a single phrase, 'Hinguar and Hubba united through the devil'. All the learned reflections and allusions of the original are similarly condensed or omitted, so that Ælfric's *Life* consists of a series of brief, dramatic scenes. The most curious point of Ælfric's method, however, is that while the manner of storytelling is so transformed, there is nevertheless in the Old English hardly a phrase which is not translated word for word from the Latin.

The hagiographical form was the dominant narrative kind in the Old English period. Not only are the saints' lives more abundant in extant Old English literature than any other kind of story, but also many other narratives seem to have been influenced by them. Among the poetry, this can be seen in *Judith*, which, in its invention of the malignity and licentiousness of Holofernes and its stress on Judith's preservation of her chastity, shows unmistakably the influence of the life of the virgin martyr. In historical works the hagiographical influence can be seen, as we noticed before, in Bede's account of Cædmon or, more insidiously, in Asser's *Life of Alfred.* Whereas Einhard's *Life of Charlemagne*, which was modelled upon Suetonius's *Lives of the Emperors*, shows a reflective insight into political situations and an interest in the creation of a character-portrait, Asser's work,[5] with its emphasis on Alfred's piety, its supernatural interpretation of his illnesses, and, above all, its simplicity of approach whereby cause and effect are not sought for outside the relationship between God and man, most clearly derives from the saint's life.

Though so important, the saint's life was extremely limited by its conventions. There was in it by definition a combination of simplicity and artificiality which precluded it from transcending the bounds of

[5] These comments are not affected by the present controversy over the authorship of the work. The argument of hagiographic influence, however, supports the view that the *Life* was written by Asser rather than by a later author, for, granted the hagiographical pattern, it is difficult to believe that the work would not have ended with a description of a pious death-bed had this not been prevented by the fact that at the time of writing Alfred was still alive. The attribution to Asser could have remained, since Asser outlived Alfred by some years.

minor forms of literature. But these literary limitations derive from the Latin models and do not at all reflect upon the intellectual grasp or poetic skill of the Anglo-Saxons. Their liking for hagiography does not show them to be naive historians or naive Christians. But there is perhaps no literary form which is more likely to trespass upon the prejudices of the twentieth century. In nearly every period there is some literary form which demands from the reader the enjoyable response of a willing suspension of disbelief, but the form varies from century to century. Nowadays anyone who likes the fantasies of science fiction or the highly conventional form of the detective story would be outraged by the saint's life. Moreover, by some twist the idealised presentation of virtue today seems not only improbable but also repulsive, a deformity of taste which Graham Greene exploited in *The Power and the Glory*. All this makes it difficult for the Anglo-Saxon saint's life to be enjoyed nowadays: its conventions displease and, being only a minor form of literature, it has not the compelling power of great literature to be accepted on its own terms. Nevertheless, as the conventions grow familiar, the Old English saints' lives can be enjoyed as well-told stories, and the Old English poets can be recognised to have made a skilful development of the Latin literary genre.

INDEX